150 MOUTHWATERING RECIPES FOR GREAT GRILLED FOOD

FRED THOMPSON

The Taunton Press

The Taunton Press, Inc., 63 South Main Street, PO Box 5506, Newtown, CT 06470-5506

e-mail: tp@taunton.com

Editor: Martha Schueneman
Copy Editor: Valerie Cimino
Indexer: Heidi Blough
Jacket/Cover Design: Nick Caruso
Interior Design: Nick Caruso
Layout: Nick Caruso
Illustrator: Rodica Prato
Photographer: Ben Fink
Food Stylist: Fred Thompson

Library of Congress Cataloging-in-Publication Data

Thompson, Fred, 1953-

  Grillin' with gas : 150 mouthwatering recipes for great grilled food / Fred Thompson.

      p. cm.

  Includes bibliographical references and index.

  ISBN 978-1-60085-031-8 (alk. paper)

  1. Barbecue cookery. 2. Gas grills. I. Title.

  TX840.B3T534 2009

  641.7'6--dc22

                          2008045840

Printed in the United States of America

10 9 8 7 6 5 4 3 2 1

FOR MY GRILLING GURU, HUGH LYNN

A cookbook is never the work of one person. While I get to be the torchbearer (or would that be "tong-bearer"?) with my name on the cover, let me introduce you to the cast of characters that made *Grillin' with Gas* take life.

Thanks first to my friend and mentor, Pam Hoenig, the editor who brought me to writing cookbooks and who has been a huge part of most all my cookbooks. She saw a need for *Grillin' with Gas* and got the ball rolling. Thanks to Martha Schueneman, who had the task of editing the manuscript into the result you see today. I'm glad she likes Southerners and the way we talk, and of course the way I write. We butted heads, figured each other out, and had lots of laughs. Carolyn Mandarano headed up a great team at Taunton, and is probably the most diplomatic person I've ever worked with. Carolyn really made this book happen and I'm very thankful for her work. The rest of the team at Taunton includes Alison Wilkes, art director; Allison Hollett, trade sales and marketing manager; and the first-rate marketing department. And of course Sue Roman, the driving force behind Taunton.

The photographs by the incredible Ben Fink make this book come to life. Some of his shots make you swear that you can smell the smoke and taste the food. Thank you, Ben, for your patience, humor, hours, and hard work that you spent on this project. You are the best.

The first gas grill I bought was a Weber, and I retired it 25 years later, after writing *Barbecue Nation*. Weber-Stephens came to my aid and supplied me with several models of their gas grills to work on this book. Because of their generosity, the recipes here were tested on a wide range of grill styles, ensuring your success in your backyard.

Thanks as always to Barry and Linda Johnson, Robin and Rachel Thomas, and Henry and Nancie Wood for enduring my recipes both good and bad. Thanks to them for the flavor profile of this book. I'd also add to that group Kyle Wilkerson, an executive chef and my daughter's boyfriend, who found out that a condition of dating my daughter was putting up with my testing and giving me an extra hand at the grill and using his palate to confirm my own. A shout-out goes to my friend Hugh Lynn, who taught me the vast possibilities of the grill.

Then there are the folks who nurture me by being who they are. A special thanks to Nikki Parrish, who has always been there for word-processing issues, my complaining, and her typing skills, and who continues to tell me how much she enjoys my smart-aleck style. Cookbook author Jim Villas, who gave me encouragement. "Reverend" Bill Summers and Robin Kline, who made sure I always took time for a laugh, as did LeAnne Gault when the edits came around. My food buddies from trips to Umbria and Burgundy, whose companionship always told me I was lucky to be doing what I do. Nothing brings me more joy than a bunch of foodies all in the kitchen being inventive, tasting, and jabbering. Pableaux Johnson always made time when I was in need and was constantly checking up on me when I went "underground" developing *Grillin' with Gas*.

Kathleen Haskins Thompson, who made it possible for me to take the chances I needed to in order to get where I am today.

In the headnotes you'll meet many folks who contributed, and I am very grateful for them. My sister, Robin Tilley, always seemed to know somebody with a great recipe. And, with fond memories, Jerry Ellis—his life ended too soon.

Thanks to Danny Meyer and the Union Square Hospitality Group for letting me be a part of the Big Apple Barbecue Block Party. Thanks to Memphis in May champ Mike Mills for his council. The good members of the Southern Foodways Alliance (SFA) for the insight I've gleaned from that group and showing me how to be proud of my heritage.

Belinda Ellis, who makes me crazy and is the driving force behind me taking many leaps of faith recently. Life is more fun because of her. Thanks, BeBe, for thinking I'm worth the trouble.

And Laura—she's always proud of her daddy, and I'm damn proud of the young woman she has become.

CONTENTS

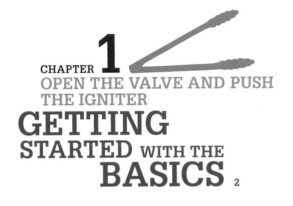

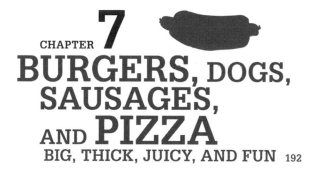

OPEN THE VALVE AND PUSH THE IGNITER

GETTING STARTED WITH THE BASICS

PEOPLE HAVE BEEN COOKING with fire since the dawn of time, but gas has been an option for only the past 50 or so years. Back in the early 1960s, gas grills were huge appliances that were tied into natural-gas lines, and they cost several hundred dollars, which was a boatload of money for the time. Over the years, gas grills became smaller, mobile, and less expensive, and they also became more efficient. In the 1970s, liquid propane (LP) stored in cylinders became the fuel of choice, and more recently grills have gone from using lava rocks and ceramic briquettes, designed to mimic charcoal (or at least to look like it), to angled metal plates (Weber calls theirs Flavorizer® bars) that keep heat more even and help to prevent flare-ups.

Gas grills in the marketplace today are for the most part extremely sophisticated, and although most are still fairly small and easy enough to move, what's old is new again: Massive gas grills are increasing in popularity as part of "outdoor kitchens," and even mid-priced grills are available with an option for natural gas.

But even inexpensive grills offer plenty of options. Multiple burners are the norm. Side burners are almost standard equipment, and most mid-range grills offer special infrared rotisserie burners, built-in smoke boxes, and separate burners that give you expert control over low-and-slow barbecuing or super hot searing. We must like what the manufacturers are producing, because 70 percent of us use gas as our medium of choice for grilling and barbecuing, and we are paying more for gas grills than ever before.

WHY GO
WITH GAS?

Okay, if you think it's wimpy to use gas over "real" fire, then think about this: Most people cannot tell a taste difference. Want more reasons to make the switch (or to defend your choice)? Gas is easier and faster to heat. You will have fewer temperature fluctuations and fewer flare-ups, which, in some schools of thought, makes gas less risky for your health. And according to many studies, gas grilling is more environmentally friendly than charcoal grilling.

BUYING
A GAS GRILL

The industry has caught up with our desire to cook fabulous food outdoors with a minimum of fuss. Whether you are buying your first gas grill or replacing an old one, here are some tips to consider before you head out to the store.

First, decide what you are really going to do with your grill. You will need a well-made grill unless you like buying one every year. If you know you are just a hamburger, hot dog, steak, and chicken breast griller, you don't need a lot of bells and whistles. A two-burner grill that has staying power is in the $300 range. But with the current grilling craze, which shows no signs of letting up, I'll bet you that you will want to get a little frisky and take your grilling to the next level. I always recommend a three-burner grill, and one in the $400 to $500 range will serve most folks very well. Grills in this price range have power ignition, have the ability to do some rotisserie cooking, produce decent smoke, and last for many years.

If you're looking to make grilling and barbecuing a hobby, then start looking for extras. A grill that will jump through hoops to help you will run about $800, and yes, that's a lot of grill. But no matter what your price point is, read through the owner's manual of each grill you're considering before you buy. This will give you a sense of the grill's ability to perform and the ease of operation. You can also compare grills online before hitting the stores.

Here are other factors to consider and features to look for when you go shopping.

- Look for heavy-gauge metal that is rust resistant or has been coated to be that way. Whether you choose

WHETHER YOU ARE
BUYING YOUR FIRST
GAS GRILL OR REPLACING AN OLD ONE,
HERE ARE SOME TIPS...

stainless steel or a powder-coated finish is a matter of preference.

- You'll want a cooking surface that's at least 400 square inches. That's the minimum, and if you think you might want to get more adventuresome than burgers and steaks, go larger.

- The lid must fit tightly and be easy to raise and lower.

- I think if you are going to do any cooking that takes longer than, say, 30 minutes, look for two or more burners, which allows for indirect cooking (see p. 8). Personally I like three burners or more.

- Btu is the unit of power that a burner has. Bigger is not always better. Look instead for efficiency ratings and total Btu in the 25,000 to 50,000 range. If you live in a windy area, or like me will be grilling in the snow, consider the higher number.

- Side burners are nice. They can keep sauces warm, or cook the eggs while the pork tenderloin cooks for breakfast. They are also good for frying and fish cookery, or for anything else that might stink up the house.

- Along with side burners I want side shelves. You can't imagine how much you will use them. Even then, having a separate table is handy.

- Rotisseries and rotisserie burners can be fun, but most anything you can do on a rotisserie you can do over indirect heat.

- If you plan to do much true low-and-slow cooking, then spend the extra money for a built-in smoke box or drawer. They used to be found only on grills that were $5,000 and up, but now can be found on grills in the $800 to $1,000 range. One of my new grills has this feature, with a separate burner for the smoke box, and it works like a champ at barbecue.

- Buy from a manufacturer that offers a good warranty, a good reputation for service, and a toll-free service that treats you like a person when you call.

- While you may think this is fussy, check for the drip pan. Is it easy to get to? Is it easy to work with? There is nothing worse than rancid fat all over you and your deck.

- If you plan to move the grill around, you'll want lockable wheels. You may want to keep your grill against your house, but check the owner's manual for recommended clearances from walls and eaves and other stuff around your house that a badly positioned grill could harm. Just because you don't see flames as you do with charcoal doesn't mean that you can't scorch or, heaven forbid, burn something.
- Plan to spend at least $400 for a grill that will last you several years if not decades. My original gas grill lived a vibrant life for 20-plus years.

TOOLS
OF THE TRADE

Gas grilling doesn't take a whole lot of special equipment, and I for one try to keep tools to a minimum. If you don't have these items at home already, then add them to your list for your next trip to the home-improvement store, the supermarket, or a kitchenware shop. Here's a list of what I think is important and an instant gift list for your friends and family:

MUST-HAVE
- A good pair of **barbecue mitts**. If you use oven mitts, choose ones that go past your wrist and are well insulated.
- Multiple pairs of **tongs**. You'll need one for raw and one for cooked to prevent cross-contamination. Ones from restaurant supply houses are good. Spring-loaded is best; the kind that break apart into a spatula and fork can be hard to work with.
- **Spatulas.** Have several sizes, and make sure all should have a sturdy blade. Long handles are nice but not necessary. I particularly like fish spatulas, which can be used for most anything else as well. I still am a metal person when it comes to spatulas and the grill.
- A sturdy, brass-bristled **grill brush** for stainless-steel and porcelain-coated grill grates; if you have cast-iron grates you will need stainless-steel bristles. Don't skimp here; you need as much help as you can get keeping the grill clean.
- **Thermometers.** Have several instant-read thermometers and make sure to calibrate them. I also like probe thermometers for long-cooking meats; those with an internal temperature alarm are convenient. An oven thermometer is much more precise to measure the internal temperature of your grill than the thermometer that may have come with your grill, and I encourage you to get one and use it frequently. Move it around on the grill—it will help you locate cool and hot spots.

- A couple of **timers**. They keep you on track through cocktails and beer.
- A few **basting brushes**. Have a small one for brushing oil on the food before grilling and a longer-handled one for basting on the grill. The new silicone brushes are easy to clean and carry a good amount of sauce or mop with one dip. There's even one out now that looks and acts like a mop brush.
- **Disposable pans** are a godsend for many chores around the grill. Use them to transport food, as drip pans, or as water pans. Keep a good supply on hand.
- **Skewers**. Have both bamboo and metal. Given a choice I will always use metal for better heat transfer, but bamboo ones are less expensive and are still acceptable. Choose flat skewers so the food doesn't spin when you turn it. You might want some double-pronged ones, but they're not a must-have. Simply use two skewers for the same effect.
- Loads of **heavy-duty aluminum foil** and 1-gallon and 2-gallon **zip-top plastic bags**.
- Don't forget an **extra propane tank**. It will at some point prevent aggravation and embarrassment.
- A restaurant-quality **half sheet pan or a jellyroll pan**. Perfect for carrying all your stuff to the grill.

- **A pepper mill**. Grind your pepper fresh—it makes a huge difference.
- **Wood chips and chunks** if you want to give that road a try.
- A good **injection syringe** if you plan to do long-cooking meats.
- **A spray bottle**, mainly for basting, but one filled with water can help control flare-ups.

NICE TO HAVE

- **Racks**. I like the new ones that hold a whole rack of any type of ribs, but the standard size is wonderful for chicken pieces, and a V-style roasting rack works for big cuts of meat (you can turn the roasting rack upside down for a quick rib rack). If you cook beer-can chickens, using a special rack will make them more stable.
- **Baskets**. Fish-fillet baskets, especially whole-fish baskets, which make turning a breeze, and a small-foods basket to use with veggies, especially if you are going to do multiple foods on the grill at the same time. These simplify turning so you can pay attention to everything else.
- An outdoor **grill light**.
- **A pizza peel**.
- **Assorted wood planks** that are 2 inches thick and at least 4 inches wide and 10 to 12 inches long. Be sure they aren't treated with chemicals

that would make them unsuitable for cooking.

- **A grill wok.**
- A couple of **pans and pots** that are very heavy-duty for use on the grill or side burner. Look to Lodge pre-seasoned cast iron for a lasting product.
- **A spice grinder.**
- **Microplane® zester.**

LET'S GET COOKING

The pros call it *mise en place*, which means "everything in its place," and your life will be a lot easier if you take a couple of minutes to think through what you will need at the grill (besides the food) when you're grilling. This is where those side shelves or an outdoor table come in mighty handy. If you are going to be yelling at someone to bring you something from the kitchen, make sure it's for a refill of your favorite beverage, not the barbecue sauce.

THE SKINNY ON TEMPERATURE

HIGH	450°–550°F
MEDIUM	350°–450°F
LOW	250°–350°F
LOW AND SLOW	200°–250°F

PREHEATING

Starting most gas grills is simply a matter of opening the valve on the propane tank, setting your burners to "Lite," and pushing an igniter button. Many of the new grills have built-in igniters on each burner's control knob. You should read the manufacturer's instructions on how to light your grill, and especially on how to light it with a match if the igniters fail. Every grill is a bit different. No matter what grill you have or what cooking method you are using, *always* heat your grill with all the burners turned on and set to high and the lid closed. Most modern gas grills can get to a temperature of about 550°F in 10 to 15 minutes, regardless of how many Btu. At this point, turn off burners and turn down the heat as necessary for the food you are preparing.

DIRECT AND INDIRECT COOKING

The methods of grilling called direct and indirect almost seem self-explanatory. Direct is just that—cooking over the direct heat source, and this is what most of us refer to as grilling. In the case of gas grills, that means that the food is placed directly over an operating burner. Direct works better for foods like steaks, hamburgers, boneless chicken breasts, fish fillets, and the like, which are thin and small enough to cook to the center before the exterior burns. With the exception of tuna steaks, direct heat involves closing the lid.

Every grill has hot and cool spots, and knowing where they are is especially important when you cook with direct heat. Once

KEEP IT CLOSED

you've learned where these spots are, you can adjust the positioning of food accordingly.

Indirect cooking is when your food is placed over burners that are turned off. Indirect methods of cooking are well known to great pit masters across the country. It's typical in a low-and-slow barbecue. George Stephen, a welder from Chicago, brought the capability to our backyards with his kettle-designed grills. Indirect cooking exponentially increases our capacity to produce delicious food with our grills. It works better with large cuts like roasts, pork shoulders, turkeys, and ribs, as

well as with smaller cuts like bone-in chicken parts. Indirect almost guarantees that foods will not burn on the outside before they are completely cooked inside. It also allows time for smoke to penetrate your food, if you so desire. Indirect comes close to eliminating pesky flare-ups, and it *always* involves the lid being closed.

How you configure your grill for indirect cooking depends on the number of burners and whether they run side to side or front to back. For a three-burner grill with burners running side to side, the front burner might be the only one turned on, and you'd place the food over the center or back burners. For a two-burner, the rear burner would be off and the food would be placed over it. For grills with burners that run front to back, you can either turn the center burners off, or for a very long-cooking food like a turkey, have one side of the grill on and the other side off. This is particularly useful when smoking, as it sets up a nice drafting relationship between heat and smoke. A water pan is also useful with the indirect method to ensure a moist finish, but only with longer-cooking items like roasts and turkeys, not necessarily with chicken parts. Refer to the owner's manual for specifics to your grill for direct and indirect cooking.

So when do you use which method? A good rule of thumb is how long the food takes to cook. If a food will be done within 20 to 30 minutes, cook it using direct heat. If it will take longer than 20 or so minutes, to be perfectly safe, use indirect. The higher side of

OUTDOOR COOKING IS MEANT TO BE AN ADVENTURE, A CHANGE OF PACE, FUN, AND A BIT CHALLENGING...

that range is for the more experienced, devil-may-care, I-like-to-live-dangerously folks.

There's a third method of cooking with a gas grill, and it's my favorite—you'll see it used throughout this book. It's a combination of direct heat for browning and indirect heat for cooking through. Here are some examples. A rack of pork ribs cooks beautifully with slow and gentle indirect heat, but 10 minutes or so before they are done, I'll flip them to direct heat to develop a little char and start brushing them with sauce. The result is a perfect rib with enough caramelization for great taste but nothing burned to spoil the experience. Or I'll sear bone-in chicken parts, including halves and quarters, or whole butterflied chickens, first over the direct section of the grill, and after they are golden brown I'll transfer them to the indirect area. Even then, after I have sauced the chicken very near the end of the cooking time, I might place it back over the direct heat to add just a bit of char.

I consistently hear folks complain about not being able to cook a steak with the same crust as a steakhouse. First you need to know that most steakhouses are cooking in the 800°F to 1,200°F range, which is hard for you to do at home, and few of us cook dozens of steaks all day, every day, to develop the expertise. If you want to get as close as possible to that steakhouse "crust" at home, first buy thick steaks, 1½- to 2-inchers. Sear the steaks over direct heat until the crust that you want has almost formed, then finish cooking the meat over indirect heat and turn your direct burner to a lower temperature. With a bit of practice you'll be the envy of the neighborhood. Of course that also means you will always be cooking the steaks for any function!

Make these cooking methods your friends and experiment with all of them. Soon you will reap accolades from your family and friends, and you'll get over-the-top taste from your gas grill.

COOK IT
TILL IT'S DONE

Grilling is more art than science, which is the beauty of why we do this. Outdoor cooking is meant to be an adventure, a change of pace, fun, and a bit challenging—and one of the biggest challenges is knowing when a food is done. The only absolute in the timing for any recipe in this book or in any other grilling recipes is that there is no absolute! Way too many variables have an effect on outdoor cooking, and you should never accept any timing guidelines as dictums. Among those variables are weather (wind, the outside temperature, rain or snow) and altitude, as well as whether the food you're cooking is a little larger or smaller than that specified in a recipe, your grill, and even how each cook defines terms like "medium" or "low" as it relates to heat level. For these reasons, take what you read in this (and any) book about grilling as guidelines, not gospel.

One of the biggest variables of all is your grill. They all cook differently and have different temperature points. A good oven thermometer is the best way to learn about your grill. But all this being said, it's much easier to adjust a gas grill to different conditions than it is to adjust a charcoal grill, whether you are dealing with hot spots or funky weather conditions.

In cold weather you will need to adjust your cooking temperatures upward to try to offset the outdoor temperature (cold weather affects the metal of the grill and drives the temperature down). But take care here, especially if you are indirect-cooking, say, a Thanks-

COMING TO TERMS

There are a few cooking terms that get tossed around a lot when it comes to a grill. They are "grilling," "grill-roasting," and "barbecuing."

- The act of **grilling** is cooking over direct heat, which you can also do on a grill pan inside; some diners look at their flattop griddle as a "grill."

- **Grill-roasting** is the process of cooking over indirect heat and is much like using an indoor oven for cuts of protein that benefit from longer cooking times in a gentler heat environment.

- **Barbecuing** is essentially grill-roasting at a super-low heat, say 225°F, and most all the time includes the addition of a smoking agent like wood chips or chunks. The setup is exactly like indirect cooking, and for gas grills that usually means only one burner running and turned to low heat. You've heard the term "low and slow" a million times, and that's just a different way of saying "barbecuing."

LITTLE STUFF TO KEEP IN MIND THAT MAKES A DIFFERENCE

- Let your food come to room temperature. It really helps the cooking process.

- For the most part, don't precook vegetables.

- Never parboil ribs—I will come talk to you if you do!

- A thermometer is your friend.

- Have a spare, full tank of propane.

giving turkey or a Christmas roast. Monitor the inside temperature of your grill (here's where that oven thermometer is invaluable). If you are grill-roasting at about 350°F, then adjust your temperature to maintain that temperature. In extreme cold this may be hard to do, so add to your cooking time and plan to baste or spray the item with broth or whatever your liquid flavoring ingredients might be to preserve moisture over the longer cooking time.

Here again each grill will vary, so if this is your first Thanksgiving turkey and it's cold outside, give yourself an extra hour. If it gets done early, don't panic, just tent it with foil and know that the hot gravy will overcome any cooling. And if Granny has to have hers steaming hot, nuke her a few slices.

Rain and snow have similar effects. A thunderstorm in the summer is going to cool the outside of your grill, but with summer rain, I tend to expect a slightly longer cooking time and make no other adjustments. Grilling in the snow is a hoot and proves to everyone what a grand grill master you are, so just follow the cold-temperature guidelines and plow your way to the grill. Wind can be your toughest adversary. If possible, place your grill so that the wind is perpendicular to the gas flow. Keep a vigil for a burner being blown out. The match light opening is a good place to look. And by all means, if the burners go out, cut off the gas, open the lid, and wait at least five minutes before trying to relight. I would like you to keep your hair and skin intact.

As in baking, grilling at higher altitudes, like in the Rockies or other high mountains, demands adjustments, too, mostly when you are cooking indirectly. You'll have to increase your cooking time. For the most part with roasts and other large cuts, increase your time by about 15 percent, but here again every grill is different.

TESTING, 1, 2, 3

So if the cooking times in a recipe are only guides, how do you know when something is done? Each recipe in this book has a few different doneness cues, and they rely on a variety of senses, but mostly sight, touch, and smell: Is the food browned, or are the juices running clear? Does the food feel firm or still a bit soft? Are the aromas having their way with you?

Touch is the way most chefs determine doneness, at least with smaller cuts (bigger cuts will be more dependent on internal temperature). Invest in a couple of instant-read thermometers, and at least one probe type. Use their temperature readings to hone your skills by learning to match touch with temperature and you'll never have to do the slice-and-peek method to check doneness again. In all of the cooking classes I teach, one of the things I get the most feedback about is how wonderful these methods are and how quickly they can be learned. I most frequently use the cheek-nose-forehead method (see below).

While you're learning to gauge doneness, *always* err on the side of undercooked. I routinely tell students in my cooking classes, kitchen assistants, and neighbors that "it's easier to put cook on than take cook off"—meaning you can always cook something longer if it isn't done enough, but you can't make something less cooked. If you aren't sure the food is done to your liking, just take the food off the grill and reduce your grill's temperature. Let the food stand or rest for however long the recipe suggests, and then check it. If it isn't as done as you prefer, return it to the grill. The beauty of the gas grill is that you still have a good heat source to return the item to and finish the cooking. You are not really wasting gas—the grill is cleaning itself by burning off any particles of protein that have adhered, which will make the job of cleaning it faster the next time you cook. Just don't forget (as I have) to cut the gas off if you don't return the food to the grill to finish cooking. You'll be very disappointed and say something like @#%*%# the next time you go to grill if your gas is gone by your own hand.

FACE METHOD FOR TESTING DONENESS

Touch your cheek—rare

Touch your nose—medium

Touch your forehead—well-done

GRILL FOR GOOD HEALTH

There is a lot of talk about grilling and its health effects. Flare-ups are the main culprits. You don't want flare-ups anyway because they affect the taste of the food adversely. Flare-ups are caused by fat dripping onto the heat source. The chemical reaction could create carcinogens, but the American Cancer Society has not yet determined the levels that might put you at risk. Here's where the new gas grills with bars over the heat source are extremely helpful in negating flare-ups and making your experience safer.

A FEW WORDS ON SAFETY

I've said that grilling is fun, and it is. But nothing will put a damper on that fun like a trip to the emergency room, a call to the fire department, or a case of food poisoning. Keep these points in mind to stay safe, healthy, and home.

FIRST THE GRILL

Gas is explosive and flammable, and you'd be wise not to forget it. Read your grill's instructions thoroughly and follow them to the letter.

- Make sure your grill is assembled properly.

- Keep your grill outside and away from overhangs. Never leave a lit grill alone for any length of time. Even when going low and slow, check on it occasionally.
- Never light a grill with the lid closed.
- Don't move a lit grill.
- Check for gas leaks routinely and every time you change a tank. It's very simple to do with a spray bottle filled with soapy water. A leak will create bubbles.
- Loose clothes and a gas grill is a bad idea.
- Watch the kids.
- Transport propane tanks in an upright fashion and store them outside, but not in an area where the temperature will reach 125°F.
- If a burner doesn't light, cut everything off including the tank, open the lid, and wait at least five minutes before trying again. If it still doesn't light, check your owner's manual for how to clear a blockage.
- Follow your owner's manual for scheduled maintenance and do it.
- Last but not least, if you smell gas, there's a problem. Shut everything down. If you still smell gas, call your friendly fire department.

NOW THE FOOD

Most, but not all, foodborne illness is caused by not handling food properly, and most often

SMOKING WITH

THE GOOD STUFF: SMOKING WOODS

WOOD TYPE	BASIC CHARACTERISTICS	GOOD WITH
HICKORY	Bacon-like, smoky	Most anything but fish
MESQUITE	Pungent, but sweet; however, burns hot so take that into account	Made for beef and lamb, but good with veggies
OAK	Mellow and is the traditional mix with hickory for barbecue of all types	Brisket, pork shoulder, pork of all types
APPLE	The darling of the barbecue circuit—mild, sweet, dense smoke; my favorite	Pork; all poultry, especially duck and turkey
CHERRY	Mild and sweet	Duck, other poultry, pork
ALDER	Light and delicate	Great with salmon and most all seafood; veggies too
PECAN	Strong and nutty; burns very cool, which makes it great for low heat	Wild game, pork, chicken
PEAR/PEACH	Woodsy and sweet, but rich	Poultry, pork, fish
GRAPEVINES	Mild and easy; great for quick-cooking foods	Small poultry, pork, turkey parts
WINE BARREL PIECES (WHISKEY TOO)	Fun and different; oak and wine nuances	Beef and poultry

those foods are protein based. Raw chicken, for example, is the source of a lot more food poisoning than raw broccoli. Keep these tips in mind to lessen the risk of making your friends, your family, or yourself sick.

- Wash your hands often in hot, soapy water.
- When I mention room temperature, the range is 65°F to 72°F, but remember that bacteria grows most rapidly between 40°F and 120°F. Minimize

the time that food spends out of the refrigerator or off the grill.

- Defrost foods in the refrigerator. Protein-based foods can be at room temperature for about 2 hours—and that's combined before and after cooking, not two hours before and two hours after—before it becomes potentially unsafe.
- Cross-contamination is real and can ruin your day. Keep tongs, cutting

boards, platters, and anything else that touches raw food away from cooked food. Wash everything that has been in contact with raw stuff in hot, soapy water.

- If reusing a marinade as a sauce or basting medium, place it in a pot over high heat and bring to a boil. Boil for *at least* a full minute (some experts recommend boiling for three minutes, others for up to five minutes). Start timing when a full boil is reached—and a full boil is one that does not go down when stirred.
- Divide a sauce that will be used for basting and for passing at the table before it comes into contact with raw or partially cooked foods. You can also bring the sauce that was used for basting to a boil like a marinade, but sometimes it radically changes the flavor, especially with cooked sauces, so I would rather divide.
- Get a clean spatula or platter for the cooked food rather than reuse the one that touched the raw. Why risk it?

ADDING FLAVOR
WITH SMOKE

What was once a disappointing aspect of gas grilling was the lack of a wood flavor. Most folks don't understand that charcoal adds such a tiny bit of smoke flavor that it has to be enhanced as well, so don't let the "charcoal snob" bully you. Grills have improved to the point that I regularly use wood for adding a bit or a lot of flavor. Many recipes in this book use wood chips, and you can certainly add this dimension to most any recipe.

Originally, charcoal was actual wood that had been burned to embers, and good barbecue joints still use this today. Charcoal as we know it, however, was Henry Ford's idea. Most of what you buy as briquettes is compressed charred wood and coal mixed with cornstarch and other chemicals. Lump hardwood is more about charred wood without fillers, and it is a much better product.

The type of wood you use to create the smoke can have a profound effect on the flavor of the food you're cooking. The box on p. 15 explains the basic characteristics of the flavors that different woods impart and offers suggestions about which foods they complement best.

If your grill is equipped with a smoke drawer or box, especially with its own burner, you're good to go. Follow the guidelines in your owner's manual. Otherwise, there are many post-purchase cast-iron smoke boxes in stores and while they are nice, they certainly aren't necessary. I used the following method for years (the same general guidelines apply for using a smoke box):

1. Soak your wood chips or chunks for at least 30 minutes. They can soak in water, or in beer, wine, or fruit juices

SMOKING GUIDELINES

- Start with a small amount for smoke until you learn your grill and your tolerance for the smoke flavor. Remember, more is not always better. Smoke is a seasoning, just like salt.

- Experiment with different woods—and different combinations of woods— to see which you prefer with which proteins. I like a mix of hickory, oak, and apple, which gives a smoky, sweet, and rich flavor.

- For more information, check out my website at www.barbecue-nation.com.

for an extra zip. I usually start with 2 to 3 cups of wood chips or several pieces of wood chunks.

2. Take a small disposable aluminum drip pan and place the drained chips inside. Cover tightly with foil, and then poke a few holes in the foil.

3. Before you preheat the grill, place this packet under your cooking grate, directly on the angled metal plates covering your burners, or on the lava rocks or ceramic briquettes, in what is generally the hottest spot on the grill. Leave it there during the heating process.

4. It really helps to have a pan of liquid in the grill when smoking. Smoking can dry food out, so some steam keeps thing moist. It can be water, beer, fruit juice, or any liquid used in the recipe. Keep the liquid in the pan for most of the cooking process (it's okay if it evaporates toward the end of the cooking time). Place the pan over the indirect-heat portion of the grill.

5. Don't start cooking until the chips have begun to smolder and smoke is present.

It has been my experience that chips will only smoke for 20 to 25 minutes, which for most indirect cooking is perfect for that smoke-kissed flavor. You can add another packet of chips if you wish, but know that every time you lift the grill's lid you are losing heat and extending the cooking time.

But what about cooking low and slow barbecue? If you are under the impression that most barbecue joints smoke food throughout the whole cooking process, get over it. Yes, there are still those that do, and there are commercial smokers that assist in this process. However, a good pit master knows that too much smoke will yield a food that tastes like a charred piece of wood, or as fellow grill master Elizabeth Karmel says, "the way an ashtray smells." Proteins tend to absorb their best smoke flavor within the first two hours. For most gas grillers, any more is a waste and you are working way too hard. If you plan to do a lot of "barbecue" cooking, I urge you to look at a grill with

QUICK CLEANING TIPS

- Use the heat of the grill to burn off food residue, and then remove it with your grill brush. Also knock off debris on the bars that cover the burners. Never use chemical solutions on either bars or burners.

- Remember to empty and clean your grease pan. It will prevent grease fires and keep critters from sniffing around your grill. Wash it with warm, soapy water.

- Once a year, clean your burners as suggested by your owner's manual.

- Clean the cooking box and inside the lid while warm with hot, soapy water. Use a scrub pad if needed.

- Wipe the outside surface occasionally. If your grill is stainless steel, use a product made for stainless.

built-in smoking capabilities. These grills know how to play the game to get perfect flavor.

Here's a trick I learned from my neighbor Robin Thomas. He soaks wood chips or chunks and places them right on the cooking grate, over the hot spot on his grill, and then preheats it. By the time his grill is heated, he's got smoke. This method is quick and easy and allows you to add chips as necessary without much effort. I use this method when quick-cooking items over direct heat and with foods that take an hour or less with indirect. Experiment with this method. You'll be surprised.

One of the most important things to do when smoking and cooking indirectly with low temperatures is to keep a pan of liquid in the cooking chamber. The dampness it creates makes the smoke more effective and helps to prevent the meat from drying out.

Remember too that "planking" is a form of smoking. Cedar planks are the norm, but there are hickory planks, and they are great with pork and beef. Cherry and maple play well with chicken, so add these to your grilling repertoire. (See the sidebar on p. 191 for more information about cooking with planks.)

And don't think it's "sissy" to wrap your hunk of meat in foil to finish cooking. What you are doing is using a "Texas Crutch." More great pit masters than you would ever imagine use this method. Wrap the meat in foil after it has had some time to absorb some smoke— usually an hour is good—then place the wrapped food back over the indirect heat of your grill or even in a heated oven. Your results will be stunning. Try Jean Lynn's Beef Brisket, by Way of Kansas City (p. 56) for the ultimate proof.

ROTISSERIE
COOKING

For centuries, humans have been cooking foods on a spit. It's funny to me that what is old is new again. A rotisserie allows you to grill food on a rotating rod with indirect heat below or beside the food. Using a rotisserie creates an incredibly moist and very evenly browned food.

If you can balance a food on a spit, you can cook it on a rotisserie. What happens during rotisserie cooking is that the protein bastes itself. As the meat turns, the melting external fat bathes the meat, keeping it moist. The method is best used on turkey, duck, chicken and other whole poultry, roasts of all types, and ribs. I love cooking whole duck and other fatty birds this way, as well as lean beef roasts. Wrapping meat (or larding) with bacon adds volumes to lean cuts of any type.

Whether your grill came with a rotisserie unit or not, most gas grills can easily accommodate a post-purchase one. Follow your rotisserie's directions for securing the meat and operating the unit. Heat your grill with all burners on high, including the rotisserie burner if your grill is equipped with one. Place the spit in the unit and the rotisserie cut out on the grill. If you have a rotisserie burner, leave it on, and set a couple of burners for indirect cooking and adjusted to low heat. If your grill doesn't have a rotisserie burner, set the burners for indirect cooking over medium heat. Remove any racks that would interfere with the rotation, place a drip pan under the meat to catch the fat as it melts, close the lid, and turn on the rotisserie motor. You can pretty much forget it at this point.

Any food that can be placed on a spit or recipe that uses a spit can be converted to this style of cooking, simply by following the direction in the previous paragraph. Also know that any rotisserie recipe can be cooked over indirect heat. The cooking time and temperature are almost exactly the same.

WHAT'S IN
THE PANTRY?

Besides techniques, the ingredients you choose can affect flavor—sometimes profoundly. This section includes products I like and used in developing and testing these recipes, as well as some suggestions for your pantry. Pick and choose, but try to have a variety of each type on hand so you can experience, for example, how different vinegars or sweeteners can affect the taste of each dish. For more suggestions and ideas for flavoring your foods, see Chapter 10.

- **Kosher salt.** preferably Morton®, and gray sea salt. I like the feel and the melt of Morton kosher, but I use a fair amount of gray sea salt since it doesn't seem to affect blood pressure so much.
- **Black pepper.** freshly ground from a pepper mill. Adds volumes of flavor.
- **Good oils.** Have an olive oil (no need to use extra-virgin in most grilling

recipes) and a canola or other neutral oil (because peanut allergies are increasingly common, you may wish to avoid peanut oil). A little truffle oil is nice for finishing a simply grilled food.

- **Composed (or compound) butters.** Make and freeze some to have on hand. Only buy unsalted butter—that way you control the seasoning.
- **Hot pepper sauces.** I use Texas Pete®, FRANK'S® RedHot®, and Tabasco®. All are excellent. Also keep an Asian hot sauce like sriracha.
- **Duke's® Mayonnaise.** If you can't find it in your area, try a southern-food website, or pick a mayonnaise that has little or no sugar. But, and this is a big but: If you are making your grandmother's recipe and she always used Hellmann's®, then you must use Hellmann's too. It's part of the flavor profile and the dish just won't taste "right" with anything else.
- **Sweeteners.** Brown sugar, honey, molasses, Splenda®, Sugar in the Raw®, maple sugar and syrup, and plain old granulated sugar.
- **Bourbon,** for the food and the cook.
- **Ketchup.** I really like the flavor of organic ketchups, Hunt's® regular ketchup, and Dickinson's®, a specialty ketchup from J.M. Smucker.
- **Tamari** instead of soy sauce. Better tasting and lower sodium. Think of it as premium soy sauce.

- **Worcestershire sauce.** Try the homemade recipe on p. 300. Many gourmet brands are excellent as well, and Lea & Perrins® is pretty good, too.
- **Apple cider** and **distilled white vinegar.**
- **Mustards.** Yellow American-style mustard, Gulden's® Brown, and Grey Poupon® or Maille® Dijon-style mustard, both grainy and smooth. I use only Colman's® Dry Mustard.
- An emergency bottled **barbecue sauce.** I use Bone Suckin' Sauce and Bull's-Eye™ when I don't have time to make my own.
- Fresh, I repeat fresh, **spices and herbs.** If they are older than six months they need to be thrown out. Within this group have a few pure chile powders, especially chipotle; smoked paprika; granulated garlic and onion; and a locally produced barbecue rub to have for emergencies (or order one from a barbecue house like Neely's or the Barbecue Shop in Memphis, Tennessee, or Magic Dust from Mike Mills's 17th Street Bar and Grill in Murphysboro, Illinois, for when you are short on time). Ground coriander and cumin mixed in equal parts is great for seafood. Crushed red chile flakes are also an important part of your spice rack.
- **Fruit preserves.** Jellies like red currant, guava, plum, and hot pepper;

THE TOP 10 KEYS TO SUCCESSFUL GRILLING

- Be patient and let your grill preheat fully.

- Keep your cooking grate clean.

- Oil the cooking grate each time you cook, and brush or spray oil on your food, especially fish, and sticking becomes a thing of the past. Oil also transfers heat quickly.

- Understand direct and indirect and when to use each or a combination.

- Always cook with the lid down.

- Shoot for caramelized, not blackened.

- Don't baste with sauces that include sugar until the end of the cooking time. That includes ketchup-based sauces.

- Turn food only once if at all possible.

- Use a thermometer for both grill temperature and internal food temperature (at least until you have mastered the "touch" method for doneness).

- Most of all, enjoy the process, and reap the rewards and praise.

peach preserves; and orange marmalade make for quick glazes and sauces. Smucker's®, Dickinson's®, and Braswell's® are my choices.

- Prepared **horseradish and wasabi** in a tube—forget the powder.
- Wickles™, the best damn **pickle** you'll ever eat.
- **Bacon,** preferably apple-wood smoked.
- Lots of **onions,** yellow and sweet; fresh **garlic;** and **shallots.**
- **Citrus fruit,** especially lemons, limes, and oranges.
- Wish-Bone® or Good Seasons® Italian salad dressing for **emergency marinades.**
- **Red and white wine and sherry.** Box wines have gotten so much better that I keep one red and one white just for cooking. The wine stays fresher in the box than in a bottle. Remember, it must be drinkable. Vermouth is also nice to have on hand for a variety of reasons, but mainly because it can double for white wine, and martinis are good when having a cookout.

21

AMERICA'S PASSION

BEEF

Absolutely Perfect **STEAKS** 34

NEW YORK STRIP STEAKS with Blue Cheese Butter 36

Allan Benton's "Frenched" **RIB-EYE STEAKS** 37

The Simplest and Best-Tasting **LONDON BROIL** in the World 38

Chinatown-Style **FLANK STEAK** 40

HANGER STEAK with Grilled Onions Tossed in Balsamic Vinegar 41

FLAT-IRON STEAK with Spicy Green Sauce 42

Kansas City–Style **BEEF RIBS** 43

Darned Good Boneless **SHORT RIBS** 44

Christmas **PRIME RIB** 47

Florentine Stuffed **BEEF TENDERLOIN** 48

Good Old Sunday **ROAST** 50

Vietnamese **BARBECUED BEEF** with Lemongrass and Peanut Sauce 52

Plain and Simple **VEAL T-BONES** 53

Dad's Americanized **GREEK KEBABS** 54

Jean Lynn's **BEEF BRISKET,** by Way of Kansas City 56

VEAL CHOPS with Worcestershire-Horseradish Glaze and Sage Butter 59

BEEF IS BACK IN A BIG WAY in the American diet, and for those of us who find the flavor of beef cooked on a grill second to none, that's a reason to celebrate—beef was always and still is king. My love affair with grilling began with a simple rib-eye steak. It was a Saturday night ritual while I was growing up. My father's steak was simple: Just salt, pepper, and fire, although the Jack Daniel's® and 7UP® was as important to the ritual as anything else. There were always some steak sauces on the table, but few were used. The true flavor of the beef always carried the meal.

We weren't alone, either. Our steak dinners might have been Saturday, but from the early 1960s on, "let's grill some beef day" was a once-a-week ritual in almost every American household.

This chapter will delve into the cuts of meat best suited for the grill and will walk you through a variety of cooking methods. Nowhere are method and cut tied as closely together as they are with beef. High temperatures and direct heat are perfect for that New York strip steak and a disaster when trying to cook a prime rib roast. You'll also learn how to tell when the meat is ready to come off the grill, as well as how to choose the best beef at the store.

Here are the steps for success for wonderful beef from the gas grill.

IN THE SUPERMARKET OR
BUTCHER SHOP

When it comes to buying beef, your eyes are your best tool, but it also helps to know grading and marketing terms and a little bit of anatomy before you even go into the store. In addition, knowing your butcher and developing a relationship with him or her is important.

In the store, look for marbling, color, and moisture. Good marbling is easy to spot. Marbling is milky white fat that "spider webs" throughout the red meat. You should avoid any cut of beef where the marbling is a brown or yellow, as this is a sign of old and very dry meat. Also avoid any large clumps of fat within the flesh. Fat melts during the cooking process, and marbling gives the beef richness and juiciness, but big chunks of fat leave a greasy taste and will give you fits with flare-ups on the grill. Fat is a good thing but too much of it is problematic. Think marbling for juiciness.

Color is another part of buying with your eyes. Beef that you see in a grocery store or in a butcher shop's case should have a light cherry red appearance. Deep, dark reds look impressive but typically are an indication that the meat came from a dairy cow. Dairy cows have their purpose—producing good milk—and everything about them goes into that. They are not bred for their meat, which is bland tasting and tough. On occasion you may see beef that is dark red, with a bit of a gray-brown tint. This indicates a couple of things. Most of the time, you're looking at a piece of meat that has just been cut and

has not been exposed to air long enough to turn that light cherry red. However, if you are in a setting that sells aged beef, like a top butcher shop or an upscale grocer, it could very well be the most flavorful purchase of the day. This is where knowing your butcher is a huge help.

The final thing that you should be looking for is moisture. Individually wrapped cuts of meat should look moist, but if condensation is apparent in the package, that indicates that the meat has probably been frozen and thawed, which is not what I want if I'm buying fresh meat! If the beef looks wet and sticky, move on to another selection. The presence of excessive moisture inhibits your ability to brown the beef to create that perfect and tasty caramelization on its exterior.

As you're developing your skills in identifying the best beef, ask questions of the

WHEN IT COMES TO BUYING BEEF, YOUR EYES ARE YOUR BEST TOOL...

LABEL
LINGO

Sell-by and use-by dates on meat labels are the lawyers' way of protecting the store and the folks who processed the meat. With the exception of ground beef, most beef is fine a few days past the sell-by date. Your nose is your best guide—if it's nearing or past the date and it smells "off," trash it. Ground beef has its own set of issues, and I never let ground meat pass the use-by date. In fact, I usually use it within one day of the sell-by date.

If you know you won't cook the beef by the use-by date, freezing it is fine, as long as you don't leave it in its original packaging or in the freezer for too long. Remove the meat from the store wrapping and put it in a freezer bag. Label the bag with the cut and the date, and then push as much air out as possible (the oxygen will speed up freezer burn). Those new vacuum sealers are great. I think after three months in the freezer beef has lost much of its flavor and juiciness, so don't let it stay frozen too long.

butcher or counterperson. That might seem easy to do in a good butcher shop, but you're probably wrong if you think it's difficult in a grocery store. The folks who work there want to pass on their expertise as much as anyone, so trust their advice and even their cooking suggestions. More and more you will also find butchers at the warehouse clubs, and these stores can be a fabulous source of meat with great deals on Choice cuts.

When buying veal, look for a pink tone to the flesh, which can sometimes be even a reddish pale pink, with milky white fat. This is formula-fed veal, and most of what is in the supermarkets today is this type. Avoid any brownish pink flesh and yellowed fat. If you are fortunate to find grass-fed veal, which has a more pronounced, somewhat beefy flavor, the flesh may be closer to red and the fat will not be as creamy white.

GRADING AND CUT

Besides looking at the beef itself, you'll need to read the label, which tells you the grade and cut of beef, as well as how fresh it is.

There are three primary grades that the United States Department of Agriculture (USDA) uses to ensure that the beef we purchase is of high enough quality for human consumption. Prime is the very top of the grading pyramid. Rough estimates suggest that only 2 percent to 5 percent of the total beef production gets this grade, and most of that is sold to restaurants. The grade most of us will

THE RIGHT CUT
FOR THE RIGHT METHOD
These are guidelines only; specific recipes may vary.

TOP-SHELF CUTS Direct Heat	LESS TENDER BUT TASTY Direct Heat	BIG CUTS TO ROAST Indirect Heat	LOWER, SLOWER, AND BRAISED Indirect Heat
Filet mignon	Hanger steak	Whole beef tenderloin	Chuck roast
Rib-eye steak	Skirt steak	Strip loin	Brisket
Porterhouse steak	Flank steak	Standing rib roast	Short ribs
New York strip	Top sirloin	Tri-tip roast	Dinosaur beef ribs
T-bone steak	Flat-iron steak	Chuck roast	
	London broil	Eye of round	

see is the second level of the USDA's system, Choice. Choice beef typically has generous marbling, which is key to a tender steak. Within this category is specialty Choice, marketed as Black Angus or Certified Angus. These designations come from the packer, not the USDA. They indicate a higher quality of Choice and are reserved for only about seven of every hundred head of cattle, which must meet strict standards for texture, firmness, and marbling. Generally, these labels do provide a more marbled piece of meat than regular Choice. When I'm shopping for beef, I seek out these specialty labels because I find their taste and tenderness to be far superior to standard Choice. The lowest grade that I will purchase is Select, and I avoid ungraded beef. Marbling is hardly noticeable on these cuts and the result is usually dry and chewy. When your pocketbook can afford it and you can find it, splurge on Prime beef, especially with what I call the glamour cuts like porterhouse steaks and prime rib roasts. The result will be superior. But in most cases Choice beef from a

reputable supermarket or butcher will supply more than enough flavor and tenderness to satisfy even the most intense beef craving.

Different cuts of beef come from different parts of the animal, and their tenderness is usually related to how the muscle is—or is not—used. The more tender and to some extent more popular are the rib, loin, and sirloin. The tenderloin muscle, for instance, is so buried into the animal's body that it very rarely has to contract to do anything, hence its extreme tenderness and mild flavor. Muscles that get lots of use, like the round (upper leg), have a stronger and more intense flavor, but the meat will also be tougher. Tenderness, even at the expense of flavor, seems to drive prices.

Veal is sometimes graded much like beef—Prime, Choice, and Good—but very little veal is graded. Look for brands like Plume de Veau® or Dutch Valley, just to mention a few, as more of an indication of quality than grade. Most likely the brand your supermarket carries is reputable and will have good flavor.

AGE YOUR OWN BEEF

SINCE DRY-AGED BEEF CAN BE PROHIBITIVELY EXPENSIVE, not to mention difficult to find, here's a method of dry-aging your beef at home that results in that improved texture, tenderness, and flavor. I borrowed this method from *Fine Cooking* magazine many years ago and find it to be extremely effective and utterly simple. I tend to do this with large cuts of beef such as a boneless rib or a strip loin roast when they go on sale. (These large cuts are also available at fairly good prices every day at the warehouse clubs.) The two caveats to doing this at home are to make sure that your refrigerator is at 40°F or below, and to cook or freeze the meat within seven days of beginning the process. Are you ready? Here we go.

Take the roast out of the store wrapping but trim nothing. Rinse it well under lukewarm water and pat it dry with paper towels. Wrap the roast lightly with a triple thickness of cheesecloth. Place this on a rack that will fit over a rimmed baking sheet. Place your dry-aging apparatus in the refrigerator for three to seven days (obviously the longer you let it age the more flavor will develop). After the first full day, carefully unwrap the beef and then re-wrap with the same cheesecloth to keep the fibers from sticking into the meat. Then return it to the refrigerator and leave it alone. When you are ready to cook the meat, unwrap it and use a sharp knife to shave off and discard any hard, dried outer layers of meat and fat. Either roast whole or slice into steaks before cooking.

The cuts most people grill are the loin and chops. Both of these cook very much like beef, especially the chops, which are really "baby steaks." Veal's internal temperature should range from 135°F for a medium-rare chop to 150°F for medium, but a well-done veal chop is a total waste of money. If you have a well-done crowd, pick another meat.

AGED TO PERFECTION

Aging affects tenderness and flavor in a massive way. Most beef is wet-aged. It is sealed in Cryovac® bags for several weeks to go through the tenderizing process with little or no moisture loss. Since moisture loss also affects poundage, many restaurants and stores that advertise aged beef use this method. Many claim that since the beef is not exposed to air, it has a fresher flavor.

The other method of aging is dry-aging, which many experts consider the gold standard. Dry-aged beef is exposed to air for three to six weeks in a very cold and controlled environment. As beef is dry-aged, enzymes in the muscle fibers break down so the meat becomes extremely tender, and the beef loses moisture, which intensifies flavor. Dry-aged beef is very hard to come by. It used to be that if you wanted to sample some of the best beef available, you had to go to a great steakhouse—a trip to Peter Luger® in Brooklyn, for example, guaranteed you Prime dry-aged beef. But more and more we have the ability to purchase high-quality dry-aged beef (though it may not be of Prime grade). Whole Foods Market, for

instance, has equipped many of its stores with dry-aging units. If I could live my life on dry aged beef, I would seriously consider it. The next time that bonus check comes through, part with some of it for a dry-aged New York strip or porterhouse and see if you don't become an aficionado.

WHAT ABOUT GRASS-FED, GRAIN-FED, AND ORGANIC?

Popular catchphrases in the beef industry today are "grass-fed," "grain-fed," and "organic." Cattle, like all things in nature, are affected by diet and lifestyle. Since the mid-1950s, almost all cattle raised in the United States gained at least 30 percent of its weight by being fed grain before slaughter; some cattle are completely grain-fed. This allows meat producers to produce beef that is consistent in flavor and tenderness.

Grass-fed animals tend to have a stronger and to a certain extent a less consistent flavor than those fed a regulated diet of grain. If you've ever had Argentine beef, for example, you've had beef that was completely grass-fed, and considering Argentine beef is world famous, that could be a hint to what we really want on our taste buds. At present, the demand for grass-fed beef in this country outstrips its supply. As better restaurateurs increase the amount of grass-fed beef that they feature on their menus, consumer demand will continue to increase. I hope that this will convince more ranchers to consider feeding their cattle only grass.

TEMPERATURE GUIDELINES

These are guidelines only; specific recipes may vary.

DONENESS LEVEL	USDA RECOMMENDATIONS	FRED'S THOUGHTS
RARE	None given	125°F
MEDIUM-RARE	145°F	135°F
MEDIUM	160°F	145°F
MEDIUM-WELL	None given	155°F
WELL-DONE	170°F	160°F and above (Larger cuts of meats cooked low-and-slow such as brisket should go to 170°F for maximum tenderness.)

Beef that is labeled "organic" is certified by the USDA National Organic Program to ensure that the cattle are fed with 100 percent organic feed, have been given no unnecessary antibiotics or hormones to promote growth, and are given access to pasture—but for no more than 200 days. Organic beef can be flavorful and slightly strong tasting and hits medium-tender on the scale. If this philosophy is important to you, organic beef is becoming easier to find and has dropped considerably in price in the past decade.

MATCHING CUT TO METHOD

All cuts of beef are delicious when the heat of a grill is applied, so long as it is applied correctly. In this chapter, you'll find recipes for many different cuts of beef. Most of the tender cuts are easy to grill quickly over direct heat. Less-tender roasts take to indirect heat, low and slow cooking, or a spin on the rotisserie. Some recipes for the tougher cuts incorporate braising or use acidic marinades to break down and tenderize the meat.

A FEW WORDS ABOUT SEARING

As you read this chapter you'll see the word "sear" many times. We throw the word around a lot but what is it actually? Searing is, in a nutshell, cooking food over high heat. Assume when you see the phrase "place over direct heat" that you'll be searing your food. No matter which cut of meat you're dealing with, it will improve when seared. Even when a recipe in this chapter engages in indirect cooking over long periods of time, at some point during the process we will sear that piece of meat to help develop flavor. Searing is what browns the outside of a cut of meat to that beautiful deep color, and the intensity of flavor comes when the sugars and the proteins within the flesh are changed by the heat to produce hundreds of nuances of flavor. Why do you think you brown ground beef before you make chili? It's simply to improve the flavor. I know that many people will tell you that searing seals in moisture, but thanks to our resident TV food scientist Alton Brown, and many government studies, we now know that theory to be untrue. Searing is about flavor.

Moisture is the biggest enemy of a good sear. When moisture is present, meat doesn't sear or turn brown, it steams—which does little to enhance flavor. (Compare the difference in flavor of steamed and grilled asparagus and you can imagine the difference in meat.) You'll see instructions throughout this book to pat the meat dry before you place it on the grill. Some of my grilling-expert friends even go as far as to wrap a piece of beef completely in paper towels and let it sit for a few minutes to soak up any moisture. Just know and understand that drier is better for a good, flavorful, intense sear.

Salt also affects searing, but in which direction is open to debate. The general consensus is that salting should take place no more than 10 minutes before grilling. Salt has a tendency to pull the juices from inside the meat, which makes the surface wet. Some chefs believe that meat should be salted two or three hours before cooking so that it can penetrate further into the flesh. I've tried both ways. Truth be known, I really can't tell much difference in flavor. The one important point about salt is that it does need to be added before you cook because it has trouble penetrating the meat afterward.

SUBLIME
OR SHOE LEATHER—
A MATTER OF DEGREE

Doneness is the key factor for total enjoyment of beef. Some cuts are at their tender best

NO MATTER WHICH CUT OF MEAT YOU'RE DEALING WITH, IT WILL IMPROVE WHEN SEARED.

when served rare to medium-rare, and others don't become tender unless they are extremely well-done.

For many years we overcooked most everything. It's taken me 20 years to convert my mother from well-done to medium. Growing up with parents who spent their childhoods on farms in rural North Carolina in the 1930s, I understand what they perceived as a need to cook items fully. Our food supply is not perfect, but it is better and safer than it was decades ago, and this allows us today to have a little variation in doneness to suit our own palates.

There is controversy even between what the USDA recommends and what many people prefer. The USDA's temperatures (see the chart on p. 30) were established in an effort to protect us from the risk of foodborne illness. If this is a concern for you, then use their recom-mendations. I personally think that these numbers are too high (note that we are *not* talking about ground beef or tough cuts like brisket but about steaks and many roasts), and my recommendations are in the same chart.

Whatever temperature you decide is best for you and your family, first understand that there is carryover cooking in almost all proteins. For instance, a 1-inch-thick steak will easily increase in temperature by 5°F during its resting period. (Resting period, you ask? That's when you let the meat stand after you remove it from the heat to allow the juices to redistribute throughout the meat.) So to hit 145°F, the steak should come off the grill when an internal thermometer registers 140°F. Larger cuts of meat can adjust themselves as much as 10°F after removal from the grill.

I for one am glad that beef is experiencing a revival in the American diet. No, we can't eat

A QUICK REFRESHER
ON COOKING TIMES
These are guidelines only; specific recipes may vary.

THE CUT	THICKNESS OR WEIGHT	TOTAL GRILLING TIME	RESTING TIME
STEAKS	1½ in. thick	12 minutes	5 minutes
FLANK STEAK	2 pounds	10–12 minutes	5 minutes
BONELESS SIRLOIN ROAST	5 pounds	50 minutes	10–15 minutes
BONE-IN RIB ROAST	6 pounds	1½–2 hours	At least 10–15 minutes

COMPOUNDING FLAVOR
WITH BUTTER

Compound butters are the sneaky little secrets in many great restaurant kitchens. Using a compound butter adds an instant burst of moisture and flavor, the combinations are limitless, and it's just so simple to do: Take a stick of butter and let it thoroughly soften at room temperature. Put the butter in a small bowl and add flavorings and a squirt or two of lemon juice. Take a fork and mash all the ingredients together. Put into a covered container and refrigerate until needed, or stick it in the freezer for up to three months.

The sky is the limit when it comes to the flavorings. Roasted garlic, fresh minced garlic, rosemary, and curry paste or powder are among my favorites. I do think that a blast of acid such as lemon juice is critical to balance all the flavors. Other than that, let your brain and your taste buds lead you down an inventive culinary path. If you're looking for a good one to start you off, check out the recipes for New York Strip Steaks with Blue Cheese Butter on p. 36.

red meat three times a day, 365 days a year. But neither should it be shunned as an unhealthy no-no. Beef should never be considered a guilty pleasure. Moderation with beef, as with all types of food, is the key to sensible enjoyment.

Updated older methods and new methods of raising cattle are being used by the boutique rancher and the industrial behemoth alike; flavor is on the upswing, and tenderness has become doable in many grades of beef. Take the recipes that follow and have fun. Be sure to experiment with the larger cuts. The beauty of a gas grill is its ability to deliver consistent and constant temperature while infusing beef with the unique flavor that can only develop from an outdoor grill. Use this tool to please your palate and bring diversity to your plate.

ABSOLUTELY PERFECT STEAKS

Four 14-ounce New York strip steaks, about 1½ inches thick

½ cup canola oil

½ cup (1 stick) unsalted butter, melted

8 teaspoons kosher salt

8 teaspoons freshly cracked black peppercorns (see sidebar, p. 111)

AT THE GRILL

Judging the doneness of steak is not as much science as it is technique and feel. Poke your index finger into your cheek at mouth level. Then press your finger into the steak. If they feel very similar, that's an indication of a rare steak. Touching the tip of your nose gives you the feel of a medium steak, and touching your forehead is a medium-well to well-done steak. Always let the meat sit for a few minutes before you serve or cut it. Juices come to the surface of the meat while it cooks. Allowing it to sit lets the meat reabsorb the juices, so they don't spill out when you cut it.

All of us want to be superior steak masters. Like all things, the quality of the end result has a lot to do with what you start with. When you crave a really great steak, seek out aged beef, and try to get your hands on Prime beef if possible. Most steaks are best when simply prepared, but knowing how to use heat is critical. With gas grills, it's easy to get a higher temperature for a great sear and then quickly lower the heat to finish cooking the steak without continuing to brown (that is, burn) the outside. Many of the newer gas grills have sear burners or separate sear plates for doing just this.

1. Remove the steaks from the refrigerator 30 to 40 minutes before cooking. Cover loosely with plastic wrap.

2. Mix the oil and butter in a 9x13-inch baking dish. Put the steaks in this mixture, turning to coat each side. Lift the steaks from the pan and allow the excess oil to drip off. Place on a platter and coat each side of each steak with 1 teaspoon of the salt and 1 teaspoon of the pepper.

3. Oil the grill racks. Preheat your grill using all burners set on high and with the lid closed for 10 to 12 minutes.

4. Place the steaks on the hottest part of your grill. Cut one burner to medium, but not the one where the steaks are. Be patient. Close the lid and cook the steaks for 3 minutes on one side, turn, and cook for an additional 3 minutes. Turn them back to the first side for an additional 3 minutes, and then finish the other side with an additional 3 minutes. Your total cooking time will be 12 minutes. This should give you a rare steak with a pretty decent char. If you desire a steak that's cooked a little more, pull the steaks to the cooler burner. Remember that the meat will continue to cook after you've removed it from the grill. Allow the steaks to rest for at least 5 minutes before serving.

NEW YORK STRIP STEAKS WITH BLUE CHEESE BUTTER

SERVES 4

DIRECT HEAT

FOR THE BLUE CHEESE BUTTER

½ cup (1 stick) unsalted butter, at room temperature

4 ounces crumbled blue cheese, preferably Maytag or Point Reyes

¼ teaspoon granulated garlic

¼ teaspoon freshly ground black pepper, or more to taste

Four 8- to 10-ounce New York strip steaks, 1 to 1½ inches thick

Olive oil

Kosher salt

Freshly ground black pepper

The stout flavor and aroma of blue cheese have always been a steakhouse staple as a salad dressing. But in recent years the blue cheese has moved from the iceberg to the red meat. This recipe gives you the basis for making compound butters, which are nothing more than butter blended with flavoring agents to add another dimension to your food. If you're not a blue cheese fan, you can totally leave it out, or use rosemary, thyme, or an even stronger cheese if you desire. Some recipes for compound butter insist that you form it into a log. Do so if you wish, but spooning it into a container works just as well.

Now what does blue cheese butter do for a New York strip steak? Ultimate steak nirvana.

1. To make the butter, blend the butter, blue cheese, garlic, and pepper together in a medium bowl. (A fork is a good tool for doing this. If you wish, you could use a hand mixer.) Pack the butter in a small container and refrigerate until needed. The butter can be made several days in advance and even frozen.

2. Allow the steaks to stand at room temperature for 30 minutes before grilling. Brush olive oil over both sides of the steaks and season generously with salt and pepper.

3. Oil the grill racks. Preheat your grill using all burners set on high and with the lid closed for 10 to 12 minutes.

4. Place the steaks on the grill, close the lid, and cook for 4 to 5 minutes per side for medium-rare. Add a minute or two to each side for medium; subtract a minute or two from each side for rare. Remove from the grill and let rest for at least 5 minutes. Smear at least a tablespoon of the butter over each steak and serve.

ALLAN BENTON'S "FRENCHED" RIB-EYE STEAKS

Allan Benton, in my and others' opinions, cures the finest country hams from his Maryville, Tennessee, "ham house." Allan once told me, "You know, I can do more than hams. Come visit and I'll cook you one of the best steaks you ever ate." So I did. "I'm not going to tell you what's in the marinade until you taste the steak," he told me on his deck overlooking the Smoky Mountains in the distance. After one bite, I could have cared less what he had marinated them in as long as he told me. "The secret ingredient is just old plain orange French dressing. Isn't that weird?" I usually don't care much for steak marinades; in most cases they cover the taste of the beef. This one does not. If anything, it doubles the impact of the beef while adding an interesting flavor note or two. Like everything Allan does, this marinade is first-rate.

SERVES 4
DIRECT HEAT

Four 12-ounce rib-eye steaks, about 1½ inches thick

¼ cup soy sauce

¼ cup canola oil

3 tablespoons bottled French dressing (the orange kind)

1 tablespoon Worcestershire sauce

½ teaspoon granulated garlic

1. Place the steaks in a baking pan large enough to hold them. Mix the soy sauce, oil, dressing, Worcestershire, and granulated garlic together in a medium bowl. Pour the marinade over the steaks. Cover with plastic wrap. Leave at room temperature for about 2 hours or refrigerate overnight.

2. Oil the grill racks. Preheat your grill using all burners set on high and with the lid closed for 10 to 12 minutes.

3. Remove the steaks from the pan and discard the marinade. Place the steaks on the grill, close the lid, and cook for 4 to 5 minutes per side for medium-rare. Add a minute or two to each side for medium; subtract a minute or two from each side for rare. Remove to a platter. Tent with foil and let rest for 5 to 10 minutes before serving.

THE SIMPLEST AND BEST-TASTING LONDON BROIL IN THE WORLD

SERVES 4 TO 6

DIRECT HEAT

One 3- to 3½-pound flank steak or thick sirloin tip (sometimes labeled London broil)

One 16-ounce bottle Wish-Bone Italian dressing

2 tablespoons dry sherry, such as oloroso

1 teaspoon Worcestershire sauce

1 Granny Smith apple, cut into thin slices

IN THE KITCHEN

Two of my favorite cuts of beef are flank steak and brisket. They're not as tender as filet mignon, but they have 10 times the flavor. They can also be ruined with sloppy knife work. Cuts of beef that are not inherently tender need to be cut against the grain of the muscle fibers. By doing this, you shorten the length of that grain and make the meat more palatable to chew. Since the grain can sometimes be difficult to see, a good rule of thumb is to slice vertically across the length of the meat.

Not everything has to be complicated or expensive to be over-the-top delicious, and here's a perfect example. London broil, as it is so labeled in many grocery stores today, is not a cut of meat. It refers to flank steak or sirloin tip that should always be marinated, cooked quickly, and thinly sliced. This recipe may look a little pedestrian to you, but don't knock it until you've tried it. This is a showy dish for a tailgate.

1. Cut shallow diagonal slits on one side of the steak. This will help it absorb the marinade better.

2. Combine the dressing, sherry, Worcestershire, and apple slices in a large zip-top bag. Add the beef, close the bag, and squish the marinade around the meat. Put in the refrigerator and marinate for at least 24 hours; 48 is better, and you can go for as long as 3 days.

3. Oil the grill racks. Preheat your grill using all burners set on high and with the lid closed for 10 to 12 minutes.

4. Remove the meat from the bag and discard the marinade and apples. Pat the meat dry with paper towels. Place on the grill, close the lid, and cook for 7 or 8 minutes. Turn, cover the grill again, and cook for an additional 8 minutes, or until the steak gives slightly to the touch and is about 140°F on an instant-read thermometer. Remove from the grill and let rest for 5 minutes. Slice very thinly across the grain and serve with any accumulated juices.

CHINATOWN-STYLE FLANK STEAK

SERVES 6
DIRECT HEAT

2 tablespoons fresh lemon juice

1 tablespoon hoisin sauce

3 tablespoons soy sauce

¼ cup Worcestershire sauce

1 teaspoon freshly ground
    black pepper

2 tablespoons chopped fresh cilantro

1 tablespoon minced fresh ginger

One 2-pound flank steak

2 tablespoons sliced fresh chives,
    for garnish

The title of this recipe's a little far-fetched, but the seasonings used to add zing to this piece of meat are true to Chinatown cooks, whether in San Francisco or on Mott Street in New York. Flank steak is one of those beautiful pieces of meat that on its own has tremendous flavor but is also a great sponge for exotic tastes. The keys to perfect flank steak are not to overcook and always to slice against the grain. Slicing with the grain and overcooking—and by that I mean past medium—yields a tough, chewy experience. A tip on dealing with fresh ginger: Use a spoon to scrape the peel from around all the knobs. It's safer than a knife and does the job beautifully.

1. Combine the lemon juice, hoisin, soy sauce, Worcestershire, pepper, cilantro, and ginger in a zip-top bag. Squish until blended. Add the steak and squish the marinade around the meat. Close the bag and marinate overnight in the refrigerator, turning the bag every time you open the refrigerator. (If you are pressed for time, you can marinate for 2 hours at room temperature, turning once or twice.)

2. Oil the grill racks. Preheat your grill using all burners set on high and with the lid closed for 10 to 12 minutes.

3. Remove the steak from the marinade and pat dry with paper towels. Discard the marinade. Place on the grill, close the lid, and cook for 5 to 6 minutes on each side for medium-rare. Add a minute or two to each side for medium; subtract a minute or two from each side for rare.

4. Transfer to a carving board and let rest for 10 minutes. Carve the meat crosswise on the diagonal. Garnish with the chives and serve immediately.

HANGER STEAK WITH GRILLED ONIONS TOSSED IN BALSAMIC VINEGAR

In the days of real butcher shops, hanger steak was the piece of meat that the employees took home for their families. Once hidden from the average consumer, it is now becoming more and more available. Long enjoyed in France and other European countries, hanger steak is extremely flavorful, but a bit chewy—not tough, just not tender. Hanger steaks are typically 1 to 2 pounds each, but more and more butchers are cutting them into smaller, serving-size pieces.

1. Make the marinade by combining the garlic, ginger, tamari, mustard seeds, both mustards, the olive oil, vinegar, pepper, and salt to taste in a nonreactive dish like a glass baking dish. Add the steaks and turn to coat. You might want to take a metal skewer or a meat fork and just poke at the steaks a little. This helps the marinade get inside the meat and tenderize it a bit. Cover with plastic wrap and refrigerate for at least 4 hours, but do not marinate this overnight—8 hours is maximum. This particular marinade will slightly "cook" the beef if left for too long

2. Thread one skewer through each onion slice. This is not absolutely necessary, but it helps to keep the onion slices from separating and falling through the grill.

3. Oil the grill racks. Preheat your grill using all burners set on high and with the lid closed for 10 to 12 minutes.

4. Remove the steaks from the marinade and pat dry. Discard the marinade. Place the steaks on the grill along with the onion slices, close the lid, and cook both for about 5 minutes. Turn and cook for another 4 to 5 minutes. This cut of meat really needs to be served medium-rare or not much past medium. Remove the steaks to a platter and let rest. Put the onions in a mixing bowl, sliding them off the skewers if necessary, and toss with the vinegar. Taste and add salt if you desire. Spoon over the steaks and serve.

SERVES 6
DIRECT HEAT

6 garlic cloves, finely minced

2 teaspoons grated fresh ginger

¼ cup tamari

1 tablespoon yellow or brown mustard seeds

2 tablespoons coarse-grained mustard

1 tablespoon Dijon mustard

¼ cup extra-virgin olive oil

¼ cup sherry or balsamic vinegar

Copious amounts of freshly ground black pepper

Kosher salt

Six 9- to 10-ounce hanger steaks

FOR THE GRILLED ONIONS

Skewers (optional; if using bamboo, soak in water for 30 minutes)

3 large red onions, peeled and sliced into thick rings

2 to 3 tablespoons balsamic vinegar

Kosher salt (optional)

FLAT-IRON STEAK WITH SPICY GREEN SAUCE

SERVES 4 TO 6

DIRECT HEAT

One 2-pound flat-iron steak

4 garlic cloves, mashed into a paste

½ cup plus 2 tablespoons
  extra-virgin olive oil

1 cup fresh flat-leaf parsley leaves

1 cup fresh cilantro leaves

2 garlic cloves, peeled

2 fresh jalapeño chiles, seeds and
  veins removed (wear gloves to
  prevent irritation)

1 tablespoon fresh lime juice

Kosher salt

Freshly ground black pepper

Flat-iron steak might be a new term, but if you're familiar with top blade, you're familiar with this cut—they're both from the shoulder, or chuck, of the steer. Top blade steak was a staple on steakhouse menus for decades, but it fell out of favor 20 or so years ago. Thanks to several chains wanting to put a reasonably priced steak on their menu, this cut came out of retirement and was rechristened the flat-iron steak. It's extremely tasty and is purported to be the second most tender steak. This sauce is intense and herbaceous and a nice foil to the char of the beef. Any leftover green sauce can be stirred into rice or mashed potatoes.

1. Place the steak on a dinner plate and rub with the mashed garlic and 2 tablespoons of the olive oil. Cover tightly with plastic wrap and refrigerate for at least 2 hours or overnight. Remove the steak about an hour before you plan to grill.

2. Put the parsley, cilantro, peeled garlic, and jalapeños in a food processor. Pulse until chopped and combined, and then, with the motor running, slowly pour in the remaining ½ cup olive oil. Let the mixture continue to process until smooth. Transfer to a small bowl. Stir in the lime juice and season to taste with salt and pepper. Let stand at room temperature for about an hour so that the flavors can meld.

3. Oil the grill racks. Preheat your grill using all burners set on high and with the lid closed for 10 to 12 minutes.

4. Remove the plastic wrap from the steak and season with salt and pepper on both sides. Place on the grill, close the lid, and cook for 4 to 5 minutes, then turn and cook for an additional 4 to 5 minutes for medium-rare to medium. The steak should give slightly when touched and an instant-read thermometer should hit about 140°F. Remove the steak from the grill and allow to rest for 5 minutes. Cut the steak across the grain into thin slices and serve with the sauce.

KANSAS CITY–STYLE BEEF RIBS

Cooks in Kansas City have always amazed me with how well they deal with cuts of beef and slow cooking. Now I won't swear to you that this method is what every pit master in Kansas City uses, but I will guarantee you great-tasting and tender ribs. Here you'll basically "steam-roast" the ribs in your oven and then finish them by searing over the flame. Just another little trick to tenderness.

1. Preheat your oven to 200°F.

2. Whisk together the Worcestershire and mayonnaise in a small bowl. Brush this mixture liberally on both sides of the beef ribs. Sprinkle heavily with the barbecue rub. Place the ribs in a disposable aluminum pan or baking dish large enough to hold them in a single layer. Add the water and cover tightly. Put in the oven and cook without peeking for 1½ hours. This step can be done one day in advance. If you do it ahead, cool the ribs in the pan with their juices, then cover and refrigerate overnight.

3. Oil the grill racks. Preheat your grill using all burners set on high and with the lid closed for 10 to 12 minutes.

4. When the grill is hot, cut off the center or back burner and adjust the heat to medium-high.

5. Remove the ribs from the baking dish and sear over the direct section of your grill for 2 to 3 minutes per side, or until some nice grill marks are showing. Move the ribs to the indirect section and brush with some of the barbecue sauce, setting aside some beforehand to serve at the table. Close the lid and cook for about 5 minutes. Turn, brush with sauce again, and cook, turning and brushing every 5 minutes for 20 minutes total cooking time. Remove the ribs from the grill. Let rest for 5 minutes, then slice into individual ribs and serve with the reserved sauce on the side.

SERVES 6 TO 8

DIRECT AND INDIRECT HEAT

½ cup Worcestershire sauce

2 tablespoons good-quality mayonnaise

Two 4-pound racks beef ribs, each cut into 3 or 4 sections

¼ cup My Quick, Simple, and Wonderful All-Purpose Rub (p. 282)

½ cup water

1 cup Surprising Kansas City–Style Sauce (p. 291)

BEEF

43

DARNED GOOD BONELESS SHORT RIBS

SERVES 4 TO 6
DIRECT HEAT

½ cup packed light brown sugar

¼ cup granulated sugar

½ cup paprika (try ¼ cup smoked paprika and ¼ cup sweet paprika)

2½ tablespoons kosher salt

2½ tablespoons freshly ground black pepper

1 tablespoon granulated onion

½ teaspoon cayenne

2 pounds boneless beef short ribs, connective tissue removed

1 cup Virginia Pruitt's Perfect Barbecue Sauce (p. 289) or your favorite thick barbecue sauce

IN THE KITCHEN

The seasoning mixture or rub makes more than you will need for this recipe, and it's fabulous sprinkled over beef brisket, pork chops, pork tenderloins, or, of course, pork ribs. Store the mixture in an airtight container for up to 2 months.

I love short ribs, but I've always been a braising person, convinced that you couldn't just grill a short rib and make it wonderful to eat. While writing this book I became obsessed with creating a simple, grilled boneless short rib recipe. The key is to trim the connective tissue that holds the bone to the meat. I found that often when you buy boneless short ribs, this tissue is still there, and it's tougher than a pair of Marine boots that have marched across Iraq. After that adjustment it's a matter of being patient at the grill. You want them nicely caramelized but you don't want to overcook them. They need to be pink inside to be tender enough to eat and enjoy. Serve with pinto beans cooked with garlic and cilantro or atop grits or mashed potatoes.

1. In a medium bowl and blend together both sugars, the paprika, salt, pepper, granulated onion, and cayenne. Sprinkle the short rib pieces liberally with this mixture until coated on all sides. Let sit at room temperature for about 30 minutes.

2. Oil the grill racks. Preheat your grill using all burners set on high and with the lid closed for 10 to 12 minutes.

3. Place the beef ribs on the grill, close the lid, and reduce the heat to medium. Turn the ribs every 3 to 5 minutes or so, so that every side gets slightly caramelized, 15 to 20 minutes total. (If your short rib pieces are small, it won't take quite this long.) The ribs should yield easily to the touch, not unlike a medium-rare steak or the way the tip of your nose feels. Reduce the heat a little more and brush the ribs with the sauce. Cover the grill and let cook for a minute or two for the sauce to set up, and then continue to turn and brush until all sides of the ribs have been glazed. Remove to a platter and let sit for 5 to 10 minutes, covered with foil. Serve.

CHRISTMAS PRIME RIB

The English have served prime rib as their Christmas dinner for centuries, and many of us are bringing that tradition home to our holiday table. Even if you live in Michigan or Maine and there's a foot of snow on the ground, taking that prime rib out to the gas grill adds yumminess to a holiday classic and gives you the added benefit of freeing up your oven for other dishes. Don't overlook the possibility of sticking a casserole on your grill while the prime rib is cooking as well.

1. Allow the roast to stand at room temperature for 30 to 45 minutes.

2. Put the garlic, rosemary, basil, salt, and pepper in a food processor and pulse to finely mince. Add the mustard and olive oil and process to form a paste. Smear the paste all over the top and sides of the roast.

3. Oil the grill racks. Preheat your grill using all burners set on high and with the lid closed for 10 to 12 minutes.

4. When the grill is hot, cut off the center or back burner and adjust the heat to medium.

5. Put the roast on the grill, bone side down, close the lid, and cook to your desired doneness, 1½ to 2 hours for medium-rare (the meat will register 135°F to 140°F on an instant-read thermometer). Transfer the roast to a cutting board and remove the bones. Loosely cover the roast with foil and let rest for 20 to 30 minutes. The internal temperature will rise 5°F to 10°F. Carve the meat into slices and serve.

SERVES 6 TO 8

INDIRECT HEAT

One 5- to 6-pound bone-in standing prime rib roast, trimmed of excess fat

6 large garlic cloves, peeled

¼ cup lightly packed fresh rosemary leaves

¼ cup lightly packed fresh basil leaves

2 teaspoons kosher salt

2 teaspoons freshly ground black pepper

3 tablespoons Dijon mustard

3 tablespoons extra-virgin olive oil

FLORENTINE STUFFED BEEF TENDERLOIN

SERVES 6 TO 8

DIRECT AND INDIRECT HEAT

FOR THE HORSERADISH SAUCE

½ cup sour cream

⅓ cup mayonnaise

3 tablespoons prepared horseradish

2 tablespoons finely snipped fresh dill

1 tablespoon fresh lemon juice

2 garlic cloves, minced

¼ teaspoon kosher salt

¼ teaspoon freshly ground black pepper

6 slices bacon

3 to 4 large garlic cloves, minced (about 1 tablespoon)

½ pound fresh baby spinach

3 tablespoons raisins

Freshly ground black pepper

One 3- to 3½-pound center-cut beef tenderloin

2 tablespoons finely snipped fresh dill

Kosher salt

For many of us, beef without the bitter, sharp contrast of spinach is just a bland experience. Well, instead of making it a side dish, we're going to put it right in the middle. While the spinach stuffing flavors the tenderloin, the juices from the tenderloin add interest to the stuffing.

1. To make the sauce, whisk together the sour cream, mayonnaise, horseradish, dill, lemon juice, garlic, salt, and pepper in a medium bowl. Cover and refrigerate for at least 20 minutes before serving.

2. Put the bacon in a large skillet. Cook over medium heat, turning occasionally, until crispy and golden, about 10 minutes. Drain on paper towels. Pour off and reserve all but 2 tablespoons of the fat. If your bacon was so lean that it did not render 2 tablespoons of fat (which I can't believe), add enough olive oil to make 2 tablespoons. Add the garlic to the fat in the skillet and cook for about 30 seconds, stirring occasionally. Throw in the spinach and cook until the spinach is wilted, 1 to 2 minutes, stirring constantly. Transfer the spinach mixture to a medium bowl, then stir in the raisins and ⅛ teaspoon pepper. Finely chop or crumble the bacon and add it to the bowl. Stir the mixture and let cool to room temperature.

3. About 30 minutes before grilling, remove the tenderloin from the refrigerator. Using a fillet knife or boning knife, trim off excess fat and the silverskin, then use a long, narrow knife to make a tunnel through the center that runs the length of the tenderloin, twisting the knife and cutting slightly with each turn to enlarge this opening. Stuff the spinach mixture into the hole from both ends using the handle of a wooden spoon. Take kitchen twine and tie the beef tightly into an even cylinder. (See drawings on the facing page.) Lightly brush the beef all over with the reserved bacon fat. Season with the dill, salt, and pepper.

4. Oil the grill racks. Preheat your grill using all burners set on high and with the lid closed for 10 to 12 minutes.

5. When the grill is hot, cut off the center or back burner and adjust the heat to medium.

6. Place the tenderloin on the grill, close the lid, and sear over direct heat for 15 minutes, turning a quarter turn once every 3 to 4 minutes.

7. Continue to grill over indirect heat until cooked to the desired doneness, 20 to 30 minutes longer for medium-rare, turning once. Remove from the grill and let rest for 5 to 10 minutes. Cut into 1-inch-thick slices and serve warm with the sauce.

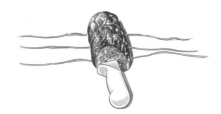

Using a long knife, cut a pocket through the center of the meat lengthwise.

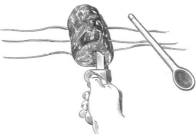

Move the knife from side to side, cutting slightly with each turn to enlarge the slot to about 2 inches.

Use your fingers to insert the stuffing and a wooden spoon to poke it through the slot.

GOOD OLD SUNDAY ROAST

SERVES 4 TO 6 OR MORE, WITH LEFTOVERS

INDIRECT HEAT

One 3½- to 4-pound bottom round or eye of round roast

1 teaspoon kosher salt

1 teaspoon coarsely ground black pepper

1 teaspoon granulated garlic

1 teaspoon dried oregano, crushed between your fingers

1 tablespoon canola oil

AT THE GRILL

Making a quick pan gravy is easy. Drain off most of the fat, leaving the rest of the drippings in the pan, then put the pan over direct heat and warm. Throw in a tablespoon or two of finely chopped onion and a couple cloves of crushed garlic. As they cook and become soft, deglaze with low-sodium beef broth, red wine, or a combination of both; you will need about 1 cup total liquid. Using a spatula, scrape the brown bits from the bottom and sides of the pan and let cook to reduce slightly. Remove from the heat and serve with the roast.

Those of us of a certain age remember when Sunday dinner centered around a beef roast. Most of the time the roasts were overcooked and tough, but the gravy, as well as all the fixings, made a meal fit for a king. Nowadays, many of us reach for more tender—and more expensive—cuts of roast beef, but this recipe shows you that you can save your money. It really is amazing what a little outdoor cookery can do for a lesser cut of beef roast.

1. Remove the roast from the refrigerator at least 1 hour before you plan to cook.

2. Oil the grill racks. Preheat your grill using all burners set on high and with the lid closed for 10 to 12 minutes. If using a rotisserie, preheat your grill using all burners set on high, including your rotisserie burner if your grill is so equipped, and with the lid closed for 10 to 12 minutes.

3. When the grill is hot, cut off the center or back burner and adjust the heat to medium-high. If you're using your rotisserie, turn the two burners at the ends to medium, cut off the middle burners, and leave the rotisserie burner running.

4. Combine the salt, pepper, garlic, and oregano in a small bowl. Completely rub the roast with the oil. Liberally sprinkle the seasoning mixture over the roast, patting the roast so that the seasonings adhere.

5. If you wish to make a pan gravy (see sidebar, left), place a rack inside a disposable aluminum pan and set the roast on the rack. Otherwise, place the roast directly on the grill, or secure the roast on the spit if you're using the rotisserie.

6. Adjust the heat to medium, close the lid, and cook for 1½ to 2 hours, or until an instant-read thermometer registers 130°F for rare or 140°F for medium. Remove the roast, tent with aluminum foil, and let rest for at least 10 minutes before carving and serving.

VIETNAMESE BARBECUED BEEF WITH LEMONGRASS AND PEANUT SAUCE

SERVES 6 TO 8 AS A FIRST COURSE OR HORS D'OEUVRE

DIRECT HEAT

An exciting finger food with the flavors of Southeast Asia, this recipe comes from an immigrant friend of mine, one of the last to get out of Saigon in the 1970s. The flavors of the lemongrass and fish sauce, the textural elements of the peanuts, and the silkiness of the peanut sauce grace the quickly cooked beef skewers in a remarkable way. These are perfect for a party—I guarantee you that your guests will remember this dish.

FOR THE CHILE RUB

1 fresh serrano chile, minced
(wear gloves to prevent irritation)

2 garlic cloves, minced

2 stalks fresh lemongrass, trimmed
and finely chopped, or
2 tablespoons dried, soaked
in water for 30 minutes

2 shallots, finely chopped

2 tablespoons fish sauce

1 tablespoon fresh lime juice

1 tablespoon toasted sesame oil

¼ teaspoon freshly ground
black pepper

1 tablespoon water

1 pound rump or eye of round roast,
trimmed of fat

12 to 16 skewers (if using bamboo,
soak in water for 30 minutes)

2 tablespoons sesame seeds, toasted

¼ cup dry-roasted peanuts, chopped

Peanut Sauce (see p. 295)

1. To make the chile rub, in a food processor, combine the chile, garlic, lemongrass, shallots, fish sauce, lime juice, sesame oil, pepper, and water. Pulse 3 to 4 times, then blend until the mixture forms a thick paste, about 1 minute.

2. Cut the beef across the grain into very thin slices. (This is easier to do if it is slightly frozen; stick it in the freezer for 15 minutes before slicing.) Place the slices in a shallow glass dish and spread with the chile rub, mixing well to coat. Cover with plastic wrap and marinate for 30 minutes at room temperature or for up to 8 hours in the refrigerator.

3. Oil the grill racks. Preheat your grill using all burners set on high and with the lid closed for 10 to 12 minutes.

4. Remove the meat from the marinade and pat dry. Thread the pieces of meat onto the skewers and sprinkle on both sides with the sesame seeds. Cook the skewers with the lid closed for 1 to 2 minutes per side for rare or medium-rare. Remove from the grill and let cool. Sprinkle the chopped nuts over the meat and serve with the peanut sauce.

PLAIN AND SIMPLE VEAL T-BONES

Veal has a lot of character just by itself, and there are many times when I don't want to add a lot of outside flavors to it, but rather just let the meat and the heat of the grill do all the talking. Veal T-bones can be expensive, and I only buy them when they're on sale. But they're a wonderful treat and an elegant meal.

1. Brush the veal with the oil. Sprinkle with the salt, pepper, and thyme. Let sit at room temperature for about 30 minutes.

2. Oil the grill racks. Preheat your grill using all burners set on high and with the lid closed for 10 to 12 minutes.

3. Place the T-bones on the grill, close the lid, and cook for about 5 minutes. Turn the chops and lower the heat to medium, cover again, and cook for another 8 minutes for medium-rare to medium. The chops should give easily when touched and register about 140°F on an instant-read thermometer. Remove from the grill, let rest for 5 minutes, and serve.

SERVES 4

DIRECT HEAT

Four 10- to 12-ounce veal T-bones, about 1½ inches thick

1 tablespoon canola oil

Kosher salt

Freshly ground black pepper

1 tablespoon chopped fresh thyme leaves

DAD'S AMERICANIZED GREEK KEBABS

SERVES 6

DIRECT HEAT

¾ cup olive oil

¼ cup fresh lemon juice

¼ cup red-wine vinegar

1 tablespoon minced
    fresh rosemary leaves

2 teaspoons sugar

1 garlic clove, minced

½ teaspoon freshly ground
    black pepper

1 pound top sirloin, cut into
    ½-inch cubes

1 zucchini, cut into half-moons

1 small Italian eggplant,
    cut into wedges

2 tablespoons canola oil

Kosher salt

Freshly ground black pepper

6 skewers (if using bamboo,
    soak in water for 30 minutes)

3 cups cooked basmati rice

Tzatziki Sauce (p. 295)

My Dad worked for Frito-Lay® for some 37 years, and at one point he won a sales contest. The prize was a kebab grill. I had never seen anything like it before and I've never seen anything like it since. It had an upright fire pit and the skewers were in an outside ring where you could turn them while they cooked. We didn't use it a lot but it was a big deal when we did. Then it sort of disappeared for over 20 years, until I cleaned out the attic and found it in almost mint condition. While today I tend to prefer lamb with Greek-style foods, Dad wouldn't allow lamb in our house. He had had too much mutton in England during World War II and refused to eat anything that came from that critter. But top sirloin roast stands in nicely for lamb, and the Greek-inspired marinade will excite your taste buds. I've added a few touches, but this is pretty close to the way I remember it from my elementary-school days.

1. In a small bowl, combine the olive oil, lemon juice, vinegar, rosemary, sugar, garlic, and pepper. Pour into a large zip-top bag, setting aside ¼ cup. Add the beef cubes to the bag, seal it closed, and squish the marinade around the meat. Marinate for at least 1 hour, but if you can refrigerate it overnight it will be much better.

2. When you're ready to cook, remove the meat from the bag, discarding the marinade. Toss the vegetables in a medium bowl with the canola oil, salt, and pepper.

3. To assemble the kebabs, thread a cube of beef onto a skewer. Then add a chunk of zucchini and a wedge of eggplant. Add another piece of meat and continue this pattern with all 6 skewers. You want 3 to 4 cubes of meat per skewer and you want to end with a piece of meat. Make sure that you leave a little room between the ingredients on the skewers.

4. Oil the grill racks. Preheat your grill using all burners set on high and with the lid closed for 10 to 12 minutes.

5. Place the kebabs on the grill and brush with some of the reserved marinade. Close the lid and cook for 3 to 4 minutes, then turn the skewers and brush with more marinade. Tongs are really the perfect tool to turn these boys. Continue cooking until the meat is rare to medium-rare, another 3 to 4 minutes. The vegetables should be cooked but still firm and the meat should give easily when pressed. Brush once more with the marinade and remove to a platter. Let sit for about 5 minutes, and then thread the meat and vegetables off the skewers onto a bed of rice. Serve with the tzatziki sauce on the side.

JEAN LYNN'S BEEF BRISKET, BY WAY OF KANSAS CITY

SERVES 10 TO 12, WITH LEFTOVERS

INDIRECT HEAT

FOR JEAN'S KANSAS CITY SAUCE

2 tablespoons margarine (not butter)

¼ cup finely chopped onion

1 garlic clove, crushed

1 cup ketchup

¼ cup packed brown sugar

¼ cup fresh lemon juice

1 tablespoon Worcestershire sauce

1 tablespoon yellow mustard

Hickory or mesquite wood chips

One 4- to 5-pound beef brisket

1 tablespoon kosher salt

½ tablespoon freshly ground black pepper

1 teaspoon granulated garlic

When Jean Lynn walks into the room, you might do a double take and swear that Catherine Deneuve is paying you a visit. With her gracious beauty and perfect manners, Jean can make you feel both at home and a friend instantly. Then you get to know the feisty and fun-loving women she actually is.

I wouldn't dream of serving this meat without the sauce. Jean tells me the original recipe came from a 30-year-old Real Lemon® cookbook, and she has tweaked it to what the sauce is today. The sweetness and the acidity marry with the boldness of the beef and its gentle smoky afternotes.

If you have never dealt with a brisket before, this recipe is a great place to start. It will ensure a superb result. You get the smoke flavor, and by using the oven you are free to do other things.

1. To make the sauce, melt the margarine in a small sauce-pan over medium heat. Add the onion and garlic and cook until soft but not colored. Add the ketchup, sugar, lemon juice, Worcestershire, and mustard. Bring to a boil, and then reduce the heat to a simmer. Cook, uncovered, for 15 to 20 minutes, or until the sauce has thickened.

2. Make a wood chip packet or two (see p. 16). Oil the grill racks. Add one packet to the grill and preheat your grill using all burners set on high and with the lid closed for 10 to 12 minutes.

3. When the grill is hot, cut off the center or back burner and adjust the heat to medium-high.

4. Sprinkle the brisket evenly and on both sides with the salt, pepper, and granulated garlic. Place the brisket on the grill away from the direct heat, close the lid, and smoke for 1 to 1½ hours.

5. In the meantime, preheat your oven to 250°F. Remove the brisket from the grill and wrap tightly in aluminum foil. Place on a baking sheet and put in the oven. (If you prefer, you can do this on your gas grill. Just make sure you have *plenty* of gas and you adjust your temperature so it is very low. Do not add any more wood chips at this point.) Roast for about 5 hours or longer, or until the brisket is tender. Let sit for 10 minutes. Unwrap the brisket carefully, because juices will have accumulated and there may be hot steam as well. Slice the brisket across the grain. Serve with the sauce.

VEAL CHOPS WITH WORCESTERSHIRE-HORSERADISH GLAZE AND SAGE BUTTER

Sometimes I think I would just as soon have a veal chop as a good steak. Bold and lively flavors are a perfect foil against veal's tender pink meat. This recipe truly shines with the House-Made Worcestershire Sauce, but a quick substitute can be regular bottled Worcestershire sauce, heated until its volume has reduced by half. Fiery yet sweet, these chops are a gift to your taste buds. Oh, and make the full amount of the sage butter. You can use it for pasta, fish, and steak, and leftovers freeze well for up to 3 months.

1. Mash the butter and sage together in a small bowl with a fork. Season with salt and pepper and mix well. Scrape the butter mixture onto a piece of waxed paper, using the waxed paper to help you form the butter into a log. Wrap and refrigerate for at least 2 hours.

2. Stir together the Worcestershire, maple syrup, and horseradish in another small bowl. Add pepper to taste. This glaze can be made up to 2 days in advance. If you make it ahead, cover and refrigerate until ready to use.

3. Oil the grill racks. Preheat your grill using all burners set on high and with the lid closed for 10 to 12 minutes.

4. Brush the veal chops with the oil. Liberally season them with salt and pepper. Place the chops on the grill, close the lid, and cook for about 4 minutes. Reduce the heat to medium, turn the chops over, and continue cooking for another 8 minutes. During the last 5 minutes, spoon on the glaze. The chops are done when they give easily to the touch and register about 140°F on an instant-read thermometer. Remove the chops from the grill and top each with about a tablespoon of the sage butter. Allow the chops to rest and the butter to start melting for about 5 minutes. Serve with any additional glaze on the side.

SERVES 4

DIRECT HEAT

¾ cup (1½ sticks) unsalted butter, at room temperature

3 tablespoons finely chopped fresh sage

Kosher salt

Freshly ground black pepper

¼ cup Jason Smith's House-Made Worcestershire Sauce (p. 296)

1 tablespoon pure maple syrup

2 tablespoons drained prepared horseradish

Four 14- to 16-ounce bone-in rib veal chops

2 tablespoons canola oil

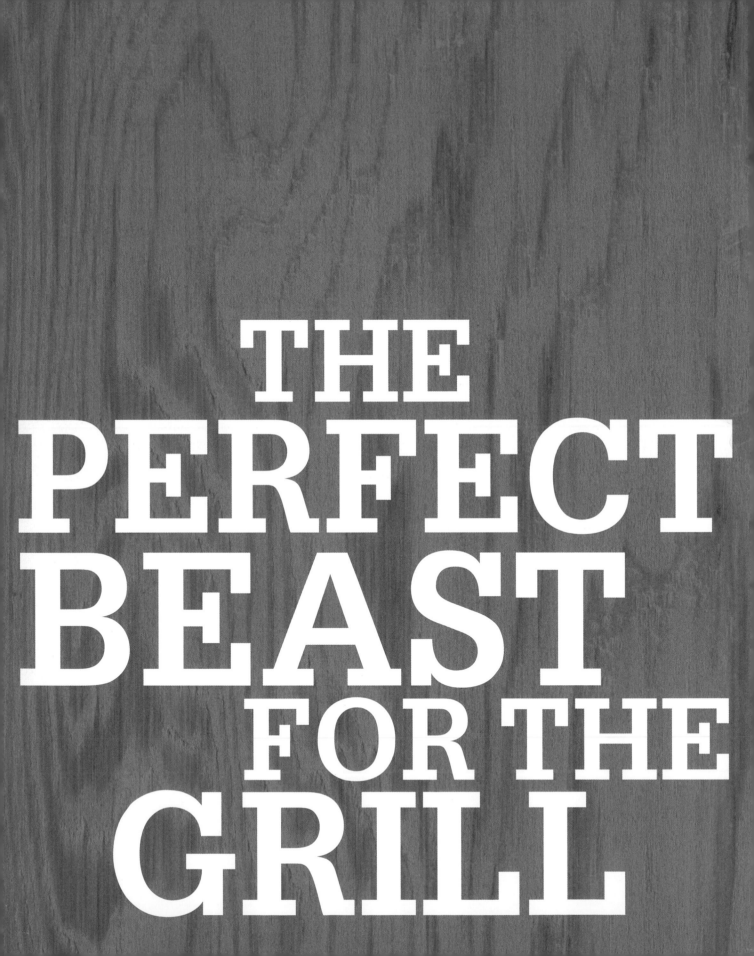

THE PERFECT BEAST FOR THE GRILL

PORK

BARBECUED SPARERIBS
with Apple Cider "Mop" 70

Sweet Heat Country-Style
PORK RIBS 72

Smoky Charred
PORK TENDERS 73

BABY BACK RIBS with
Coffee Barbecue Sauce 74

Fred's Finest
BABY BACK RIBS 76

Cuban-Style
BABY BACK RIBS with
Guava Glaze *Costillitas* 78

South Florida–Style
PORK ROAST 80

SOUTHERN TENDER 82

"YAKITORI" PORK with
Japanese Gremolata 84

Tamarind-Glazed
PORK TENDERLOIN with
Pear Marmalade 86

Robin Kline's Surprising
PORK TENDERLOIN 89

Smoky Charred
PORK TENDERS 73

Fred's Ultimate **SMOKED
PORK SHOULDER** 91

Western Tennessee–Style
BONE-IN PORK RIB CHOPS
94

Maple-Kissed **PORK CHOPS**
96

Laughing Cheese-Stuffed
PORK CHOPS 97

ALL CUTS OF PORK are the gas griller's ideal canvas. You can rub pork, brine it, sauce it, smoke it, and paint it in so many different "colors" of flavor. It's impossible to sum up in one chapter or even in a lifelong study all of the ways to cook all of the different cuts of pork. This is the ultimate chapter for experimentation, and I hope that you will do just that. And contrary to what many aficionados believe, a gas grill can hold its own with a charcoal grill on just about any pork preparation.

This gold standard of the grill takes on many forms and shapes as well as textures and flavors. From the leanest and most tender loin to the hind quarter of ham and shoulder, pork absorbs the rustic spices of an American barbecue as well as the gentle nuances of European- or Asian-inspired enhancements and the heady garlic-lime mojo from Cuba and other Hispanic cultures. Pork is naturally juicy, yet fear of fat has created breeding methods that produce leaner pigs, so pork isn't quite as forgiving as it once was, and care must be taken to match the cut of pork to the grilling method. Whether you are cooking pork chops, ribs, or a butt, developing your pork-grilling skills will yield meals of significant joy.

Where I come from, "barbecue" is a noun, a word for pork that is cooked slowly over low heat and often smoked. (I've always thought it was interesting that hickory wood seems to be the preferred smoking medium, since for de-

cades before hogs were domesticated and commercially raised, their diet was primarily hickory nuts.)

Barbecue is critical to southern politics. In the core southern states, any candidate running for office, whether local, state, or national, will eat his or her weight in some form of barbecue by campaign's end. Barbecue, and for the most part all facets of pork, crosses all social, cultural, and economic boundaries. It is the most democratic of meats.

Like the blues, barbecue is about as American as you can get. While we've integrated many foods from around the world, the idea of cooking a pig over an open flame is truly ours. Barbecued pork and the seasonings that go with it are sources of huge regional pride and constant bickering. Here's my plan to stop all this. Good barbecue is good barbecue, no matter where it's from or how it's prepared. To deny yourself great Memphis ribs

...DEVELOPING YOUR PORK-GRILLING SKILLS WILL YIELD MEALS OF SIGNIFICANT JOY

because you were born in eastern North Carolina is not only stupid, it's a sin. Our job as grillers of excellence is to rid the world of badly cooked pork. Wander through this chapter to find nirvana at the grill. Everything on the hog is good.

IN THE MARKET

When shopping for pork you won't find grades like Prime, Choice, and Select. The USDA grades pork from 1 to 4, with 1 being the top and 4 being the lowest grade. This grading system is about fat-to-lean ratio, and grade 1 is the leanest group of pork. The good news about this grading system is that most all pork sold at the butcher shop or your supermarket is number 1 grade.

Look for pork that ranges from a white-pink to a reddish pink and has been well trimmed, with almost no grain. The fat should be creamy white. The exception is some of the larger cuts of pork like the butt or picnic, where the grain is noticeable and the meat is a darker pink to almost red. Any pork that is super-pale or wet looking needs to be avoided.

Shop the sales for pork. Many cuts, like baby back and spareribs, Boston butt, picnics, hams, and even pork tenderloins and whole loins are shrink-wrapped in Cryovac, making them perfect candidates for the freezer. Most of these cuts will freeze nicely for three to four months. And believe me, baby back ribs that cost $1.99 a pound just seem to taste better than the ones you paid for at $3.99 a pound.

MATCHING CUT TO METHOD

The most important key to success with pork is knowing how different parts of the animal react with different cooking methods. The loin, which is located on either side of the backbone from the shoulder to the hind leg, is the most expensive but also the leanest and most tender

THE RIGHT CUT
FOR THE RIGHT METHOD These are guidelines only; specific recipes may vary.

THE TENDER CUTS Direct Heat	THE TENDER LARGE CUTS Use a combination of direct and indirect heat	RIBS Use a combination of direct and indirect heat	LOW AND SLOW Low Indirect Heat
Pork tenderloin Bone-in pork chop Boneless pork chop Country-style ribs Ham steak Shoulder blade steak Sirloin chop	Boneless pork loin roast Rack of pork Sirloin roast Cured ham	Baby back ribs Spareribs	Boston butt Picnic shoulder Fresh ham Pork belly

of all the cuts. This is not what you use to make barbecue. Here you will find my personal favorites, rib chops, T-bone pork chops, and the tenderloin, as well as the super-popular baby back ribs. With the exception of baby backs, cuts from the loin typically benefit from direct heat and quick cooking, but because of their leanness they also get happy when brined.

Along the side of the pig we find the belly. Gourmet chefs are "discovering" this cut and it is fast becoming their darling, but when you smoke it, it's America's favorite breakfast treat—bacon. Pork belly is a fatty and rich cut that can take to the grill with a little indirect cooking in a flavorful liquid.

Also from this area are the spareribs, which usually have flank or brisket attached. When the flank or brisket is removed, spareribs magically become St. Louis ribs. I tend to buy spareribs, not St. Louis ribs, although when I cook spareribs I will remove the flank from the rear of the rib to promote even cooking. (I'll then throw these half-pound pieces in

a freezer bag to save for another day. They're delicious seasoned as you would ribs but cooked over direct heat, or cook them as you would boneless pork chops.) Both styles of ribs demand an indirect cooking method. Spareribs are longer than baby backs and have less meat, but what they lack in meat they more than make up for in flavor. To be honest with you, I buy what's on sale, because baby backs and spareribs are both delicious.

You will also see pork ribs labeled "country-style," which I approach in a totally different manner. These ribs have more in common with a pork chop than with other ribs, and I cook them as I would most leaner pork chops, over direct heat.

From the hindquarter of the hog we find the ham, and from the front quarter, the shoulder. The shoulder in most supermarkets is divided into two pieces, the butt end or Boston butt as it is sometimes called, and the picnic or, if it's sold already smoked and cured, picnic ham. I know that the "butt" sounds like it

HERITAGE PORK

DURING THE DARK YEARS when "fat" was considered an ugly word, many pork producers began to breed hogs with leaner meat. They did a great job of producing lean, pinky white cuts of pork—which at the same time significantly reduced the flavor and moisture content of the meat. It's funny how things run in a circle, because today heritage pork is the most sought after of any hog. Heritage pork is simply from older breeds of pig that are being raised in a very natural environment with diets similar to those of a century ago. These hogs have a higher fat content and more flavor than most commercially raised hogs. Cuts from these animals are also more expensive and demand a trip to a specialty butcher shop or a farmers' market, or they can be ordered online. One of the best sources for heritage pork is Flying Pigs Farm in the Batten Kill River Valley area of New York. Check out their website at www.flyingpigsfarm.com or, if you're in New York City, look for them at the Union Square Greenmarket in Manhattan and the Grand Army Plaza Greenmarket in Brooklyn. Also check with your state's agricultural department. Many heritage pork farms are cropping up throughout the country.

Don't confuse heritage pork with premium producers like Niman Ranch. The farms that produce for the Niman Ranch brand are held to strict methods of raising their animals that result in superior pork in flavor and texture, much like certified Angus beef is superior to regular supermarket beef. But this premium pork is not necessarily from heritage breeds of pig.

A BASIC
BRINE

Combine 4 cups water (or a mixture of water, beer, vinegar, or fruit juice) with ¼ cup kosher salt and ¼ cup sugar or other sweetener, such as molasses or honey, in a small saucepan. Place over medium heat and stir until the sugar has dissolved. Remove from the heat and add 1 cup ice cubes. Let the brine cool, then pour over up to 5 pounds of meat in a large zip-top plastic bag. If you're brining chops or a tenderloin, refrigerate for no more than two hours. Larger cuts can be brined overnight. You can also use this as an injecting solution, but cut the amount of salt in half.

should come from the rear of the pig, not the front, but I wasn't consulted when they were naming these cuts! Shoulder cuts as well as the ham were made for low and slow cooking, and lots of smoke. Their high fat content keeps them moist and juicy during the long cooking time, with no loss of flavor. Here's where that delicious meal of pulled pork originates—what, for me anyway, is barbecue.

BRINES AND INJECTIONS

Throughout this chapter you'll see recipes that use brines and injection solutions. Both add flavor and tenderness to a variety of pork cuts, but brines work from the outside in and take more time to work their magic. Brining and injecting give you a little fudge factor on keeping a lean and typically dry cut of pork moist and tender.

Brines are not much more than salt, sugar, and water, but you can adjust the proportions or add other flavorings and seasonings if necessary. I tend to use a ratio of 1 part salt and 1 part sugar to 16 parts liquid and let the pork sit in this solution, refrigerated, for no longer than 24 hours. Smaller pieces of meat such as tenderloins and pork chops benefit from a briefer brining of one to two hours. I don't always brine pork loin chops and tenderloins, but many folks do. Never season any brined food with additional salt until after you've cooked it, unless you like your tongue fat and your joints puffy.

Injections are the new secret weapon on the competitive barbecue circuit. When Chris Lily of Big Bob Gibson's Barbecue in Decatur, Alabama, took home the crown with pulled pork at the Memphis in May International Festival℠ (the Super Bowl of barbecue contests) by injecting his shoulders with a solution of vinegar, apple juice, salt, and sugar, he set a new standard. When grilling shoulders or butts for pulled pork barbecue, I highly recommend using an injection of some kind. While the new gas grills are fantastic at being able to replicate

A QUICK REFRESHER
ON COOKING TIMES

Also be sure and see p. 68. Those are guidelines only; specific recipes may vary.

THE CUT	THICKNESS OR WEIGHT	TOTAL GRILLING TIME	INTERNAL TEMPERATURE (Before Resting)	RESTING TIME
CHOPS	About 1 in. thick	10-15 minutes	160°F New thinking: 145°F	5 minutes
FRESH HAM	12-17 pounds	4-6 hours	160°F	20 minutes
BONELESS LOIN ROAST	3-5 pounds	1-1¼ hours	160°F New thinking: 145°F	10-15 minutes
BONE-IN RIB ROAST	4-6 pounds	1½-2 hours	160°F New thinking: 145°F	At least 10-15 minutes
RIBS	3-4 pounds	1½-2 hours	160°-170°F	5 minutes
WHOLE TENDERLOINS	¾-1 pound	20-30 minutes	160°F New thinking: 145°F	5 minutes

the taste of old-fashioned smoked barbecue, the additional liquid introduced through the injection is the backyard grill meister's key to perfect barbecue. Be sure and check my personal recipe on p. 91 for an even more interesting twist on the phenomenon.

SMOKING IS GOOD STUFF

Real barbecue is pork shoulders or whole hogs cooked over wood that has been burned down to embers, which slowly cooks the meat. The inherent factor of the wood smoke infuses the pork with flavor. Fortunately, we don't have to go through this difficult process to flavor with smoke. Wood chips and chunks, soaked in liquid and drained, come to our rescue as they smolder with the heat of the gas burners. Truth be known, this is the way most commercial barbecue is produced today.

While most of us think hickory when we think of smoked pork, hickory is in fact a bit strong. Try mixing some hickory and apple wood for a fabulous smoke tone to your pork. Check out p. 16 for more information about smoking.

...IF THE RIBS BEND EASILY, ALMOST 90 DEGREES, YOU'RE READY TO EAT.

WHEN IS IT DONE?

The USDA recommends that all pork be cooked to well-done, or about 170°F. Again, this is to protect us from anything that might cause us ill. All bacteria (including trichinae, the nasty bug from our parents' day that causes trichinosis) die at temperatures around 140°F. Most chefs and cooking school instructors agree that pork today, particularly loin and chops, is best served in the 150°F to 160°F range, which means that there is still some pink in the center and the juices have not all been driven out by excess heat. Don't forget that the temperature will increase by 5°F to 10°F during the resting time.

This temperature range does not apply when you're in the act of low and slow cooking. On a smoked pork shoulder, 160°F will not give you the falling-off-the-bone tenderness that's expected for barbecue, nor will you be pleased with the results of ribs at that temperature. You can experiment with your own likes, but 170°F to 190°F seem to be the best internal temperature for these items.

You really don't need a thermometer to know when a rack of ribs is done. Judge it exactly the way the pit masters of Memphis would do: Lift the rib with a pair of tongs, and if the ribs bend easily, almost 90 degrees, you're ready to eat (see the photo on the facing page).

BARBECUED SPARERIBS WITH APPLE CIDER "MOP"

SERVES 4
INDIRECT HEAT

1 tablespoon kosher salt

1 tablespoon chili powder

2 teaspoons granulated garlic

2 teaspoons paprika

1 teaspoon dried oregano

½ teaspoon freshly ground
  black pepper

Two 3- to 4-pound racks spareribs

FOR THE
APPLE CIDER MOP

1 cup apple cider

¼ cup apple-cider vinegar

¼ cup mustard (use your favorite)

2 tablespoons tamari

2 tablespoons Worcestershire sauce

1 teaspoon kosher salt

1 teaspoon hot sauce
  (use your favorite)

In barbecue circles, the word "mop" has a different meaning: It isn't what you do to the kitchen floor, it's what championship barbecuers do to the meat as it cooks. A mop is really nothing more than a thin basting sauce, with a consistency not unlike what you brush on your Thanksgiving turkey. A mop does add magnificent essence to many grilled items, especially pork shoulders and ribs, and most barbecue champions view it as their secret weapon. This recipe is fairly straightforward and a good one for honing your "championship" grilling skills.

1. In a small bowl, combine the salt, chili powder, garlic, paprika, oregano, and pepper and stir with your fingertips or a spoon.

2. Put the spareribs, meaty side up, on a baking sheet. Following the line of fat that separates the meaty ribs from the tougher tips at the base of each rack, cut off the tips. Turn each rack over. Cut off the flap of meat attached in the center of each rack. Also cut off the flap of meat that hangs below the shorter end of the ribs. (Reserve the tips and meaty flaps and cook as you would boneless pork chops.) Remove the thin membrane from the back of each rack.

3. Heavily sprinkle the rub mixture on both sides of the ribs. (You probably won't use all of it. Store any leftovers in an airtight container for 6 weeks.) Then give your ribs a massage, working the spices into the surface of the meat. Allow the ribs to stand at room temperature for 20 to 30 minutes before grilling.

4. Oil the grill racks. Preheat your grill using all burners set on high and with the lid closed for 10 to 12 minutes.

5. When the grill is hot, cut off the center or back burner and adjust your heat to low.

6. Place the ribs, bone side down, over the indirect section of your grill. Close the lid and cook the ribs for 1 hour.

7. While the ribs cook, put your mop together. Combine the cider, vinegar, mustard, tamari, Worcestershire, salt, and hot sauce in a medium saucepan. Place the pan over high heat and bring to a boil. Remove the pan from the heat and reserve. After the ribs have been grilling for an hour, baste them with the mop. Continue to baste every 30 minutes for another 1½ to 2 hours, or until the meat has shrunk back slightly from the rib bones and a rib can be easily torn off with your fingers. The total grilling time will be 2½ to 3 hours.

8. Transfer the ribs to a clean baking sheet and lightly brush with some of the remaining mop. Tightly cover with aluminum foil, allowing the ribs to steam a bit, then remove the foil and let the ribs rest for 30 minutes. Cut the ribs between the bones and serve hot or at room temperature.

AT THE
TABLE

Mops are great ways to lightly flavor food and keep the food super moist while grilling. Use with chicken, thick pork chops, pork roasts, and ribs.

Leaving out the apple cider and replacing with bourbon develops an excellent mop for beef roasts.

SWEET HEAT COUNTRY-STYLE PORK RIBS

SERVES 6 TO 8
DIRECT AND INDIRECT HEAT

2 very ripe papayas, peeled, seeded, and coarsely chopped

½ cup dry white wine

¼ cup fresh lime juice

3 tablespoons grated fresh ginger

2 tablespoons tamari

2 teaspoons Chinese five-spice powder

2 teaspoons hot Hungarian paprika

5 to 6 pounds country-style pork ribs

Country-style pork ribs are almost a pork chop by virtue of where they are cut from the animal. The rib is small, with abundant meat, and the taste leans more toward a pork chop. It's just a different animal entirely from spareribs or baby backs. In this version sweet and hot combine to make an interesting and delicious grilling experience.

1. Put the papayas, wine, lime juice, ginger, tamari, five-spice powder, and paprika into a food processor. Pulse the mixture 4 or 5 times until combined and smooth, then let the machine run for about 30 seconds to smooth the paste a little more.

2. Remove the membranes from the back of the ribs. Put the ribs in a jumbo-size zip-top bag and pour in the papaya marinade, squishing to coat the meat. Close the bag. Put in the refrigerator for at least 4 hours and up to overnight. Turn the bag every time you open the refrigerator.

3. Oil the grill racks. Preheat your grill using all burners set on high and with the lid closed for 10 to 12 minutes.

4. When the grill is hot, cut off the center or back burner and adjust your heat to medium-high.

5. Remove the ribs from the marinade and pat the ribs dry. Discard the marinade. Place the ribs, meat side down, over the direct heat of the grill. Close the lid and cook for about 10 minutes, until good caramelization begins to show. Remove the ribs to the indirect section of the grill, close the lid, and continue cooking for about 1½ hours, turning every 15 minutes. The ribs are done when firm to the touch or, since these ribs are so meaty, check the internal temperature for 160°F. Remove from the grill to a cutting board, cut apart the ribs, and serve.

SMOKY CHARRED PORK TENDERS

Cocoa powder and cinnamon aren't just for desserts or sweet beverages. When you use cocoa powder in savory recipes, it gives an added depth to the dish rather than a chocolate taste, and here the cinnamon rounds out the chipotle and cumin. Together, they are the big ingredients in this awesome dish. I first developed this recipe for a story I was writing about tailgating.

1. Put the pork in a large zip-top bag. Put all the remaining ingredients in a food processor. Pulse to combine, and then run the machine for about a minute to puree. Pour the marinade over the pork and close the bag. Squish the marinade around the pork to coat. Let stand at room temperature for 45 minutes, or stick the pork in the refrigerator for up to 4 hours.

2. Oil the grill racks. Preheat your grill using all burners set on high and with the lid closed for 10 to 12 minutes.

3. Remove the pork from the bag and discard the marinade. Pat dry with paper towels. Drizzle each tenderloin with a little oil and brush or rub over the surface. Place on the grill, close the lid, and cook, turning occasionally, so that all sides are evenly browned, 15 to 20 minutes. The pork is done when it yields slightly when pressed and an instant-read thermometer reads 145°F to 150°F. Remove the tenders to a cutting board and let rest for at least 5 minutes before slicing. Slice at an angle into ¼-inch-thick slices. Serve.

SERVES 4 TO 6
DIRECT HEAT

2½ to 3 pounds pork tenderloins, silverskin removed

1 canned chipotle chile in adobo sauce

¼ cup fresh orange juice

2 tablespoons sugar

1 tablespoon canola oil, plus more to brush on the pork

1 teaspoon ground cinnamon

1 teaspoon ground cumin

1 teaspoon unsweetened natural cocoa powder

1 teaspoon kosher salt

¼ teaspoon freshly ground black pepper

BABY BACK RIBS WITH COFFEE BARBECUE SAUCE

SERVES 6

INDIRECT HEAT

6 racks baby back ribs, roughly
    12 pounds

Kosher salt

Freshly ground black pepper

¼ cup water

**FOR THE COFFEE
    BARBECUE SAUCE**

¼ cup vegetable oil

1 medium onion, chopped

20 to 30 garlic cloves,
    coarsely chopped

¼ cup chopped fresh cilantro leaves

1 fresh jalapeño chile, seeded
    and chopped (wear gloves
    to prevent irritation)

1 teaspoon ground cumin

1 teaspoon chili powder

1 teaspoon crushed red chile flakes

¾ cup roasted coffee beans

Grated zest of 1 lemon

Juice of 1 lemon

¼ cup packed dark brown sugar

¾ cup red-wine vinegar

1 cup ketchup

1 tablespoon kosher salt

1 tablespoon freshly ground
    black pepper

Three 6-ounce cans tomato paste

Many of this country's greatest chefs are now flavoring their barbecue sauces with coffee. Of course, according to my friend "Cotton" Morgan of Katy, Texas, folks in that area have been throwing leftover coffee into barbecue sauces for years. Cotton thinks that it harkens back to the old chuck-wagon days, and although coffee sauces are usually paired with beef, Cotton uses this sauce on pork and quail, too. This recipe is an amalgamation of two or three different barbecue sauce recipes. It's bold and fun and I think you'll like it.

1. Oil the grill racks. Preheat your grill using all burners set on high and with the lid closed for 10 to 12 minutes.

2. When the grill is hot, cut off the center or back burner and adjust your heat to medium-high.

3. Remove the membranes from the back of the ribs. Liberally season the ribs with salt and pepper. Combine the ribs with the water in a disposable roasting pan and cover loosely with foil, or wrap the ribs and water in a double layer of heavy-duty foil. Place the ribs on the indirect section of your grill and close the lid. Adjust the heat to medium and monitor your temperature with an oven thermometer, maintaining a temperature close to 300°F. Let the ribs cook for about 1½ hours. Remove from their packaging and place on a baking sheet.

4. While the ribs are cooking, make the sauce. Heat the oil in a large saucepan until it just shimmers. Add the onion, garlic, cilantro, jalapeño, cumin, chili powder, crushed red chile flakes, coffee beans, and lemon zest. Cook this mixture, stirring, for about 2 minutes. Add the lemon juice, brown sugar, vinegar, and ketchup to the pot. Cook the mixture, stirring occasionally, until the liquid has reduced by one-quarter to one-half, about 15 minutes. Add the salt, pepper, and tomato paste. Stir to combine well. Cover and reduce the heat to a simmer. Cook for 1 to 1½ hours. Strain the solids from the sauce and set aside.

5. Turn all the burners on your grill to medium, including the ones you've cut off. Place the ribs, meat side down, on the grill, close the lid, and cook for about 5 minutes. Turn the ribs over and baste with the barbecue sauce. Cook for another 5 minutes. Repeat this process for a total of 20 minutes. Remove the ribs from the grill, cut into serving portions, and serve. Pass the remaining sauce at the table.

COOK
AHEAD

Most all ribs can be cooked until they are almost done and reserved at room temperature for an hour or so, or even refrigerated for three or four days or frozen for three months. Keeping some partially cooked ribs around is smart entertaining and good weeknight planning. Just finish the ribs with the sauce until heated through. And if you're craving ribs but the weather is not cooperating with using your grill, you can do step 2 in your oven. Just preheat it to 300°F and cook as directed.

FRED'S FINEST BABY BACK RIBS

SERVES 6

DIRECT HEAT, OR A COMBINATION OF DIRECT AND INDIRECT

6 racks baby back ribs, roughly 12 pounds (spareribs will also work)

¼ cup Dijon mustard

1 tablespoon brown sugar

1 tablespoon paprika

1 teaspoon chili powder

¼ teaspoon cayenne

¼ teaspoon kosher salt

Freshly ground black pepper

¼ cup water

1 cup barbecue sauce (use your favorite)

2 tablespoons honey, or as needed

No offense to those chicken folks, but here's the *real* "finger lickin' good" meal. These ribs are mouth-happy perfection. The recipe is my most requested (usually in a panic) from my newspaper column and took about 20 years to get the way it is today, yet I still tinker with it and encourage you to do the same. The key is slow-roasting heat combined with moisture to create steam that melts away some of the fat and softens the meat. I like to start these in the oven, so that's how I've written this recipe. If you prefer to do it entirely on the grill, try the method in the sidebar on the facing page. I also like to use thick tomato-based sauces with a little heat (Bull's-Eye and Kraft® bottled sauces work well), and some smoke flavor won't hurt. The final finish gives the ribs character.

1. Preheat your oven to 300°F.

2. Rinse the ribs and pat them dry. Remove the membranes from the back of the ribs. Place the ribs on a baking sheet and brush the ribs generously with the mustard. Combine the sugar, paprika, chili powder, cayenne, and salt in a small bowl. Sprinkle this mixture over both sides of the ribs. Grind fresh pepper over the ribs.

3. Place the ribs in an aluminum roasting bag and add the water. Seal the bag tightly, place on a baking sheet, and put in the oven. Slowly cook the ribs for 45 minutes to 1 hour. Remove the bag from the oven and let the ribs cool in the roasting bag for 30 minutes. Open the bag away from you in case there is residual steam. (You can do this several days ahead and even freeze them at this point. If you do freeze them, let them cool completely in the roasting bag, then drain off any liquid, seal the bag well, and stick it in the freezer. Thaw before continuing with step 4.)

4. Oil the grill racks. Preheat your grill using all burners set on high and with the lid closed for 10 to 12 minutes.

5. When the grill is hot, reduce the heat to medium and place the ribs, meaty side down, on the grill. Close the lid and cook for about 15 minutes, then turn. Brush the seared side with the barbecue sauce, cover again, and cook for another 10 to 15 minutes. Turn, brush with sauce, cover, and let them enjoy the heat for another 10 minutes. Brush the same side with sauce again, cover, and cook for no more than 5 minutes. Uncover, drizzle the ribs with the honey, and let them stay on the heat a couple of minutes more to allow the honey to glaze. Remove and serve to hoots and hollers.

AT THE GRILL

In the past few years I've added a wrinkle to these ribs, and if you have the time, give this a try. Set your grill for indirect cooking. Add some wood chips or hunks of wood, like hickory or oak, to your smoke box, or make a foil-smoking packet. Let some smoke build in your grill, then place the ribs (brushed with the mustard and rub) on the grill, bone side down, and adjust the temperature to low. You want the temperature to stay at about 200°F, so check with an oven thermometer. Smoke for about 3 hours, replenishing the wood chips as needed. About every 45 minutes, spray the ribs with apple cider. The ribs are ready for the next step when you can grab them with a pair of tongs, lift them up, and they bend easily. Place them over direct heat and proceed with the sauce and honey, cooking the ribs for about 15 more minutes.

CUBAN-STYLE BABY BACK RIBS WITH GUAVA GLAZE *COSTILLITAS*

SERVES 4 TO 6

INDIRECT AND DIRECT HEAT

2 to 3 racks baby back ribs,
    4 to 6 pounds

2 cups packed light brown sugar

Juice of 2 lemons (reserve the rinds)

Juice of 2 limes (reserve the rinds)

2 tablespoons ground allspice

5 garlic cloves, crushed

1 medium onion, sliced

1 teaspoon kosher salt

2 cups water

FOR THE GUAVA GLAZE

½ cup guava jelly

½ cup packed light brown sugar

Juice of 1 lime

1 teaspoon apple-cider vinegar

1 teaspoon ground cumin

½ teaspoon kosher salt

This inspired Cuban recipe comes from my friends Lorenzo and Tracy. Here's another example where a gas grill is superior to charcoal in its ability to become two tools. We're actually going to use the grill as an oven in the beginning, and then as a grill to cook them over direct heat to get the caramelization that's so tasty from outdoor cooking. (If you are low on gas or if it's just cold outside, you can always use an oven heated to 300°F for the first part of the cooking process.) The guava glaze is extremely versatile. Use it on just about any form of pork, including tenderloin, loin roast, or chops, as well as on boneless, skinless chicken breasts or thighs—the list is long. Many supermarkets now stock guava jelly in their Hispanic foods sections, and believe it or not Smucker's also makes it. You can order it from their website.

1. Remove the white membrane from the back side of the ribs. If you desire, cut the racks in half.

2. In a 3-quart saucepan over medium heat, combine the brown sugar, lemon juice, lemon rinds, lime juice, lime rinds, allspice, garlic, onion, salt, and water. Cook for 3 to 5 minutes, stirring until the sugar has completely dissolved.

3. If using your oven, preheat it to 300°F. Otherwise, oil the grill racks. Preheat your grill using all burners set on high and with the lid closed for 10 to 12 minutes. Cut off one burner for indirect cooking and lower the heat to medium.

4. Place the ribs in a large baking dish (I use disposable aluminum pans for this) and pour the juice mixture over the ribs. Cover tightly with foil and put in the oven or on the indirect section of your grill. Close the lid and cook for 1 hour. Then remove the ribs from the pan, discard the juices and solids, and reserve the ribs until ready to finish on the grill. You can do this step up to 3 days in advance.

5. To make the guava glaze, combine the jelly, brown sugar, lime juice, vinegar, cumin, and salt in a small saucepan. Place over high heat and bring to a boil, stirring constantly. Reduce the heat to a simmer and cook for about 15 minutes, uncovered, stirring occasionally. Let cool to room temperature. Divide the mixture in half so that some of the glaze can be used to baste and you'll have some to pass at the table.

6. Relight the burner you turned off and place the ribs, meat side down, on the grill over direct heat. Close the lid and cook for about 5 minutes. Turn the ribs over and grill for another 5 minutes. Flip one more time and brush generously with the guava glaze. Cook for 2 to 3 minutes, turn over again, and brush the other side with the glaze. Cook for 2 to 3 minutes and remove to a platter. Cut into individual ribs if desired. Pass the reserved guava glaze at the table.

AT THE TABLE

These ribs are awesome when served with smashed and sautéed plantains. Just slice the fruit in ³⁄₄-inch pieces, flatten them slightly with the palm of your hand, and cook in canola oil or butter until warmed through and nicely browned on both sides. The sweet-no-sweet flavor is a natural with pork.

SOUTH FLORIDA–STYLE PORK ROAST

SERVES 8 TO 10

INDIRECT HEAT

One 5-pound boneless pork shoulder
    roast or Boston butt

Zest of 2 navel oranges

Juice of 2 navel oranges
    (about ¾ cup)

2 fresh jalapeño chiles, seeded,
    ribs removed, and diced
    (wear gloves to prevent irritation)

2 tablespoons coarsely chopped
    fresh thyme

2 tablespoons coarsely chopped
    fresh cilantro

1 tablespoon coarsely chopped
    fresh sage

5 to 6 garlic cloves, minced

2 tablespoons kosher salt

1 tablespoon freshly ground
    black pepper

¼ cup olive or canola oil

From the southern Caribbean to south Florida, a pork shoulder roast is a special-occasion dish. This one marries the flavors of the region and gives you something to celebrate, or lets you take a mini-vacation without leaving your grill. The pork can be served either shredded or sliced. It reheats beautifully, so don't hesitate to make this in advance or over the weekend to serve a few days later. Black beans and yellow rice are the ideal side dishes.

1. Make ¼-inch diagonal cuts on all sides of the pork roast. Using a blender or food processor, combine the orange zest, orange juice, jalapeños, thyme, cilantro, sage, garlic, salt, and pepper, pulsing until well combined. With the machine running, slowly pour in the oil until the marinade has emulsified.

2. Pour some of the marinade over the roast and massage into the meat, taking care to work it down into the slits. Put the roast in a large zip-top bag, pour the remaining marinade over the roast, close the bag, and marinate in the refrigerator for 4 to 6 hours.

3. Take the roast out of the refrigerator at least an hour before you plan to cook. Remove from the bag, discarding the marinade. Place the roast on a rack inside a disposable roasting pan.

4. Oil the grill racks. Preheat your grill using all burners set on high and with the lid closed for 10 to 12 minutes.

5. When the grill is hot, cut off the center or back burner and adjust your heat to medium-high.

6. Place the pan over the indirect section of the grill. Reduce the heat to medium and close the lid. You want to maintain a temperature inside the grill of about 325°F. Cook without peeking for about 2 hours. Then cover the roast with aluminum foil and continue cooking for another 2 hours, or until the internal temperature has reached 180°F and the meat is fork-tender.

7. Remove from the grill and place on a platter. If shredding, allow the pork to cool for about 5 minutes, and then use two forks to shred the meat. If slicing, let the roast sit for 10 to 15 minutes before carving.

8. In the meantime, add a little water or additional orange juice to the roasting pan and place back over the heat. Using a spatula, scrape up the brown bits, and then pour these juices back over the shredded or sliced pork.

AT THE TABLE

Both Robin Klein's Surprising Pork Tenderloin on p. 89, and the one for Smoky Charred Pork Tenders on p. 73, are perfect for a tailgate. To adapt the recipes, for cooking on the road simply season the tenderloins before you leave home, put the sauce in a Thermos® bottle, and take 18 little mini sandwich buns along with you. After you cut the pork, put 3 to 4 slices in each little sandwich bun, sprinkle with cilantro, and garnish with a dollop of sauce. Your friends will be well fed and the folks around you in the parking lot will be jealous.

SOUTHERN TENDER

SERVES 4 TO 6
DIRECT HEAT

½ cup soy sauce

¼ cup packed brown sugar

½ teaspoon granulated garlic

½ teaspoon ground cinnamon

2 tablespoons dry sherry,
   such as oloroso

2 to 3 pounds pork loin,
   cut into 1-inch cubes

One 10-ounce jar currant jelly

1 tablespoon yellow or
   brown mustard

Green bell peppers, cut into squares
   (optional)

Cherry tomatoes (optional)

Onions, quartered (optional)

White or cremini mushrooms
   (optional)

Skewers (if using bamboo, soak in
   water for 30 minutes)

4 tablespoons (½ stick) unsalted
   butter, melted

At first glance this looks like just another pork kebab recipe. It's not. The currant jelly is the key to taking what could be a commonplace entrée and making it regal. Don't pass this recipe by. The judges at the North Carolina Pork Cookout praised this recipe that I've adapted from contestant John Adams.

1. Combine the soy sauce, brown sugar, granulated garlic, cinnamon, and sherry in a small bowl. Mix well. Put the pork cubes in a large zip-top bag and pour the marinade over the pork. Close the bag and squish the marinade around the meat. Put in the refrigerator for 4 hours, turning the bag occasionally.

2. Combine the currant jelly and mustard in a small saucepan. Set over low heat and gently cook until the jelly melts, but don't stir until it's almost entirely melted. Set aside at room temperature.

3. Oil the grill racks. Preheat your grill using all burners set on high and with the lid closed for 10 to 12 minutes.

4. Thread pork cubes and your choice of vegetables onto the skewers in an alternating pattern. Brush with the melted butter.

5. Place the skewers on the grill. Cook, turning every 3 to 4 minutes and basting with the jelly sauce. Lower your temperature if necessary to keep the jelly from burning. Grill for a total of about 15 minutes or until the pork is fairly firm to the touch. Remove from the grill, slide off the skewers, and serve immediately.

"YAKITORI" PORK WITH JAPANESE GREMOLATA

SERVES 4 TO 6
DIRECT HEAT

2 cups dry sherry, such as oloroso

1 cup tamari

4 tablespoons granulated sugar

2 tablespoons light brown sugar

4 tablespoons grated fresh ginger

3 garlic cloves, minced

3 scallions, coarsely chopped

2½ to 3 pounds pork tenderloins, silverskin removed

1 cup plum preserves, preferably red plum

1 tablespoon grated lemon zest

¼ cup dry roasted unsalted peanuts, chopped

¼ cup fresh cilantro leaves

IN THE KITCHEN

When you see the phrase "coats the back of the spoon," here's how to determine the sauce's thickness. Dip the spoon into the sauce, let most of it drip off, and then run your index finger across the back of the spoon. (Be careful—it may be hot!) If the trail your finger leaves holds, then the sauce is done.

Yakitori houses are so common in Japan that there's one section of Tokyo that has street after street full of these tiny restaurants, and each one might have 16 seats. Yakitori is basically anything cooked on a stick. The typical sauce used with it works extremely well with a whole pork tenderloin, which quite frankly is easier than all that skewering. Gremolata is an Italian garnish made of parsley, lemon zest, and garlic that is traditionally sprinkled over ossobuco. Here I have an Asian "gremolata" with peanuts, cilantro, and ginger. Don't skip this step. It adds volumes to the flavor of this dish.

1. In a medium saucepan, combine the sherry, tamari, both sugars, 2 tablespoons of the ginger, the garlic, and scallions. Place over high heat, bring to a boil, and then reduce the heat to medium-low and simmer for about 10 minutes. You want this sauce to reduce slightly, just barely coating the back of a spoon. Pour the sauce through a strainer and let cool. Divide the yakitori sauce in half.

2. Put the pork tenderloins in a large zip-top bag, then pour half the yakitori sauce over the pork. Close the bag and squish the marinade around to coat the pork. Put in the refrigerator and marinate for 1 to 2 hours.

3. Pour the remaining yakitori sauce into a small saucepan. Whisk in the plum preserves. Set over medium heat and bring to a simmer, whisking until the preserves dissolve. Reduce the heat so it is very low and cook the sauce slowly for about 20 minutes, stirring occasionally. The sauce should readily coat the back of a spoon, or have the viscosity of honey.

4. Oil the grill racks. Preheat your grill using all burners set on high and with the lid closed for 10 to 12 minutes.

5. Remove the pork tenderloins from the bag and discard the marinade. Place the pork on the grill and adjust the temperature to medium-high. Close the lid and cook, turning the tenderloins every 4 minutes. After 16 minutes, brush the tenderloins on all sides with some of the yakitori-plum sauce so that they are completely coated. Reserve the remaining yakitori-plum sauce for dipping. The tenderloin is done when it gives slightly to the touch or registers 145°F to 150°F on an instant-read thermometer. Remove from the grill to a cutting board and let rest for 5 to 10 minutes.

6. While the pork is resting, mix the lemon zest, peanuts, cilantro, and the remaining 2 tablespoons ginger in a small bowl. Slice the pork on the diagonal, transfer to a platter, and sprinkle with the gremolata. Serve with the reserved yakitori-plum sauce on the side.

TAMARIND-GLAZED PORK TENDERLOIN WITH PEAR MARMALADE

SERVES 4
DIRECT HEAT

FOR THE PEAR MARMALADE

One 2-inch piece fresh ginger, peeled and grated

½ cup water

Grated zest of 1 orange

2 tablespoons fresh orange juice

½ cup packed brown sugar

½ teaspoon pure vanilla extract

1 cinnamon stick, or ½ teaspoon ground cinnamon

1 tablespoon unsalted butter

4 Asian pears, or a combination of Bartlett and Asian pears, peeled, cored, and chopped into ½-inch pieces

FOR THE TAMARIND GLAZE

2 tablespoons tamarind paste

1 tablespoon water

1 tablespoon orange marmalade

½ teaspoon ground cinnamon

¼ cup Chardonnay or other dry white wine

Kosher salt

Freshly ground black pepper

Two 1-pound pork tenderloins, silverskin removed

1 tablespoon olive oil

I was a happy boy when tamarind paste and dried tamarind showed up in my local supermarket. No more trips to New York's Chinatown to find this interesting and amazing ingredient. You've been consuming tamarind since long before it was fashionable, most notably as a main ingredient in Worcestershire sauce. Tamarind crosses many cultures, and thanks to our melting pot, it has finally become part of the norm in this country. Another thing I like about this recipe is the pear marmalade. Quickly made marmalades and chutneys always enhance the flavors of grilled foods.

1. To make the marmalade, take a medium saucepan and combine the ginger, water, orange zest, orange juice, sugar, vanilla, cinnamon, butter, and pears. Place the pan over medium-high heat and bring to a boil. Reduce the heat, cover, and simmer for 3 to 5 minutes. Uncover and continue cooking, stirring occasionally, for 15 minutes or until the pears are soft but not mushy. Remove and discard the cinnamon stick. Let cool. The marmalade can be made up to 3 days in advance. Keep in the refrigerator, covered, but bring to room temperature before serving.

2. To make the glaze, combine the tamarind paste, water, marmalade, cinnamon, wine, salt, and pepper in a small bowl. Put the tenderloins in a large zip-top bag and pour the glaze over the meat. Squish the bag, coating the meat with the glaze. Close the bag and leave at room temperature for 1 hour, but no more than 1½ hours. Otherwise, refrigerate for up to 8 hours.

3. Oil the grill racks. Preheat your grill using all burners set on high and with the lid closed for 10 to 12 minutes.

4. Remove the tenderloins from the glaze and pat dry. Discard the glaze. Lightly brush the tenderloins with the oil and place them on the grill. Close the lid and cook the meat for about 30 minutes, turning every 10 minutes or so. The tenderloins are done when they are firm but yield to the touch, they are slightly pink in the center, and a meat thermometer registers 145°F to 150°F.

5. Remove the tenderloins to a platter and let sit for 10 minutes. Cut into medallions and serve with the pear marmalade.

ROBIN KLINE'S SURPRISING PORK TENDERLOIN

Fellow food writer Robin Kline lives in Iowa, where pork is king. This recipe was a surprise hit of my book *Barbecue Nation*. People would look at the sauce and go, "How in the world can that be good?" But one bite was all it took. In fact, I remember doing this recipe at the NBC affiliate in Knoxville, Tennessee, and the weather guy came and pigged out on this tenderloin. I knew it had to be good when the producer told me, "He never eats anything anybody cooks on TV. Ever." Seems like a pretty good recommendation to me.

1. Pat the tenderloins dry with paper towels. In a small bowl, combine the paprika, salt, both sugars, chili powder, cumin, and pepper. Rub about 2 tablespoons of this mixture on each tenderloin, giving it a good massage with the spices.

2. In a small saucepan, stir together the barbecue sauce and dressing. Set over low heat, stirring until just warm. Set aside.

3. Oil the grill racks. Preheat your grill using all burners set on high and with the lid closed for 10 to 12 minutes.

4. Place the pork on the grill and cook for 15 to 20 minutes total, turning occasionally to brown evenly on all sides. The pork is done when it yields slightly to pressure or an instant-read thermometer reads 145°F to 150°F. A few minutes before removing the pork from the grill, brush each tenderloin with the jelly and allow it to glaze. Transfer the pork to a cutting board and let stand for 5 to 10 minutes. Slice on the diagonal and arrange on a platter. Sprinkle the meat with the cilantro and serve with the sauce on the side.

SERVES 6 TO 8
DIRECT HEAT

Three 1-pound pork tenderloins, silverskin removed

2 tablespoons paprika

2 teaspoons kosher salt

2 teaspoons light brown sugar

2 teaspoons granulated sugar

2 teaspoons chili powder

2 teaspoons ground cumin

2 teaspoons freshly ground black pepper

½ cup smoky, tomato-based barbecue sauce, such as East Tennessee–Style Barbecue Sauce (p. 288) or bottled sauce (use your favorite)

½ cup ranch salad dressing

½ cup hot pepper jelly, at room temperature

½ cup chopped fresh cilantro leaves

FRED'S ULTIMATE SMOKED PORK SHOULDER

Few of us will ever cook a whole hog, but we all have the ability to smoke a pork shoulder. This recipe started out as strictly a North Carolina–style barbecue—remember, *barbecue* is a noun—and over the years it has evolved from low-and-slow–cooked smoked pork in a vinegary sauce to a meat that works as a base for all the regional sauces, including Memphis and Georgia as well. The rub is more Memphis, and it helps produce a better "outside brown," those prized bits of char that get chopped into pork barbecue. You may find the use of a Cuban ingredient weird here, but smoked or roasted pork shoulder is a favorite in Cuba. Like so many good recipes, this happened almost by mistake, but as I continued to tinker with it and serve it to a multitude of different people, I found that indeed I might have hit on the ultimate recipe.

You could use a whole shoulder, a Boston butt, or a fresh picnic here. Injecting whole hogs and pork shoulders is all the rage now, with good reason. It helps to keep the pork moist and get flavor from the inside out. This makes a lot, but it freezes beautifully.

1. Mix the paprika, sugar, salt, both peppers, granulated garlic, and mustard together in a small bowl. Rub this mixture all over the pork. Wrap in plastic wrap and refrigerate overnight. (I like to reserve a tablespoon or more of this rub before using it on the pork so that I can sprinkle the finished pulled pork with it.)

2. At least 1½ hours before you plan to put the pork on, remove it from the refrigerator. Take an injection syringe and pull the mojo up into the tube. Plunge the injector into the pork and then slowly push in the mojo as you move the needle back toward you and out of the meat. You want to do it this way so that you don't have these huge puddles and so that the mojo is more evenly distributed. Repeat this several more times at random spots until the mojo is gone.

SERVES 12 TO 15

INDIRECT HEAT

1 tablespoon paprika

1 tablespoon sugar

1 tablespoon kosher salt

1 tablespoon freshly ground black pepper

1 teaspoon freshly ground white pepper

1 teaspoon granulated garlic

1 teaspoon dry mustard

One 5- to 7-pound bone-in Boston butt or picnic shoulder

1 cup prepared Cuban mojo marinade, strained (I prefer Nellie and Joe's brand)

6 to 8 cups hickory or apple wood chips, soaked in water for at least 1 hour

Your choice of barbecue sauce, such as Eastern North Carolina (p. 290), Lexington (p. 290), Memphis (p. 293), or Kansas City (p. 291)

3. Oil the grill racks. Preheat your grill using all burners set on high and with the lid closed for 10 to 12 minutes.

4. When the grill is hot, cut off the center or back burner and adjust your heat to medium-high.

5. Drain the wood chips. If your grill is equipped with a smoke box, fill it with the chips. If not, divide your wood chips among six foil packets (see p. 16), and place one packet at one end of the grill while it preheats. When the grill is ready, cut off all but one burner and turn it to low. Place the pork away from the direct heat. Place a disposable 9x13-inch aluminum pan opposite the smoke source and fill the pan halfway with water. If your grill has a smoke box with its own separate burner, cut off all the burners except that one and turn it to low. Cover the grill and go drink a beer.

6. Typically, smoking chips or even chunks will last 15 to 20 minutes. The pork will gather most of its smoke flavor in the first 2 hours of cooking. Every 20 minutes, working as quickly as you can to keep the smoke from escaping, replace your smoke packet or the chips in the smoker box and add water to the aluminum pan if necessary. When you've used all the chips, try not to open the grill again until the barbecue is close to being done, which will take 4 to 5 hours longer. The best clue that the barbecue is done is to take a pair of tongs and grab the flat bone that runs through the center of the meat. If it moves easily or you can pull it out, then the pork is done. Sometimes in windy conditions or when it's cold, it can take up to 7 hours for a shoulder to magically become barbecue. The internal temperature should be 180°F to 190°F.

7. When you've determined that the barbecue is ready, pull it off the grill into a large roasting pan and let rest for about 20 minutes. Then with forks or tongs, begin to pull the meat

IN THE KITCHEN

Barbecue reheats nicely in a microwave at medium power. Don't nuke this stuff full bore or it will dry out. Another way I like to reheat pork is to put about an inch of water in a 3-quart saucepan and then insert a vegetable steamer. As the water begins to simmer and steam, pile the barbecue on top of the vegetable steamer and cover. Steam the 'cue for 5 to 10 minutes or until heated through.

so that it comes off in stringy chunks. Separate out the skin and as much fat as you desire. Any of the outside brown, which is crispy, should be set aside and finely chopped, then stirred back into the meat. You can leave the barbecue pulled as it comes off the shoulder, or you can chop it a little finer if you desire. At this point I like to sprinkle the pulled pork with the rub that I reserved before using it on the outside, tossing the barbecue to blend.

8. Some people like to sauce their barbecue at this point, and I tend to do that with about ½ cup of the barbecue sauce that I intend to serve. Again, toss to combine. Serve hot with one of the cole slaws (see p. 246) and additional barbecue sauce on the side.

WESTERN TENNESSEE–STYLE BONE-IN PORK RIB CHOPS

SERVES 6
DIRECT HEAT

FOR THE MOLASSES-KISSED SAUCE

½ cup ketchup

3 tablespoons molasses

1 tablespoon distilled white vinegar

1 tablespoon yellow mustard

1 tablespoon light brown sugar

2 teaspoons Worcestershire sauce

½ teaspoon kosher salt

¼ teaspoon hot pepper sauce

¼ teaspoon granulated garlic

Freshly ground black pepper

½ cup water, or more as necessary

FOR THE PORK RUB

2 teaspoons freshly ground
    black pepper

1½ teaspoons paprika

1½ teaspoons light brown sugar

1½ teaspoons kosher salt

1 teaspoon dry mustard

1 teaspoon granulated garlic

1 teaspoon granulated onion

Pinch of cayenne

Six 10-ounce bone-in pork rib or
    T-bone chops, at least 1 inch thick

What makes something western Tennessee–style? First, you've got to have a dry rub. And this one is great not only for pork chops, but for just about any kind of pork. Second, West Tennesseans like their meat to be cooked on the bone, but you could substitute boneless chops if you desire. The last sign of western Tennessee grilling is a dose of molasses in the sauce. This recipe has all three. Make yourself some sweet "ice" tea and enjoy this trip to Graceland . . . because barbecue is akin to a state of grace.

1. To make the sauce, whisk together the ketchup, molasses, vinegar, mustard, brown sugar, Worcestershire, salt, hot pepper sauce, granulated garlic, pepper, and water in a medium saucepan. Place over medium heat and bring to a boil. Reduce the heat and simmer for 10 minutes or until slightly thickened, stirring occasionally. Remove from the heat and set aside.

2. To make the rub, in a small bowl combine the pepper, paprika, brown sugar, salt, mustard, granulated garlic, onion, and cayenne. Mix together well with your fingers.

3. Remove the pork chops from the refrigerator and let sit at room temperature for at least 30 minutes. Lightly brush each chop on all sides with the oil and then sprinkle liberally with the rub, massaging the mixture into the meat.

4. Oil the grill racks. Preheat your grill using all burners set on high and with the lid closed for 10 to 12 minutes.

5. Place the chops on the grill, close the lid, and cook for 5 to 7 minutes. Turn the chops (if you wish, you can separate out some of the sauce and brush the chops with it to create a bit of a glaze) and cook for another 7 to 8 minutes, or until the pork chops are firm to the touch and the internal temperature is around 150°F. Remove from the grill and let rest for about 5 minutes. Serve with the sauce.

MAPLE-KISSED PORK CHOPS

SERVES 6

DIRECT HEAT

1 cup apple cider or unsweetened
    apple juice

⅓ cup apple-cider vinegar

3 tablespoons pure maple syrup

2 tablespoons drained prepared
    horseradish

2 teaspoons Worcestershire sauce

Freshly ground black pepper

Six 8-ounce loin pork chops,
    about 1½ inches thick

Pork has always enjoyed a great relationship with sweet and spicy ingredients. The marinade for these pork chops is a balance of sweet and hot, with the added attraction of the woodsy flavor of real maple syrup. Do try to get the real thing, not just pancake syrup. And if you can find Grade B, you'll get an even more intense taste experience. Use boneless or bone-in chops, as you prefer.

1. Whisk together the cider, vinegar, maple syrup, horseradish, Worcestershire, and pepper in a small bowl. This can be made up to 2 days in advance. Cover and refrigerate.

2. Remove any excess fat from the pork chops. Massage pepper into both sides of the meat. Put the pork chops in a large zip-top bag and pour the marinade over the meat. Squish the marinade around the meat and close the bag. Put in the refrigerator and marinate overnight. Turn the bag every time you open the refrigerator.

3. About 30 minutes before cooking, take the pork chops out of the refrigerator and remove them from the marinade. Pat dry. Pour the marinade into a small saucepan and bring to a boil over high heat. Continue to cook at a rolling boil for 3 minutes. Remove from the heat and set the sauce aside.

4. Oil the grill racks. Preheat your grill using all burners set on high and with the lid closed for 10 to 12 minutes.

5. Place the pork chops on the grill and cook for about 5 minutes. Turn them over and brush with the sauce. Cook for an additional 5 minutes, then turn and brush again with the sauce and cook for another 5 minutes. Turn one more time and brush again with the sauce. Cook for another 5 minutes or until firm to the touch and the internal temperature is about 150°F. Remove from the grill and let rest for about 10 minutes before serving. Serve any additional sauce at the table.

LAUGHING CHEESE-STUFFED PORK CHOPS

Sometimes in the middle of the week you need something quick, good, and different. These pork chops fit the bill, and they couldn't be simpler. We're going to shove a little cheese in the middle of thick-cut chops to give them flavor and moisture without going through the brining process. By using wedges of The Laughing Cow® cheese, you don't even have to wash a utensil to cut your cheese. Be sure you buy the semisoft wedges and not the firmer rounds. I like the French onion flavor for these chops, but feel free to use your favorite.

SERVES 4
DIRECT HEAT

Four 8- to 10-ounce bone-in pork loin chops, about 1½ inches thick

Kosher salt

Freshly ground black pepper

4 wedges The Laughing Cow cheese

1. Take the pork chops from the refrigerator at least 30 minutes before cooking. Using a boning knife, cut a lateral slit about 2 inches long into the center of the meat to form a pocket. Season each chop with salt and pepper and then push one wedge of the cheese as far into the pocket of each chop as you can. You can close the pocket with a toothpick if you desire, but it's not really necessary.

2. Oil the grill racks. Preheat your grill using all burners set on high and with the lid closed for 10 to 12 minutes.

3. Place the chops on the grill and adjust the heat to medium. Close the lid and cook for about 5 minutes. Turn, cover again, and cook for an additional 5 minutes. Press on the chop to check for doneness. It should be firm but give slightly. If not, continue to cook the chops, checking at 2-minute intervals until firm but slightly giving. Remove to a platter. Let rest for 5 minutes. Serve to oohs and aahs.

ON THE
LAMB

LAMB AND GAME

LET'S TAKE A WALK ON THE WILD SIDE—well, really not so wild anymore. Although the meats in this chapter may have stronger flavors than those in other chapters, they're often less gamey than they were in the past, and our palates are adjusting to bolder flavors.

If your ancestry is northern European, lamb possibly might not be your favorite thing. People in northern climates raised sheep for their wool more than for their food, and any sheep that appeared on tables as mutton were most likely very old, with very tough and very gamey meat. My father's experience with mutton during World War II meant that during my childhood, lamb of any description never graced our dinner table. It's a shame that I went through most of my youth without ever tasting lamb, and now I continue to crusade for people to understand and appreciate lamb. No, I'm not talking about that leg of lamb that your grandmother roasted to death and served with mint-flavored apple jelly. Most lamb is raised domestically now, and the gamey, strong taste is muted, but the tenderness and depth of flavor has remained. It's a rich meat that takes well to a large number of seasonings from an array of culinary traditions and, when cooked medium-rare or less, is juicy and expressive. If you're like me, you'll find that nothing is more seductive than the smell of lamb cooking over open flame. It will absolutely drive you crazy.

Venison has a well-deserved reputation for being a heart-healthy red meat. Domestically raised venison is lean and has a milder flavor than the gamey deer meat that my dad brought home from his annual hunt. Venison also is a sponge, willing to work and play well

A WORLD OF FLAVOR

Have you ever wondered why lamb is so popular all over the world? Sheep are easy to herd and not difficult to handle. They are also not real picky when it comes to hilly countryside, sparse pasture, and wild changes in temperature. Lamb also pairs with a wide variety of robust seasonings; from the garlic, mustard, and rosemary of the Mediterranean to the curries of India or the tagines of North Africa, lamb's underlying sweetness is a classic to use with any number of ethnic ingredients.

with a wide variety of seasonings to bring a superior experience to the table.

American ranch-raised bison is also having newfound glory. Bison is lean as well, but not at all dry, and it is richer in taste than beef. It eats much like a steak, only better. The flavor notes of bison remind me of grass-fed Argentine beef, which is considered the best in the world. Sure, it's a bit pricey, but it's worth it for an occasional treat. And by the way, if you have squeamish eaters, just tell them it's steak until they've swooned once or twice over the flavor.

IN THE
STORE

Lamb, venison, and bison carry many of the characteristics of beef. When buying lamb, look for nice white marbling and some external fat, but not too heavy. Avoid any dark-colored meat—an indication that the animal was probably older and may be approaching the mutton category. Lamb should be light red, and from experience I've learned that all your chops should be at least an inch thick. Lamb is best cooked to medium-rare doneness, and anything thinner than an inch just seems to carbonize too quickly. If you're paying for rib chops, don't be bashful about asking your butcher to french them. You're paying a premium for these, so get premium service.

With venison there will be very little marbling, but the color should be deep red, almost claret. Many times venison will only be available frozen, and as long as the package looks as if it has been handled properly, I wouldn't shy away from it.

Bison, or buffalo, is primarily sold cut into steaks. While leaner than beef, bison still has a

THE RIGHT CUT
FOR THE RIGHT METHOD
These are guidelines only; specific recipes may vary.

TOP-SHELF CUTS Direct Heat	LESS TENDER BUT TASTY Direct Heat	BIG CUTS TO ROAST Indirect Heat	LOWER, SLOWER, AND BRAISED Indirect Heat
Lamb tenderloin	Lamb shoulder chops	Leg of lamb	Lamb ribs
Lamb rib chops	Lamb leg steaks	Boneless leg of lamb	Bison ribs
Lamb loin chops	Deer leg steaks	Deer ham	
Venison loin chops		Venison sirloin roast	
Venison tenderloin		Venison tenderloins	
Bison rib-eye steaks		Lamb crown roast	
Bison filet mignon			
Bison sirloin			

WHAT THE HECK IS SPRING LAMB?

The term refers to animals born in the spring and originally was supposed to indicate freshness and quality. Today consider it more of a marketing label than a true indication of anything else. Modern breeding allows lambs to be born all year.

in a similar fashion. Chops and tenderloins react best to direct heat. A butterflied leg of lamb works both sides of the fence, with a little direct heat and finished over indirect. Bone-in legs of lamb and deer hams are more comfortable with entirely indirect cooking. Again, you have to pair the method to the cut for success.

As with other forms of protein, the amount of time your lamb, venison, or bison stays on the grill will depend on a variety of factors, from the thickness of the meat to the weather where you are.

presence of marbling, which should be white and not yellow. The color of bison will be more like the darker red color of venison or Argentine beef, definitely much darker than American beef. Bison can be treated to any seasoning or cooking method that you would use for beef, and because of its leanness tends to like the medium-rare to medium doneness levels.

MATCHING CUT TO METHOD

Whether you're cooking lamb, venison, bison, or another form of game, the secret to success is to not overcook it. Most cuts are similar to beef and pork and can be handled

DONE TO TASTE

Since I led a lamb-free childhood, my education with this meat mostly took place in restaurants. I would order lamb in a restaurant and let the waitstaff and chef be my guides, and I discovered the incredible taste that comes from lamb that is cooked no more than medium. I encourage you to follow suit.

Checking for doneness with lamb is exactly like beef: pushing your cheek for rare, the tip of your nose for medium. Even if your mother or grandmother cooked lamb beyond medium, try it just once done less and see if you prefer it. You can also use a meat thermometer; be sure to factor in that most meat will increase by 5°F to 10°F during the resting time.

A QUICK REFRESHER
ON COOKING TIMES
Also be sure and see the sidebar below. These are guidelines only; specific recipes may vary. All doneness levels are medium-rare.

THE CUT	THICKNESS OR WEIGHT	TOTAL GRILLING TIME	RESTING TIME
LAMB LOIN CHOPS	1½ in. thick	12 minutes	5 minutes
LAMB RIB CHOPS	1 in. thick	8–10 minutes	5 minutes
LAMB SHOULDER CHOP	1 in. thick	12 minutes	5 minutes
BONE-IN LEG OF LAMB	5–7 pounds	1½–2¼ hours	10 minutes
BONELESS LEG OF LAMB, NOT ROLLED OR TIED	4 pounds	40 minutes	10 minutes
RACK OF LAMB	1½–2 pounds	40–50 minutes	10 minutes
VENISON FILET STEAKS	1½–2 pounds	8–10 minutes	5 minutes
VENISON T-BONE STEAKS	1½ in. thick	About 10 minutes	5 minutes
WHOLE VENISON TENDERLOIN	3–4 pounds	1½ hours	5 minutes

TEMPERATURE
GUIDELINES
These are guidelines only; specific recipes may vary. I believe lamb should never be cooked past a medium doneness for maximum flavor and enjoyment.

DONENESS LEVEL	USDA RECOMMENDATIONS	FRED'S THOUGHTS
RARE	140°F	125°–130°F
MEDIUM-RARE	150°F	130°–140°F
MEDIUM	160°F	140°–150°F

NIKKI'S BUTTERFLIED LEG OF LAMB

One 4- to 5-pound butterflied
    leg of lamb

¾ cup vegetable oil

½ cup red-wine vinegar

1 small onion, chopped

2 garlic cloves, crushed with the
    flat side of a knife

2 teaspoons Dijon mustard

2 teaspoons kosher salt

½ teaspoon dried oregano

½ teaspoon dried basil

1 bay leaf

⅛ teaspoon freshly ground
    black pepper

My friend Nikki Parrish shared this recipe with me many years ago, and it remains one of my favorite lamb preparations. Have your butcher bone the leg of lamb and cut into a butterfly shape. The butcher does not need to roll and tie this roast. This recipe is actually easier to do on a gas grill than a charcoal grill because of the magnificent heat control that you have with a gas grill. I would normally suggest cooking most large pieces of meat indirectly, but lamb only improves with the char of a direct fire. The scent of this as it cooks is mesmerizing, and even lamb haters tend to sing praises over this dish.

1. Combine the oil, vinegar, onion, garlic, mustard, salt, oregano, basil, bay leaf, and pepper in a large zip-top plastic bag. Add the lamb. Squish the marinade all around to coat the meat and put the bag in the refrigerator. Marinate for 48 hours, turning the bag over occasionally. About 30 minutes before grilling, remove the lamb from the marinade, pat it dry, and let it sit at room temperature.

2. Pour the marinade into a saucepan and place over high heat. Bring to a full boil. Reduce the heat slightly and continue to boil for 5 minutes. Remove from the heat and let cool.

3. Oil the grill racks. Preheat your grill using all burners set on high and with the lid closed for 10 to 12 minutes. Adjust your burners to medium.

4. Place the lamb over direct heat. Close the lid and cook for about 10 minutes, then turn, baste with the marinade, and cook for another 10 minutes. Cut all the burners to medium-low. Continue cooking and basting, turning every 5 minutes, until an instant-read thermometer registers 135°F in the thickest part of the roast. Remove the roast from the grill and let rest for 10 minutes before serving. The lamb will be crusty on the outside, and will have areas of different doneness to please everyone at your table.

SIMPLE GRILLED RACK OF LAMB

There are times that I rue the day that I first had rack of lamb at La Residence restaurant in Chapel Hill, North Carolina. Seasoned with rosemary and cooked to perfection, it was a great dining moment. What I didn't need was to develop a taste for a luxury meat. Rack of lamb can be costly, but it is a fabulous, fantastic, celebratory treat. Be sure to let it stand alone and show its true flavors—simple is best with rack of lamb. And if I've spoiled you with this recipe, I'm sort of sorry. Cut this recipe in half and it's an awesome intimate dinner for two.

1. Trim the lamb of any excess fat, but take care to leave a coating of fat over the meaty loin section of the ribs. Rub both sides of the racks with the olive oil, then sprinkle with the rosemary and pepper, rubbing them into the meatiest parts.

2. Oil the grill racks. Preheat your grill using all burners set on high and with the lid closed for 10 to 12 minutes.

3. When the grill is hot, cut off the center or back burner and adjust the heat to medium-high.

4. Grill the lamb, meat side down, with the lid closed and over direct heat for 4 or 5 minutes, or until the temperature of the meatiest part reaches 100°F. Move the lamb to the indirect section of the grill, close the lid, and cook for 15 to 20 minutes longer, or until the thickest part of each rack yields easily to pressure from your finger or the internal temperature reaches 135°F for medium. Remove the lamb from the grill and let it rest for about 5 minutes before cutting between the ribs into individual chops. Serve immediately.

SERVES 6 TO 8

DIRECT AND INDIRECT HEAT

Two 1¾- to 2-pound racks of lamb, approximately 8 chops each, frenched (see sidebar, below)

¼ cup plus 2 tablespoons olive oil

1 tablespoon chopped fresh rosemary

Freshly ground black pepper

AT THE MARKET

Frenching is the removal of the membranes, fat, and meat around the rib bones of the chop to expose part of the bone. Have your butcher french the chops for a more elegant presentation.

SALTED AND SAUCED LAMB RIBS

3 to 4 pounds lamb spareribs, about 4 racks total

Seasoned salt, such as Lawry's®

Freshly ground black pepper

Smoked paprika (optional)

1½ cups barbecue sauce

½ cup water, if using a thick barbecue sauce

Lamb ribs are becoming more and more available in supermarkets across the country, and you should take advantage of them. They are a fascinating change of pace from pork ribs and cook much faster. I like the ribs basted with a semisweet, thin, vinegar-based sauce. But you can also go with a heavier Kansas City–type sauce, or even baste them with something as simple as bottled Italian dressing.

1. Sprinkle the lamb ribs evenly and liberally on both sides with equal amounts of salt, pepper, and paprika, if using. Place them in a shallow pan and cover, then refrigerate overnight. Remove the ribs from the refrigerator and let stand at room temperature for at least 30 minutes before grilling.

2. Oil the grill racks. Preheat your grill using all burners set on high and with the lid closed for 10 to 12 minutes.

3. When the grill is hot, cut off the center or back burner and adjust the heat to medium.

4. Place the ribs, meaty side down, over the indirect section of the grill. Close the lid and cook for about 2 hours, turning every 30 minutes.

5. Remove the ribs from the grill and place in a disposable aluminum pan. Pour the barbecue sauce over the ribs (if you're using a thicker sauce, stir the water into it before adding), cover tightly with foil, and return to the grill to cook for about 20 more minutes, or until the ribs are extremely tender. Remove the pan from the grill and cut the ribs into individual pieces. Pour the sauce into a separate bowl and pass at the table.

LAMB CHOPS WITH MINT CHIMICHURRI

Chimichurri, the green and herbaceous condiment of Argentina, steps away from its normal parsley, oregano, onion, and garlic to pick up some fresh and spicy flavors that are perfect with lamb chops. Don't be afraid to use this sauce on other proteins as well. It's extremely good with simply grilled fish like salmon or swordfish. This chimichurri should be eaten the same day it's made.

1. Put the cilantro, parsley, mint, jalapeño, vinegar, lime juice, honey, and a sprinkling of salt in the bowl of a food processor. Pulse to combine and form a thick paste. With the motor running, gradually add 4 tablespoons of the olive oil and process until the sauce is smooth. Stop at least once to scrape down the sides of the bowl. If the sauce is still thick, stir in a little more olive oil. Pour the sauce into a bowl and cover with plastic wrap. Refrigerate until needed, but bring to room temperature about 20 minutes before serving.

2. Oil the grill racks. Preheat your grill using all burners set on high and with the lid closed for 10 to 12 minutes.

3. Season each lamb chop with salt and pepper. Combine the rosemary and garlic and mash to a paste with your knife on a cutting board. Use your knife to scoop it into a small bowl, then stir in the remaining 2 tablespoons olive oil and smear this paste over both sides of the lamb chops. Place the chops on the grill, close the lid, and sear quickly on both sides for about 2 minutes. Reduce the heat to medium and continue cooking the lamb for another 4 to 5 minutes per side. These chops are best when medium-rare to medium. The chops are done when they give slightly to the touch or an instant-read thermometer registers 135°F to 140°F. Remove to a platter, let rest for about 5 minutes, then drizzle the chimichurri on top of the chops. Serve immediately.

SERVES 4 TO 6

DIRECT HEAT

1 cup tightly packed
    fresh cilantro leaves

½ cup tightly packed
    fresh flat-leaf parsley leaves

¼ cup tightly packed
    fresh mint leaves

1 fresh jalapeño chile, halved
    and seeded (wear gloves to
    prevent irritation)

4 tablespoons white-wine vinegar

Juice of 1 lime

1 tablespoon honey

Kosher salt

6 tablespoons olive oil,
    plus more if necessary

Six 6- to 8-ounce double-cut lamb
    loin chops, about 1½ inches thick,
    trimmed of excess fat

Freshly ground black pepper

3 tablespoons chopped
    fresh rosemary leaves

4 garlic cloves, minced

SIMPLY LUXURIOUS LAMB CHOPS WITH RHUBARB-CHUTNEY SAUCE

SERVES 6

DIRECT HEAT

If you're not a lamb eater, this is a good recipe to start with. Nothing could be more straightforward, more elegant, and more delightful to the tongue than these lamb chops.

FOR THE RHUBARB-CHUTNEY SAUCE

4 cups thawed and drained frozen rhubarb, or about 6 stalks fresh rhubarb

1 large onion, chopped

⅓ cup honey, or more to taste

¼ cup apple-cider or sherry vinegar

½ cup golden raisins

1 fresh jalapeño chile, seeded and coarsely chopped, or more to taste (wear gloves to prevent irritation)

4 garlic cloves, finely minced

8 whole cardamom pods (white or green), tied together in cheesecloth or in a tea ball

½ cup water

1 cup chopped fresh cilantro

Twelve 4-ounce loin or rib lamb chops, trimmed of fat and cut about 1 inch thick

2 garlic cloves, cut into slivers

1 teaspoon olive oil

1 teaspoon freshly cracked black peppercorns (see sidebar, p. 111)

1. To make the chutney, stir together the rhubarb, onion, honey, vinegar, raisins, jalapeño, garlic, and the cardamom bag in a medium saucepan. Add the water, place over medium-high heat, and bring to a boil. Lower the heat to a simmer. Cover and cook for about 15 minutes, or until the rhubarb is extremely tender. Taste it to see whether you want it sweeter or hotter. If the rhubarb is especially tart, add more honey. Stir in a teaspoon and then taste. If the chutney seems mild, add 1 or 2 more chopped jalapeños. If you add either, continue cooking for another 5 minutes to blend the flavors. Remove from the heat, fish out the cheesecloth bag, and stir in the cilantro. Serve this chutney warm, at room temperature, or cold.

2. Pat the lamb chops dry. Insert slivers of garlic into each one by making small cuts with a paring knife and poking in the garlic. Brush the tops lightly with half the olive oil, and pat on half the cracked peppercorns. Turn the chops over, brush with the remaining oil, and press in the remaining pepper. Let sit at room temperature for about 30 minutes or up to 1 hour.

3. Oil the grill racks. Preheat your grill using all burners set on high and with the lid closed for 10 to 12 minutes.

4. Place the lamb chops on the grill and cook for 3 to 4 minutes per side. The lamb should give slightly when touched with your finger, indicating medium-rare to medium, or the internal temperature should register 135°F to 140°F. You don't want to overcook. Remove to a platter and pass the rhubarb chutney.

THAI MARINATED LAMB CHOPS WITH CURRY VINAIGRETTE

SERVES 6

DIRECT HEAT

1 teaspoon coriander seeds, crushed
(see the facing page)

1 teaspoon black peppercorns,
cracked (see the facing page)

⅛ teaspoon cayenne

1 tablespoon grated fresh ginger

2 tablespoons Thai fish sauce

¼ cup fresh lemon juice

1 tablespoon sugar

Six 6- to 8-ounce lamb T-bone chops
or rib chops

FOR THE CURRY VINAIGRETTE

1 tablespoon curry powder

2 teaspoons Dijon mustard
(grainy is nice)

2 tablespoons fresh lemon juice

2 tablespoons rice vinegar

½ cup extra-virgin olive oil

¼ cup canola oil

Kosher salt

Freshly ground black pepper

My friend Nancie McDermott, who spent time in the Peace Corps in Thailand and is one of our country's great experts on Asian cooking, tells me that lamb is widespread in Asia and takes well to most Asian seasonings. Its assertiveness stands up to the sweet, sour, hot, and salty flavors of Asian cooking. The curry vinaigrette is good on grilled vegetables and any simply grilled firm fish.

1. Combine the coriander, peppercorns, cayenne, ginger, fish sauce, lemon juice, and sugar in a large zip-top bag. Squish to combine. Add the lamb and squish the marinade all around the lamb. Close the bag and refrigerate for 12 hours, turning occasionally.

2. To make the vinaigrette, in a small bowl whisk together the curry powder, mustard, lemon juice, and vinegar. Take a paper towel, dampen it, roll it up, shape it into a circle, and place your bowl on the paper towel. (This will help give you stability as you whisk in the oil.) Slowly drizzle in the olive oil, and then the canola oil, whisking constantly. Of course, if you have a blender, food processor, or immersion blender handy, by all means feel free to use it. Taste and add salt and pepper to your needs. Pour into a covered jar and refrigerate until needed. If the emulsion breaks, shake well.

3. Oil the grill racks. Preheat your grill using all burners set on high and with the lid closed for 10 to 12 minutes.

4. Remove the lamb from the refrigerator and the bag, and discard the marinade. Pat the lamb dry. Place on the grill, close the lid, and cook for 7 to 8 minutes. Turn and cook for another 7 minutes. The meat should be firm but with a little give when you touch it, giving you a rare to medium-rare doneness, which is perfect for this kind of chop. Remove to a platter, drizzle with the curry vinaigrette, and serve. Pass additional vinaigrette at the table.

CRACKED PEPPERCORNS

THE FLAVOR AND TEXTURE OF FRESHLY CRACKED PEPPERCORNS—or any whole spice—can add volumes of taste and texture to any dish, and you won't get the same result by just using your coarse setting on your pepper mill or by purchasing cracked peppercorns. Pour out the whole peppercorns onto a cutting board or flat surface. Grab a heavy skillet or saucepan and place it directly over the peppercorns. Using your weight, lean hands first into the skillet or pan until you hear a little cracking. This is only the first step. We flatten the peppercorns out enough so that they won't go rolling all over the kitchen counter. Using the edge of the skillet or pan and leaning your weight into it, continue cracking the peppercorns several at a time until you've gone through all of them. It's a simple process, and after you've done it a few times you probably won't have to sweep the kitchen floor afterward.

OHIO-STYLE VENISON STEAKS

Four 4- to 6-ounce boneless venison loin steaks, about 1 inch thick

1 cup cranberry-orange crushed fruit for chicken, such as Ocean Spray®

½ cup dry red wine, such as Pinot Noir or Burgundy

2 tablespoons Dijon mustard

4 garlic cloves, minced

2 tablespoons fresh rosemary leaves, chopped

½ teaspoon freshly ground black pepper

AT THE TABLE

What goes with game? Some of the classic dishes to pair up when you're cooking wild game or even domestically raised wild critters are turnips, cabbage, chestnuts, mushrooms, and onions. In the South, a bowl of hot, heavily buttered grits or rice is always welcome, and most any chutney or pepper relish is extremely good. Cranberry sauces of any description are always a positive addition to most game or wild poultry; try it with quail. Cumberland sauce is another classic.

Venison is one of those "new" healthy meats. It's extremely lean, whether farm-raised or wild, so you have to be careful about how you cook it to prevent it from drying out. I'm amazed at the number of hunters who still pine for the beginning of deer season, and this is especially true north and west of Akron, Ohio. Here's a favorite way that they have with venison steaks. Look for the crushed fruit with the canned fruit in your supermarket.

1. Put the steaks in a large zip-top bag. Pour in ½ cup of the crushed fruit, the red wine, mustard, garlic, rosemary, and pepper. Close the bag and squish the marinade to combine and coat the steaks. Refrigerate for at least 4 hours, or up to overnight. Turn your bag occasionally.

2. Oil the grill racks. Preheat your grill using all burners set on high and with the lid closed for 10 to 12 minutes.

3. Pull the steaks from the bag and discard the marinade. Lightly pat the steaks dry and place on the grill. Cook for 5 minutes, then turn and cook for 4 to 5 minutes longer. You don't want to overcook venison. A nice medium-rare to medium doneness is perfect. The steaks should give easily when touched but offer some resistance, and an instant-read thermometer should register 140°F. Remove the steaks to a platter and serve with the remaining crushed fruit.

BARBECUED VENISON TENDERLOIN

Marinating venison, especially if it's wild, softens the gaminess of its flavor, and most wild game responds well to a little infusion of fruit. The barbecue sauce that I'm suggesting here is one that I developed for squab, with its rich, complex, dark meat. I think you'll find it as pleasing with venison as with the bird.

1. Trim any silverskin or excess fat from the venison. Put it in a large zip-top bag. In a medium bowl, blend the oil, tamari, vinegar, lemon juice, Worcestershire, mustard, parsley, pepper, salt, and garlic. Pour this mixture over the tenderloin. Close the bag and squish the marinade around the meat. Refrigerate for at least 4 hours but not much longer than 6 hours.

2. Oil the grill racks. Preheat your grill using all burners set on high and with the lid closed for 10 to 12 minutes.

3. Pull the tenderloin from the marinade and discard the marinade. Place the venison on the grill, reduce the heat to medium-high, and cook for about 10 minutes, turning to evenly brown the tenderloin. An instant-read thermometer should register 150°F for medium doneness and the meat should give slightly to the touch. During the last minute or two of cooking, brush the tenderloin with barbecue sauce. Remove to a platter and let rest for at least 10 minutes. Cut the tenderloin on the diagonal into ½-inch-thick slices and serve with more barbecue sauce.

SERVES 4
DIRECT HEAT

One 1½- to 2-pound venison tenderloin

½ cup canola oil

¼ cup tamari

¼ cup balsamic vinegar

¼ cup fresh lemon juice

2 tablespoons Worcestershire sauce

1 tablespoon dry mustard

1 tablespoon chopped fresh flat-leaf parsley

1 teaspoon freshly ground black pepper

½ teaspoon kosher salt

1 garlic clove, minced

About 1 cup Blueberry Barbecue Sauce (p. 146)

SAUERBRATEN-MARINATED VENISON LOIN

SERVES 8

DIRECT AND INDIRECT HEAT

5 bay leaves

2 sprigs fresh thyme,
    or 1 tablespoon dried thyme

20 black peppercorns

5 whole cloves

Two 3-inch cinnamon sticks

10 juniper berries or ½ cup gin

1 medium onion, finely chopped

1 carrot, finely chopped

1 rib celery, finely chopped

2 garlic cloves, crushed

2 cups dry red wine,
    such as Pinot Noir or Burgundy

½ cup red-wine vinegar

One 4-pound boneless venison loin

Kosher salt

Freshly ground black pepper

Olive oil

Sauerbraten is warming and hearty on a cold winter's evening. This cousin of the long-braised real thing combines the flavors in a marinade and then gives it a new dimension by using the grill as a heat source. Although beef is traditionally used in sauerbraten, venison's lean texture makes it a good source of healthy protein, and it becomes flavorful and tender after a night swimming in this marinade. Serve with braised red cabbage and egg noodles topped with crumbled gingersnaps to deepen the German experience.

1. Put the bay leaves, thyme, peppercorns, cloves, cinnamon sticks, juniper berries, onion, carrot, celery, garlic, wine, and vinegar in a large heavy saucepan. Place over medium heat and bring to a boil. Remove from the heat and allow to cool completely.

2. Trim any silverskin from the venison. Put the venison in a large zip-top bag and pour the marinade over the meat. Close the bag and marinate in the refrigerator for at least 24 hours for a mild taste; 36 hours gives you a bolder flavor.

3. Oil the grill racks. Preheat your grill using all burners set on high and with the lid closed for 10 to 12 minutes.

4. When the grill is hot, cut off the center or back burner and adjust your heat to medium-high.

5. Remove the venison from the marinade and pat dry with paper towels. Discard the marinade. Season with salt and pepper, brush lightly with olive oil, and place on the grill. Close the lid and cook for 5 minutes, then turn and cook for another 5 minutes. Turn again and cook for 5 more minutes. Move to the indirect part of the grill and close the lid. Cook for about 1½ hours longer, or to an internal temperature of 140°F (the meat should feel like the tip of your nose). Remove and let rest for 10 minutes before slicing and serving.

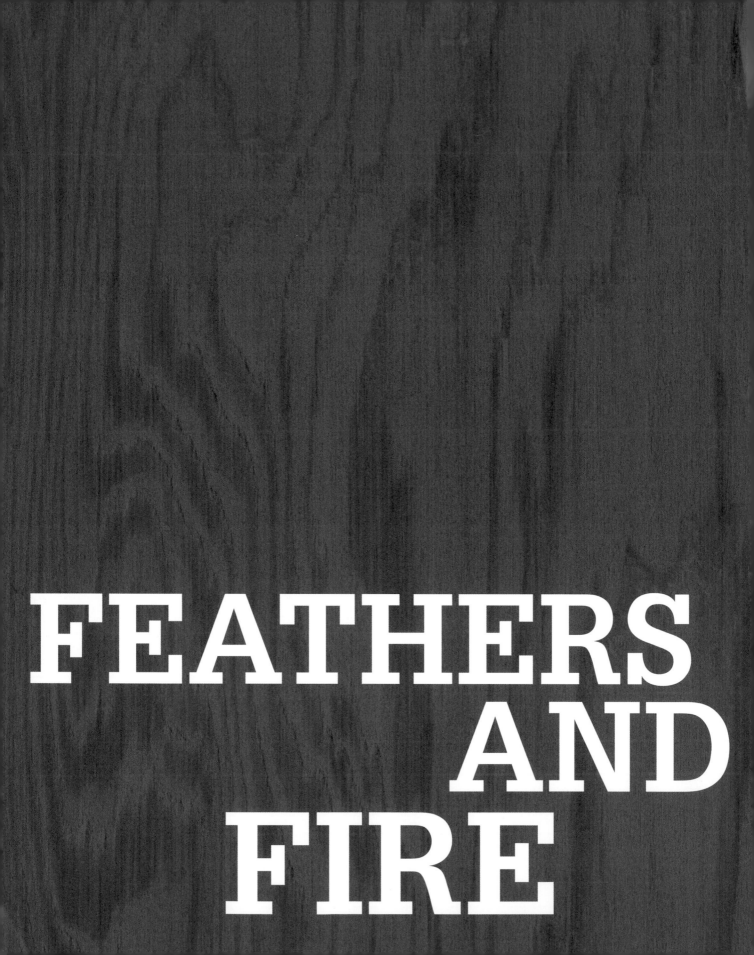

FEATHERS AND FIRE

POULTRY AND GAME BIRDS

Smoky **CHIPOTLE CHICKEN** 126

Kansas City **BARBECUE-GLAZED CHICKEN** 127

CURRIED CHICKEN with Mango-Curry Chutney 128

Caribbean Rubbed **CHICKEN BREASTS** 130

Grilled **CORIANDER CHICKEN** with Cilantro-Walnut Pesto 131

Nikki Parrish's **SMOKE-ROASTED CHICKEN LEGS**, Alabama-Style 132

Grilled **CHICKEN WITH GOAT CHEESE** 135

CHICKEN *SPIEDINI* 136

THAI BARBECUE CHICKEN THIGHS with Peanut Sauce 138

Forget the **FRIED CHICKEN WINGS** 141

Super-Moist Buttermilk-Brined **CHICKEN BREASTS** 142

Grilled Moroccan-Style **CORNISH GAME HENS** 143

Hickory-Smoked **BOURBON TURKEY** 144

"BLUE" CHICKEN 146

ROTISSERIE DUCK with Chipotle-Tamarind Barbecue Sauce 148

Grilled **DUCK BREASTS** with Hot Pepper Jelly Glaze 150

Asian Grilled **QUAIL**, Savannah-Style 152

BACK IN THE 1950s and early 1960s, flimsy charcoal-fueled braziers became the backyard accessory that no home could be without. Chicken, slathered with barbecue sauce and, quite frankly, usually burned, soon became part of the American landscape. We've learned a lot about grilling chicken since then, and grills, especially gas ones, have come a long way, too. If you're still turning out charred chicken, pay attention.

Poultry is indeed one of the most versatile of all meats that we can put on the grill. It just waits for us, soaking up all kinds of flavor. It can become elegant or down-home and everything in between. In this chapter, we're going to learn the fine points of cooking chicken on the grill, and then we'll explore beyond chicken and delve into turkey, duck, and quail. (Most of these recipes can be easily extrapolated to work for capon, squab, poussin, and goose.) Each bird has its own special characteristics after being kissed by an outdoor flame. After you've cooked your way through this chapter, you'll no longer reserve turkey just for Thanksgiving, but you will enjoy it throughout the year. Your barbecued chicken parts will become golden brown and slightly caramelized but never burned. You'll delight in fast-cooking quail, much more available now than ever before, with its rich meat that's a

POULTRY IS ONE OF THE MOST VERSATILE OF ALL MEATS THAT WE CAN PUT ON THE GRILL.

A CHICKEN IS A
CHICKEN, OR IS IT?

Most of the chicken and turkey available today has a flavor problem. Mass-produced birds raised in cages are just boring. But like all the other proteins throughout this book, there is a national push to produce better-tasting chickens that can carry the value-added premium label. The most prevalent marketing term is "free range." Free-range birds are just that, birds that are allowed to run around, we hope outside, but at least through the indoor houses, for part of every day. Allowing the birds to move contributes to a firmer and more flavorful meat. Not all free-range poultry is equal, but all have a much richer flavor than caged birds. Some free-range birds come from old-fashioned breeds, and this is the best of both worlds, much like heritage pork and grass-fed beef. Unfortunately, like all things that are not mass produced, these fowl cost more, but quite frankly they're worth it.

wonderful foil for so many seasonings. And you'll turn a duck from that frozen hunk that you find in so many markets into a new delight for your friends and family.

The biggest thing to remember when cooking poultry is cleanliness. Working with poultry, especially when it's raw, is messy and can be germy. Wash your tools and your hands *often* with hot, soapy water. Make sure that raw and cooked never mingle—don't put cooked chicken on the plate you carried the raw stuff out to the grill on, and don't use the same tongs or forks for raw and cooked, either. This doctrine of cleanliness also applies to your grill. Keep your cooking grate as clean as

humanly possible. Poultry loves to stick to proteins left behind from previous grilling experiences, and you don't want to lose any of that beautiful flavor that's happening as the birds transform themselves into golden treats.

IN THE
MARKET

Chicken pieces and parts are easy to come by. Every large supermarket chain carries at least one national brand plus the store's private label. Most are low in fat, and they cook quickly and are tender by most standards, but unless you opt for a "premium" bird (see "A Chicken Is a Chicken, or Is It?" on p. 119), chicken has a flavor problem. That's where our gas grill, some seasonings, and a great sauce can elevate these birds.

When looking for fresh poultry, make sure that the skin fits the body—that is, that it covers the meat—and that it doesn't look splotchy or dried out. This applies whether you're buying loose parts or looking at parts in pre-wrapped containers. Either way, if you get poultry home and it smells funny, make a return trip. Any off odors are a warning that trouble lurks. Whole turkeys, duck, goose, and quail come to most of us in a frozen state, so I tend to look for freezer cases that are well maintained and buy from supermarkets that have good traffic. How these birds were treated in transport makes all the difference in the world, and sometimes it is hard to discern whether freezer burn is lurking. Ninety percent of the time I find frozen ducks, goose, and quail to be of exceptional quality. Frozen turkeys are okay in a pinch, but fresh is better.

CUTTING CHICKEN

With the breast down and the tail of the chicken facing you, use poultry shears to cut along one side of the backbone down the entire length of the chicken.

Turn the chicken so the neck end is facing you and cut along the other side of the backbone; remove and discard the backbone.

Turn the chicken breast side up and open up the chicken. Flatten it with the palm of your hand.

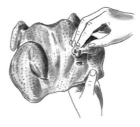

Make ½-inch-deep slits on either side of each breast, about 1 inch from the end of the neck. Tuck the legs into the slits. Use the smooth side of a mallet to pound the chicken to an even thickness.

If you are fortunate enough to live in a community where fresh turkey, duck, and quail are available, the same guidelines apply as for chicken. Don't be concerned about the fat layer that lies under most duck skin. It's absolutely the best basting medium you'll ever have for anything and much of it cooks away as you grill it. And once it renders away, ounce for ounce skinless duck breast is leaner than chicken breast.

THE PIECES, THE PARTS, THE WHOLE, AND THE
RIGHT METHOD

Just about every variety of bird can be cooked using every method your gas grill can handle, from simple quick grilling to a combination of direct and indirect to totally indirect for a wonderful grill-roasted result to spit-roasted on a rotisserie, that spinning bar of intense flavor. Using smoke chips with these methods adds an interesting flavor note. The length of time most poultry cooks is perfect for smoking (big birds like turkey should be smoked using the method described in the first chapter).

Chicken basically comes whole, quartered, in pieces, boneless, and skinless, and each needs a different arena. Whole is best grill-roasted over indirect heat or put on a spit. Pieces benefit most from a quick turn over direct heat before moving to indirect heat. The same applies for quarters, butterflied chickens, or halves. Boneless, skinless chicken breasts,

THE COMBO
MAMBO

Combination grilling, and by that I mean using direct heat to sear and develop some brownness and then transferring food to an indirect section of the grill to finish cooking, is a magnificent way to create volumes of flavor and keep items moist and tender. Nowhere is this technique more necessary than in dealing with poultry, especially poultry pieces, to prevent the dreaded rare-inside, charred-outside condition. You'll see this method used over and over again in this chapter, and I would make it part of your grilling arsenal for any item that needs to cook longer than 20 minutes. Adding indirect heat will make the cooking time longer, but the result will be something that you're glad to put in your mouth.

the go-to meat for our harried present-day life, is the only type of chicken that I recommend cooking completely over direct heat. Other poultry that is better over direct heat includes split Cornish game hens and quartered duck

THE RIGHT BIRD
FOR THE RIGHT METHOD
These are guidelines only; specific recipes may vary.

FAST AND FURIOUS Direct Heat	SEAR IT QUICK, COOK IT SLOW Direct and Indirect heat	THE WHOLE BIRD Indirect Heat	ROTISSERIE Indirect heat or your grill's rotisserie burner
Boneless, skinless chicken breasts Boneless, skinless chicken thighs Turkey cutlets Butterflied quail Duck breasts	Cut-up fryers Chicken quarters or halves Bone-in chicken pieces Chicken wings Turkey drumsticks Boneless turkey roasts Cornish game hen halves Butterflied chickens, turkeys, or ducks Squab	Chickens Turkeys Ducks Hens Capons Cornish game hens Goose	Whole chickens Whole ducks Whole hens Cornish game hens Capons Goose Turkey breasts Turkey halves

or duck parts, although when cooking duck breasts or legs, it might be necessary to turn off one or more burners and use a little indirect roasting because of the amount of fat under the duck's skin.

Fresh turkey is available in many parts of the country year-round, although you may have to order a whole bird. Breasts (both bone in and boneless) and turkey parts such as legs, halved turkey breasts, or rolled and tied boneless turkey breasts that are sometimes labeled "turkey London broil" are all great additions to the grill. All forms of turkey need indirect heat

for the bulk of their cooking, but pieces you can do much like chicken, with a combination of direct for its quick-searing potential and indirect to finish the meat.

Small birds like quail need to be cooked quickly over direct heat and are best cooked only to a medium doneness. Quite frankly, a quail grilled to well-done is not much of a treat.

Pair the cooking method to the right cut of poultry. Don't be that slacker backyard griller who completely blackens the outside of poultry while leaving much of the inside dead raw. With a gas grill, there's absolutely no excuse

BRINING AND DINING

Most any brine in this cookbook will work well with poultry. One I particularly like is from Jamie Purviance, the executive chef and chief cookbook author for Weber-Stephen Products Co. Jamie uses a combination of pickling spices and kosher salt. I've adapted that a little bit to include 1/4 cup pickling spices, 1/4 cup kosher salt, 2 tablespoons sugar or another sweetener, and 2 quarts water. If you wish you can heat this brine, stirring for a few minutes to get everything to dissolve. Put the poultry in a large zip-top bag, pour the brine over, and refrigerate for at least 30 minutes but no more than 2 hours. On larger pieces such as a whole turkey, an overnight brine is acceptable. This much brine will take care of a whole chicken or 4 pounds of chicken parts. It's easily doubled or even tripled to handle a turkey. Be sure and use a non-injected turkey if you're going to brine. You don't want to double the water and salt content. Buying fresh, natural, and free-range is always the best option.

for this taking place except that you got more interested in the beer than the cooking. And even then, your gas grill is there to be your friend and helper. Great grilled chicken is an awesome experience—do it often.

NO WHINING—THINK BRINING

In the past decade or so, you might have started a new Thanksgiving tradition of brining your turkey. If you haven't adopted this tradition, you might want to—especially if you think that turkey tends to be dry and bland. The biggest reason we brine turkeys is to help with moisture and to add a bit of fla-

vor. I think it's funny that brining became popular as we shifted to "non-injected at the processing plant" turkeys. At least when we do the brining, we control the chemistry in the brine. Always read the label on a turkey, especially a frozen one—you don't want to brine a bird that's already been injected with sodium! That would be a salty mess. Never brine kosher poultry either, as they are always brined at slaughter.

Chickens were the next bird to hit the brine, both in their whole incarnation as well as quarters and parts, especially bone-in, skin-on breasts. I routinely brine chicken quarters

GREAT GRILLED CHICKEN IS AN AWESOME EXPERIENCE— DO IT OFTEN.

and large pieces when I intend to smoke them, because smoke tends to dry out protein.

Usually with duck or quail a flavorful marinade is used, so brining tends not to be necessary, and besides, these birds—with the inclusion of squab—are fattier and have richer, moister meat.

The one cut that I think benefits the most from a brine is a boneless, skinless chicken breast, but brining takes time, so it defeats their purpose as a fast-cooking, easy dinner. That said, even a 15- to 30-minute brine can make a massive amount of difference in moisture and tenderness with probably what is the most overcooked item that hits our plates today.

WHEN IS IT DONE?

The USDA of course has its recommendations for poultry. Breast meat should be cooked to about 170°F and thigh meat to 180°F. Again, I side with many chefs and other culinary profes-sionals in thinking that this is a bit high, especially when it comes to free-range and more natural poultry products. I believe breast meat should be in the 160°F to 165°F range and thigh meat at about 175°F to have splendid, juicy results. All the bad critters are dead. If you cut into poultry and still find it pink to red at the joints, then introduce it to the microwave for further cooking. Remember, too, that as the pro-tein rests it continues to cook, and the internal temperature can rise as much as 10°F.

I also like to do another little test by taking a small paring knife and cutting into the area be-tween the joint of a drumstick and a thigh or the wing and its breast. The juices should run clear and in most circumstances there should be no pinkness around the bone. (The exception is if you are buying an organic bird—some pink color around the joint often remains.) If you are buying a turkey or a whole chicken from a natural-foods store, discuss doneness temperature and done-ness indicators with the butcher. Also use the touch test; both breast and thigh should be firm to the touch (like your forehead, see p. 13).

A QUICK REFRESHER
ON COOKING TIMES

Also be sure and see p. 12. These are guidelines only; specific recipes may vary.

THE CUT	THICKNESS OR WEIGHT	GRILLING TIME GUIDE	RESTING TIME
BONELESS, SKINLESS CHICKEN BREASTS	4–8 ounces	12–18 minutes	5 minutes
BONE-IN CHICKEN BREASTS	8–10 ounces	30 minutes	5 minutes
BONE-IN CHICKEN THIGHS AND DRUMSTICKS	4–8 ounces	20–25 minutes	5 minutes
WHOLE CHICKEN	3–4 pounds	60–80 minutes	10 minutes
DUCK BREASTS	6–8 ounces	15–20 minutes	5 minutes
WHOLE DUCK	5–6 pounds	1–1¾ hours	10 minutes
BONELESS TURKEY ROAST	Roughly 5 pounds	1½ hours	10 minutes
BONE-IN TURKEY BREASTS	3–4 pounds	1½ hours	10 minutes
WHOLE TURKEY	12–14 pounds	2½–3½ hours	At least 20 minutes

SMOKY CHIPOTLE CHICKEN

SERVES 6 TO 8
DIRECT HEAT

4 garlic cloves, peeled

3 canned chipotle chiles in adobo sauce

¼ cup red-wine vinegar

2 teaspoons salt

Grated zest of 1 lemon

Juice of 1 lemon

Two 3- to 3½-pound chickens, cut into 8 pieces each

Chipotle chiles are nothing more than dried jalapeños that have been smoked, but that's saying a lot. Smoking this chile enriches its aroma and flavor and adds depth to all types of food. Nowhere is this more evident than with chicken. Canned chipotle chiles in adobo sauce are readily found in your supermarket.

1. Combine the garlic, chiles, vinegar, salt, lemon zest, and lemon juice in a food processor. Pulse 4 or 5 times to combine, and then let the machine run for about a minute to make a smooth paste.

2. Put the chicken pieces in a large zip-top bag and pour the paste over the meat. Close the bag and place flat on the counter. Squish the paste around to thoroughly coat the meat. Put in the refrigerator and marinate for at least 4 hours, but overnight will give you a better taste experience.

3. Oil the grill racks. Preheat your grill using all burners set on high and with the lid closed for 10 to 12 minutes.

4. Remove the chicken from the marinade and pat dry. Pour the marinade into a small saucepan and place over medium-high heat. Bring to a boil and cook for at least 3 minutes. Remove from the heat and let cool.

5. Brush the pieces lightly with oil. Place the legs and thighs on the grill, close the lid, and adjust the burners to medium-high. Turn the pieces frequently, cooking for about 15 minutes. Place the breasts and the wings, skin side up, on the grill. Cook for about 5 minutes and turn. Cook all of the chicken for about 25 minutes longer, turning frequently. During the last 10 minutes baste frequently with the marinade. The chicken is done when the juices run clear when the thickest section is pierced with a sharp knife, or when an instant-read thermometer registers 180°F when inserted into the thigh and 170°F in the breast. Serve with marinade.

KANSAS CITY BARBECUE-GLAZED CHICKEN

Kansas City is one of this country's great barbecue meccas. Here, sauce is king, and that sauce better be thick, tomatoey, and sweetened with an essence of molasses. Now, somebody from Kansas City might argue with this recipe. I'll think you'll just find it darned good. Indirect heat and the temperature control that you have with a gas grill allow for this sauce to glaze, not burn.

1. For the sauce, heat the oil in a medium saucepan over medium heat. Stir in the garlic, tomato paste, chili powder, crushed red chile flakes, allspice, and cloves and cook, stirring, until the paste is dark brick red, about 3 minutes. Add the ketchup, water, vinegar, molasses, brown sugar, 1½ teaspoons of salt, the soy sauce, Worcestershire, mustard, pepper, and bay leaf. Adjust the heat to maintain a gentle simmer and cook until the flavors come together, about 30 minutes. Remove and discard the bay leaf.

2. Oil the grill racks. Preheat your grill using all burners set on high and with the lid closed for 10 to 12 minutes.

3. When the grill is hot, cut off the center or back burner and adjust the heat to medium-high.

4. Position a drip pan under the grate on the indirect side.

5. Season the chicken with salt and pepper. Place on the grill, skin side down, over direct heat. Close the lid and cook until the skin is crisp, turning as needed, about 5 minutes. Dip each piece of chicken in the sauce, letting any excess sauce drip off, then return the chicken to the grill on the indirect side, over the drip pan. Arrange the dark-meat pieces closer to the fire than the white meat. Close the lid and cook, basting once more, until nicely glazed and an instant-read thermometer inserted in the thickest part of each piece registers 170°F, 25 to 30 minutes longer. Remove from the grill and serve immediately.

SERVES 4 TO 6
DIRECT AND INDIRECT HEAT

1 tablespoon vegetable oil

3 garlic cloves, smashed with the flat side of a knife

1 tablespoon tomato paste

2 teaspoons chili powder

1½ teaspoons crushed red chile flakes

⅛ teaspoon ground allspice

Pinch ground cloves

1 cup ketchup

1 cup water

¼ cup apple-cider vinegar

2 tablespoons dark molasses

1 tablespoon dark brown sugar

Kosher salt

1½ teaspoons soy sauce

1½ teaspoons Worcestershire sauce

1 teaspoon dry mustard

Freshly ground black pepper

1 bay leaf

3½ pounds mixed chicken parts

CURRIED CHICKEN WITH MANGO-CURRY CHUTNEY

SERVES 6
DIRECT HEAT

FOR THE CURRY PASTE RUB

Vegetable oil cooking spray

½ cup curry powder

2 tablespoons chopped fresh ginger

2 garlic cloves, chopped

1½ teaspoons crushed coriander
    seeds (see sidebar, p. 111)

3 tablespoons fresh orange juice

2 tablespoons water

Kosher salt

Two 3- to 3½-pound chickens, cut
    into 8 pieces each and skinned

**FOR THE MANGO-CURRY
    CHUTNEY**

1 tablespoon canola oil

1 small onion, chopped

1 small fresh serrano or jalapeño
    chile, chopped (wear gloves
    to prevent irritation; if you're
    worried about heat, discard
    the seeds)

1 mango, peeled, pitted, and cubed

2 tablespoons fresh orange juice

1 teaspoon apple-cider vinegar

Freshly ground black pepper

2 tablespoons chopped fresh cilantro

Chicken loves flavor, and this recipe will satisfy most any bird. The recipe has three distinct flavor steps—the chicken is first marinated, then rubbed with a curry paste, and finally served with a mango chutney. The chutney's purpose is to balance the flavor of the chicken, kind of like how we put ketchup on a hamburger, and it is critical to the enjoyment of the dish. If time is short, at least pick up a mango-based chutney from the supermarket to integrate with the headiness of the chicken.

1. To make the rub, coat a small skillet with the cooking spray, and then add the curry powder, ginger, garlic, and coriander seeds. Place the skillet over medium-low heat. Cook this concoction, stirring, for 2 to 3 minutes, or until the smell fills the room. Pour in the orange juice and water and stir gently until the liquid is absorbed by the spices. The mixture will tend to be dry, almost like biscuit dough, but it should hold together when pinched. Season with salt to taste, cover, and refrigerate until ready to use, or for up to 3 days.

2. Place the chicken pieces on a rimmed baking sheet. Remove the curry rub from the refrigerator and reserve 1 tablespoon. Massage the rest of the rub onto the chicken pieces. Either cover or transfer the pieces to a zip-top bag and put in the refrigerator for at least 1 hour and up to 4 hours.

3. Meanwhile, make the chutney. Heat the oil in a small skillet over medium heat. Add the onion and cook for 3 or 4 minutes, or until it begins to soften. Add the chile and cook for about 30 seconds, or just until fragrant. Add the mango, orange juice, vinegar, and the reserved tablespoon of curry rub and cook, stirring occasionally, for 5 to 7 minutes, or until the mango softens but still retains its shape. Season with pepper to taste and stir in the cilantro. Cook for about 1 minute longer and then transfer to a small bowl. Cover and refrigerate until chilled. The chutney will keep for up to 3 days.

4. Oil the grill racks. Preheat your grill using all burners set on high and with the lid closed for 10 to 12 minutes.

5. Adjust your burners to medium-high heat. Place the chicken legs and thighs on the grill, skin side up, close the lid, and cook for about 15 minutes, turning every 3 to 5 minutes. Place the breasts and wings on the grill, skin side up. Cook all the chicken for an additional 25 to 30 minutes, turning each piece every 3 to 5 minutes. The chicken is done when the juices run clear when the thickest sections are pierced with a knife, or when an instant-read thermometer inserted into the thickest part of the thigh registers 180°F and the thickest part of the breast registers 170°F. Transfer the chicken pieces to a platter and serve immediately with the chutney.

CARIBBEAN RUBBED CHICKEN BREASTS

SERVES 4

DIRECT HEAT

2 tablespoons granulated sugar

1 tablespoon light brown sugar

1 tablespoon ground allspice

2 teaspoons granulated garlic

⅛ teaspoon cayenne

Kosher salt

Freshly ground black pepper

Four 6-ounce boneless, skinless
  chicken breasts, trimmed

2 teaspoons canola oil

America's favorite convenience food—boneless, skinless chicken breasts—always needs some help. With the addition of a sweet-hot rub and quick cooking, we can turn this weeknight quickie into a weeknight favorite. Serve this with black beans and rice.

1. Mix both sugars, the allspice, garlic, cayenne, and a sprinkling of salt and black pepper together in a small bowl. Set aside.

2. You can skip this step, but the 5 minutes you put in here will make your chicken breasts cook much more evenly. Put the chicken breasts, one at a time, into a heavy-duty zip-top bag. Using a meat mallet or rolling pin, pound the chicken until it is an even thickness, usually about ½ inch.

3. Pat the chicken breasts dry with paper towels and brush with the oil. Evenly sprinkle the spice mixture on both sides of the chicken and then massage it into the meat.

4. Oil the grill racks. Preheat your grill using all burners set on high and with the lid closed for 10 to 12 minutes.

5. Place the chicken on the grill, close the lid, and cook for 4 to 5 minutes on each side. The chicken should be firm to the touch and just cooked through. Remove from the grill to a platter and let rest for about 5 minutes before serving.

GRILLED CORIANDER CHICKEN WITH CILANTRO-WALNUT PESTO

Southwestern taste with a little Italian know-how creates a multicultural delight.

1. For the marinade, heat a small dry skillet over medium heat. Add the coriander, cumin, and peppercorns and stir constantly until fragrant, 1 to 2 minutes. Transfer to a spice grinder and grind to a fine powder.

2. In a food processor, combine the ground spices, garlic, ginger, olive oil, water, cayenne, saffron, lemon juice, and salt. Process: transfer the paste to a large glass baking dish. Add the cilantro and stir to combine. Add the chicken and thoroughly coat with the spice paste. Cover with plastic wrap and refrigerate for at least 4 hours or overnight.

3. For the pesto, in the food processor, combine the cilantro, garlic, jalapeño, walnuts, lemon juice, salt, pepper, and cumin. Process to a paste. Add the water and process to combine. Pour into a serving container and set aside.

4. Remove the chicken from the refrigerator 30 minutes before cooking. Oil the grill racks. Preheat your grill using all burners set on high and with the lid closed for 10 to 12 minutes.

5. When the grill is hot, cut off the center or back burner and adjust the heat to medium-high.

6. Place the thighs and the drumsticks on the grill over direct heat. Close the lid and sear for 5 minutes, turning once. Move the chicken to the indirect section of the grill and cook for 10 minutes more. Sear the breasts and wings over direct heat for 5 minutes, then move to the indirect section with the thighs and drumsticks and cook for 25 minutes. When done the juices should run clear when pierced with a knife, and the internal temperature on the thighs should be 180°F and the breasts 170°F. Serve with the pesto and pita.

SERVES 4

DIRECT AND INDIRECT HEAT

FOR THE CORIANDER MARINADE

2 tablespoons coriander seeds

1 teaspoon cumin seeds

2 teaspoons black peppercorns

8 garlic cloves

One 2-inch piece fresh ginger, peeled and thinly sliced

3 tablespoons olive oil

¼ cup water

1 tablespoon cayenne

Pinch saffron

2 tablespoons fresh lemon juice

2 teaspoons salt

½ cup chopped fresh cilantro

1 whole chicken, cut into 8 pieces (3½ to 4 pounds)

FOR THE CILANTRO-WALNUT PESTO

1 cup chopped fresh cilantro

4 garlic cloves

1 fresh jalapeño, seeded and cut into chunks (wear gloves to prevent irritation)

½ cup walnuts, toasted

½ cup fresh lemon juice

1 teaspoon salt

1 teaspoon freshly ground pepper

¼ teaspoon ground cumin

¼ cup water

Warm pita bread, for serving

NIKKI PARRISH'S SMOKE-ROASTED CHICKEN LEGS, ALABAMA-STYLE

Hickory wood chips, soaked in water for at least 30 minutes

4 chicken leg quarters (about 3½ pounds)

Salt

Freshly ground black pepper

½ cup vegetable oil

1 cup mayonnaise

1 cup apple-cider vinegar

1 tablespoon fresh lemon juice

1 tablespoon prepared horseradish

1½ tablespoons freshly cracked black peppercorns (see sidebar, p. 111)

½ teaspoon kosher salt

¼ teaspoon cayenne

Only in northern Alabama will you see anything like this recipe, whose defining characteristic is mayonnaise. Most all of the barbecue joints in this part of Alabama have a take on this recipe, which is one of the true regional specialties left in barbecue land. My friend Nikki Parrish, from Cullman, Alabama, prefers to showcase her hometown delicacy with game hens, but chicken legs (sometimes called leg quarters, but whatever they're called they have the thigh and drumstick still joined together) are a little easier to find sometimes. Don't snicker about the mayonnaise until you've tasted this.

1. Prepare two smoking chip packets (see p. 16). Oil the grill racks. Preheat your grill using all burners set on high and with the lid closed for 10 to 12 minutes.

2. When the grill is hot, cut off the center or back burner and adjust your heat to low. Season the chicken legs with salt and pepper. Place the legs over the indirect section of your grill. Close the lid and smoke for 2 to 2½ hours, basting with the oil and seasoning with additional salt and pepper after an hour. Cook until the internal temperature is 170°F.

3. Meanwhile, in the largest mixing bowl you have, combine the mayonnaise, vinegar, lemon juice, horseradish, cracked pepper, salt, and cayenne. Refrigerate until the legs are done (this can be made up to 4 days in advance).

4. Ladle out a little of the mayonnaise sauce for serving. Place the smoked legs in the bowl with the remaining sauce and toss to coat. Let them sit for a few minutes, then drain and serve with the reserved sauce. Discard the sauce where the chicken rested.

GRILLED CHICKEN WITH GOAT CHEESE

Here in North Carolina we have a wonderful goat cheese dairy called Celebrity Farms, near Silar City. Their success and attention to quality have spawned many artisanal goat cheese makers throughout the state. Ben Barker, the award-winning chef of the Magnolia Grill, in Durham, North Carolina, used to serve a chicken breast stuffed with goat cheese, and the combination was ethereal. I'm making life a little easier with boneless, skinless chicken breasts and by melting the goat cheese on top of the chicken at the very end.

SERVES 6

DIRECT HEAT

Three 8-ounce boneless, skinless chicken breasts, halved and trimmed

¼ cup olive oil

Freshly ground black pepper

6 ounces soft goat cheese

3 tablespoons sliced chives

Kosher salt

1. Place the chicken breasts on a large platter. Rub them with the olive oil and pepper. Cover and refrigerate for at least 30 minutes or up to 6 hours.

2. In the meantime, combine the goat cheese and chives in a small bowl. Season with salt and pepper to taste and make sure the mixture is well blended.

3. Oil the grill racks. Preheat your grill using all burners set on high and with the lid closed for 10 to 12 minutes.

4. Turn your grill's burners to medium-high and place the chicken on the grill. Close the lid and cook for about 5 minutes. Turn the breasts over and spread about 1 tablespoon of the goat cheese mixture in a thin coat on each breast half. Cook for an additional 7 to 11 minutes, without turning the chicken, or until the chicken is cooked through. Remove from the grill to a platter and serve immediately with the remaining goat cheese–chive mixture on the side.

CHICKEN *SPIEDINI*

½ cup extra-virgin olive oil

¼ cup coarsely chopped fresh
    marjoram, oregano, or thyme

3 tablespoons white-wine vinegar

1 shallot, finely chopped
    (about 3 tablespoons)

2 garlic cloves, coarsely chopped

4 teaspoons kosher salt

Freshly ground black pepper

1¼ pounds boneless,
    skinless chicken breasts,
    cut into 1½-inch cubes

¾ pound pancetta or slab bacon,
    cut into 1-inch cubes

2 cups dry fine breadcrumbs

8 skewers (if using bamboo,
    soak in water for at 30 minutes)

Every nation has a word for chunks of meat roasted on a stick. *Spiedini* is that word in Italian. What could be bad about this recipe? Quick-cooking boneless, skinless chicken breasts cut into cubes, marinated in a garlicky-herby fluid, and alternated on a skewer with pork. There is one little Italian twist that many of us in this country probably are not familiar with—coating the chicken pieces in breadcrumbs before placing them on the grill. It adds another dimension of texture to this already delicious yet simple preparation.

1. Whisk the olive oil, marjoram, vinegar, shallot, garlic, 2 teaspoons of the salt, and pepper in a large bowl. Add the chicken and turn to coat evenly. Cover and marinate at room temperature for 1 hour, stirring once, or refrigerate for up to 4 hours. If you choose to refrigerate, you might want to pour everything into a large zip-top bag to take up less space.

2. Oil the grill racks. Preheat your grill using all burners set on high and with the lid closed for 10 to 12 minutes.

3. Put the pancetta or bacon into a saucepan with enough cold water to cover. Bring to a boil over high heat, then immediately drain off the liquid. Set aside.

4. Remove the chicken from the marinade and discard the marinade. Put the breadcrumbs in a shallow bowl and season with the remaining 2 teaspoons salt. Roll the chicken pieces in the breadcrumbs to coat.

5. Alternate threading the chicken and pancetta onto the skewers, starting and ending with chicken. Leave space around the meat so the heat gets to all sides.

6. Place the skewers on the grill. Close the lid and grill, turning every few minutes, until the chicken is cooked thoroughly and the breadcrumbs are crispy, 8 to 10 minutes. Serve hot.

THAI BARBECUE CHICKEN THIGHS WITH PEANUT SAUCE

SERVES 6

DIRECT HEAT

4 garlic cloves, minced

¼ cup chopped fresh cilantro leaves

¼ cup plus 2 tablespoons Asian fish sauce

1 teaspoon freshly ground black pepper

1 teaspoon curry powder

3 cups unsweetened coconut milk ("lite" is fine)

4 pounds bone-in chicken thighs

1½ teaspoons green curry paste

1 teaspoon paprika

1 garlic clove, smashed and worked into a paste

2 tablespoons creamy peanut butter

1 tablespoon seedless tamarind paste

2 tablespoons light brown sugar

¼ cup chopped unsalted dry-roasted peanuts

2 limes, cut into wedges

Think of that tasty standby, Thai chicken satay, and transfer those flavors to a moist chicken thigh and you've got a general idea of how good this recipe is. Nowadays most all of the ingredients needed for this recipe can be found at your local supermarket. If not, Asian markets definitely have them. Although we're working with chicken thighs in this recipe, the marinade and the sauce are exceptional on pork and even lamb. The peanut sauce will keep for several days in the refrigerator. For a really funky side dish later on in the week, toss the sauce with Chinese noodles and a few minced scallions for a cold noodle salad. Serve these thighs with steaming jasmine rice.

1. In a large zip-top bag, combine the minced garlic, cilantro, ¼ cup of the fish sauce, the pepper, curry powder, and 1 cup of the coconut milk. Add the chicken thighs, close the bag, and squish the marinade to coat the chicken. Refrigerate for at least 4 hours and up to 8 hours.

2. While the chicken is marinating, make the dipping sauce. Take a medium saucepan and add the curry paste, paprika, garlic paste, peanut butter, tamarind, brown sugar, peanuts, the remaining 2 tablespoons fish sauce, and the remaining 2 cups coconut milk. Place over medium heat and bring to a simmer, stirring to blend the ingredients. Let the sauce cook until thickened and reduced by half, 15 to 20 minutes. The sauce can be served warm or at room temperature.

3. Oil the grill racks. Preheat your grill using all burners set on high and with the lid closed for 10 to 12 minutes.

4. Remove the chicken from the refrigerator 30 minutes before you plan to cook. Pull the chicken thighs from the marinade and pat dry. Pour the remaining marinade into a small saucepan. Bring to a full boil over high heat and let boil for 1 minute. Remove from the heat and let cool.

5. Place the chicken on the grill and close the lid. The chicken will need to cook for 25 to 35 minutes. You want to turn the pieces frequently and baste with the reserved marinade. About halfway through the cooking time, you will need to reduce the temperature of your burners to medium so that the thighs don't turn into crispy bits of carbon. During the last 5 minutes or so, do not baste with the marinade. When the thighs are firm to the touch and an instant-read thermometer hits 165°F to 170°F, remove the thighs to a platter. Let rest for about 5 minutes, and then serve with the dipping sauce and lime wedges on the side.

FORGET THE FRIED CHICKEN WINGS

As legend has it, back in October of 1964 Buffalo's Anchor Bar owner Teressa Bellissimo fried her first chicken wings and then smothered them in a hot sauce. Since then, they have become America's favorite finger food. How do you improve on them? I'll take that challenge by leaving the fryer under the counter and taking the wings to the grill. Once you've added that sear of instant caramelization, I'm willing to bet that the fryer may not see the light of day again.

1. Place the wings in a large bowl and drizzle with the canola oil. Toss the wings until they are well coated. Sprinkle the rub over the wings and toss to coat. Cover and put in the refrigerator overnight. About an hour before you're ready to cook, remove the wings and make the hot sauce.

2. Take a large skillet and melt the butter over medium heat. Add the garlic and cook for about 2 minutes, just long enough for the garlic flavor to infuse the butter. Pour in the hot sauce, vinegar, and celery seeds. Stir to combine and remove from the heat.

3. Oil the grill racks. Preheat your grill using all burners set on high and with the lid closed for 10 to 12 minutes.

4. Place the chicken wings on the grill, close the lid, and cook for 15 to 20 minutes, turning frequently, until all sides are brown and have grill marks. Transfer the wings to the skillet with the hot sauce and place over low heat, tossing to completely coat the wings. Let the wings and the sauce meld for about 5 minutes. Remove the wings to a platter, and pour any additional sauce over them. Serve with the dressing, celery sticks, and plenty of napkins.

SERVES 6 TO 8 AS AN APPETIZER

DIRECT HEAT

3 pounds chicken wings, tips removed

3 tablespoons canola oil

2 tablespoons My Quick, Simple, and Wonderful All-Purpose Rub (see p. 282) or your favorite barbecue rub

½ cup (1 stick) unsalted butter

6 garlic cloves, minced

½ cup Frank's RedHot Sauce or your favorite variety

1 tablespoon distilled white vinegar

⅛ teaspoon celery seeds

Blue cheese or ranch dressing, for serving

Celery sticks, for serving

SUPER-MOIST BUTTERMILK-BRINED CHICKEN BREASTS

SERVES 4

DIRECT AND INDIRECT HEAT

2 cups low-fat buttermilk

1 tablespoon kosher salt

Four 1-pound bone-in chicken breasts

1 tablespoon ground cinnamon

1 tablespoon ground cumin

1 tablespoon ground coriander

1 tablespoon sugar

1 tablespoon granulated garlic

1 tablespoon onion powder

1 tablespoon freshly ground
    black pepper

1 teaspoon ancho chile powder

1 teaspoon chipotle chile powder

1 teaspoon ground ginger

1 teaspoon ground sage

Your favorite sauce for chicken,
    barbecue or otherwise (optional)

Sometimes developing recipes for a cookbook is a bit like being a mad scientist. You have dreams in smidgens of flavor profiles that somehow or another you want to work together. This recipe started out in my head as grilled fried chicken and resulted in one of the moistest, most tender chicken breasts I've ever cooked on the grill.

1. Pour the buttermilk into a large zip-top bag. Add the salt and the chicken breasts. Close the bag and squish the liquid around the chicken breasts. Put in the refrigerator and let sit overnight, turning the bag several times.

2. Combine the 11 herbs and spices in a small container with an airtight lid. You won't use all of this mixture for this recipe, but use the extra within 6 months.

3. Oil the grill racks. Preheat your grill using all burners set on high and with the lid closed for 10 to 12 minutes.

4. When the grill is hot, cut off the center or back burner and adjust your heat to medium-high.

5. Remove the breasts from the bag and discard the brine. Pat the breasts dry and then sprinkle about a tablespoon of the rub on each breast, gently massaging the rub into the meat.

6. Place the chicken breasts, skin down, over the direct heat section of your grill, close the lid, and cook for 3 or 4 minutes or until nicely seared. Turn and sear the other side for 3 to 4 minutes. Move the chicken breasts to the indirect area, cut your burners to medium, and close the lid. You want to maintain about a 325°F temperature. Grill-roast for about 45 minutes or until an instant-read thermometer reads 170°F in the thickest portion of the breast. During the last 5 minutes glaze the chicken breast with your choice of sauce on the skin side only. Remove the breasts from the grill to a platter and let rest for about 5 minutes. Serve.

GRILLED MOROCCAN-STYLE CORNISH GAME HENS

Cornish game hens are perfect for entertaining or for an elegant dinner. The little hens, which are actually a variety of chicken, become an individual portion for each person. In this recipe we gamble a little bit and cook the hens over direct heat, replicating what the Moroccan nomads might have done over an open pit. I think you'll find the end result interesting and appetizing.

1. Combine the oil, lemon juice, cilantro, parsley, garlic, paprika, cinnamon, turmeric, allspice, ginger, and lemon zest in a small bowl and stir until well mixed.

2. Put the hens in one or two large zip-top bags and pour the marinade over them, dividing equally if using two bags. Squish it all around the hens and close the bags. Refrigerate for at least 6 hours, but preferably overnight.

3. Oil the grill racks. Preheat your grill using all burners set on high and with the lid closed for 10 to 12 minutes.

4. Remove the hens from the marinade, pat dry, and discard the marinade. Adjust the burners on your grill to medium heat. Place the hens, breast side down, on the grill, close the lid, and cook for about 15 minutes. Turn and grill for an additional 25 to 30 minutes, or until the juices run clear when the thickest part of the thigh is pricked with a knife and an instant-read thermometer inserted in the thigh registers 170°F. Take care with your temperature, adjusting the burners' heat as necessary. The bird should be grilled, not burned. Let rest for at least 5 minutes before serving.

SERVES 4
DIRECT HEAT

½ cup peanut oil

¼ cup fresh lemon juice

2 tablespoons chopped fresh cilantro

2 tablespoons chopped fresh flat-leaf parsley

2 garlic cloves, minced

1 tablespoon paprika

2 teaspoons ground cinnamon

2 teaspoons ground turmeric

2 teaspoons ground allspice

2 teaspoons minced fresh ginger

2 teaspoons minced lemon zest

Four 1- to 1¼-pound Cornish game hens

HICKORY-SMOKED BOURBON TURKEY

SERVES 12 TO 14

INDIRECT HEAT

One 12-pound fresh turkey

8 cups water

2 cups pure maple syrup

1 cup bourbon

½ cup plus 1 tablespoon kosher salt

1 tablespoon pickling spice

1 large carrot, peeled and
    halved crosswise

1 rib celery, halved crosswise

1 medium onion, peeled and halved

1 lemon

2 teaspoons freshly ground
    black pepper

Hickory wood chips, soaked in water
    for 1 hour

This turkey gets smoked. Yeah, the low and slow way to magnificent results. Armed with a brine and hickory chips, a plain-Jane turkey turns into outdoor cooking nirvana. If bourbon is not your thing, cut back by half or cut it out entirely, replacing it with another cup of water. You can buy specially designed turkey brining bags, but it's just as easy to use turkey oven-cooking bags for brining. Plan ahead for the 6-hour cooking time.

1. Remove the giblets and neck from the turkey; reserve for other uses, if desired. Rinse the turkey thoroughly with cold water and pat dry.

2. To make the brine, a large stockpot is usually a good container. Pour in the water, maple syrup, bourbon, ½ cup of the salt, and pickling spice. Place your turkey in a brining bag and pour the brine over the bird. The turkey needs to be completely submerged, so add additional water if needed. Close the bag tightly; like to put it in another bag just for insurance. Put in the refrigerator for at least 24 hours, but no more than 36 hours or the brine will begin to make the meat mushy.

3. Oil the grill racks. Preheat your grill using all burners set on high and with the lid closed for 10 to 12 minutes.

4. When the grill is hot, cut off the center or back burner and adjust the heat to medium-low.

5. Remove the turkey from the brine, discarding the water mixture. Pat dry inside and out and set it on a baking sheet. Stuff the cavity with the carrot, celery, and onion. Slice the lemon in half and squeeze the juice over the turkey, then place the rinds in the cavity. Season the turkey with the remaining 1 tablespoon salt and the pepper, rubbing it into the skin. Fold the wings under and tie the legs together with kitchen twine.

6. Drain the wood chips and place in a smoker box (follow your manufacturer's instructions) if your grill is so equipped. If not, see pp. 16–17 for directions on making a wood-chip packet. Place a small disposable pan on the grill and fill halfway with water. Place the turkey on the grill, close the lid, and be patient. The turkey will need to cook and smoke for about 6 hours, or until a meat thermometer registers 170°F when inserted into the thickest part of the thigh or the juices run clear when nicked with a knife. During this time you will need to add additional water and wood chips. Wood chips tend to burn for 15 to 20 minutes. So about every 30 minutes, quickly add more wood chips. Every time you lift the grill's lid you're losing precious heat and smoke.

7. When the turkey is done, remove it from the grill and let rest for at least 30 minutes before carving.

"BLUE" CHICKEN

SERVES 4
DIRECT AND INDIRECT HEAT

1 pint fresh blueberries

¾ cup red-wine vinegar

Two 1- to 1½-pound Cornish
   game hens, backbones removed
   and split in half

¼ cup olive oil

1 bay leaf

¼ teaspoon dried thyme

1 garlic clove, minced

FOR THE BLUEBERRY
BARBECUE SAUCE

1 tablespoon olive oil

1 small onion, minced

1 fresh jalapeño chile, stemmed,
   seeded, and finely chopped
   (wear gloves to prevent irritation)

1 cup fresh blueberries

2 tablespoons rice vinegar

2 tablespoons ketchup

4 teaspoons brown sugar

4 teaspoons Dijon mustard

½ teaspoon hot sauce

2 tablespoons unsalted butter

Kosher salt

Freshly ground black pepper

That's what my daughter calls this poultry dish because the first time I served it, when she was about 10 or 11, she was intrigued at how the marinade had turned the flesh a light blue color. The concept for this dish came from a dinner at the Inn at Little Washington. The blueberry barbecue sauce has great applications not only here but also with duck, venison, quail, or squab. It makes about a cup and will keep in the refrigerator for 4 days. Reheat it slowly, stirring, before serving. Poussins are fun, but Cornish game hens work well, too.

1. For the marinade, combine the blueberries and vinegar in a 2-quart saucepan. Set over medium heat and bring just to a boil. Remove from the heat and let steep for 1 hour at room temperature. Strain, discarding any solids.

2. Place the Cornish hens in a large zip-top bag. Pour in the vinegar mixture, oil, bay leaf, thyme, and garlic. Close the bag and squish the mixture around to combine and coat the game hens. Let stand at room temperature for about 1½ hours or refrigerate overnight.

3. Meanwhile, make the barbecue sauce. In a medium skillet, heat the oil over medium-high heat. When it shimmers, add the onion and jalapeño. Stir constantly until both vegetables are tender. Add the blueberries, vinegar, ketchup, brown sugar, mustard, and hot sauce to the pan. Bring to a boil, then reduce the heat to low and simmer for 15 minutes. Stir the mixture often. Remove the mixture from the heat and let cool slightly. Pour into a blender or food processor and process by pulsing until smooth. You might need to scrape down the sides once or twice while doing this. Strain the blueberry mixture into a small saucepan, pressing hard against the solids to get out all the liquid. Place the saucepan over medium heat and whisk in the butter. Add salt and pepper to taste, then remove from the heat.

4. Oil the grill racks. Preheat your grill using all burners set on high and with the lid closed for 10 to 12 minutes.

5. When the grill is hot, cut off the center or back burner and adjust your heat to medium-high.

6. Remove the hens from the bag and discard the remaining marinade. Place on the direct heat portion of your grill, close the lid, and sear each side for about 2 minutes. Place the birds over the indirect heat portion of the grill and cook for a total of about 1¼ hours, or until an instant-read thermometer inserted in the thigh registers 180°F or the juices run clear when pierced with a knife. During the last 5 minutes, brush the game hens with a bit of the barbecue sauce. Remove to a platter and serve with additional sauce on the side.

147

ROTISSERIE DUCK WITH CHIPOTLE-TAMARIND BARBECUE SAUCE

SERVES 4

INDIRECT HEAT

FOR THE CHIPOTLE-TAMARIND BARBECUE SAUCE

One 6-ounce can tomato paste

¼ cup water

½ cup tamarind paste

⅓ cup packed dark brown sugar

3 canned chipotle chiles in adobo sauce, chopped

2 tablespoons sherry vinegar

1 garlic clove, smashed with the flat side of a knife

1 tablespoon kosher salt

One 5-pound duck

Kosher salt

Freshly ground black pepper

1 orange, quartered

1 red onion, quartered

4 garlic cloves, smashed with the flat side of a knife

Like the black-and-white cows of television-commercial fame that implore you to "eat more chickin," I'm on a campaign to eat more duck. It's a rich and luscious meat that takes to the grill better than almost any other poultry item. Duck can stand up to assertive flavors as in this preparation. The tamarind and dark brown sugar combine in the sauce to give you volumes of flavor and a wonderful hue. I will warn you that when this duck is finished it's going to be a deep, dark mahogany—almost black—color. If you don't have a rotisserie, then cook the duck like you would any other poultry over indirect heat.

1. For the barbecue sauce, blend the tomato paste, water, tamarind paste, sugar, chipotles, vinegar, garlic, and salt until smooth with a hand blender or in a food processor. If you aren't using it immediately, cover and refrigerate for up to 1 week. (This sauce yields about 2 cups, and you won't use all of it for this recipe. Brush the remainder over some boneless, skinless chicken breasts the next time you throw those on the grill.)

2. Preheat your grill with a rotisserie attachment using all burners set on high and with the lid closed for 10 to 12 minutes.

3. Remove the giblets and neck from the cavity of the bird and discard. Trim the neck flap and excess fat from around the cavity. Rinse the bird inside and out and pat dry. Pierce the skin all over with a small knife or skewer at ½-inch intervals, taking care not to poke into the fat. Season the cavity generously with salt and pepper and stuff it with the orange, onion, and garlic.

4. Thread the duck onto the rotisserie spit through the cavity. Attach the spit to the rotisserie. Cook the duck until most of its fat has rendered and the meat is almost cooked.

This should take 50 to 60 minutes. At this point, brush the duck with about ½ cup of the barbecue sauce. Continue cooking until the duck has a rich mahogany glaze and an instant-read thermometer register 180°F when inserted into the thickest part of the thigh, about 20 minutes longer, basting once more about 10 minutes before it is done.

5. When the duck is cooked, transfer to a cutting board and let it rest for 10 minutes. Don't cover it or you will lose the crisp skin. Remove the duck from the rotisserie spit. Carve the duck and arrange the pieces on a warm serving platter. Drizzle more of the sauce over the pieces and pass the rest at the table.

ROTISSERIE
COOKING

Rotisserie cooking has become the rage in the past few years, and personally I'm glad this method of cooking is back. It cooks large items more evenly than any other method and, because of the constant turning, it's almost self-basting. You don't need to use your rotisserie all the time. Heck, you don't even need to have a rotisserie, but it's kind of a fun way of cooking every now and again. Most manufacturers of better gas grills today at least have designed the capability to incorporate a rotisserie into their product, and rotisseries are readily available as accessories for most grills. Higher-end grills such as the Weber Summit®, Viking® gas grills, and several other models now include an infrared rotisserie burner, which makes life even easier.

Since many grills with rotisserie attachments are four- and six-burner models, you should turn the two burners at the end to medium, cut off the middle burners, and leave the rotisserie burner running. If your grill is not equipped with a rotisserie burner, don't worry. On a three-burner grill, cut off the center and back burner. For those grills without the rotisserie burner, you may have to add another 15 to 20 minutes to your cooking time.

GRILLED DUCK BREASTS WITH HOT PEPPER JELLY GLAZE

SERVES 4

DIRECT HEAT

Four 6- to 8-ounce boneless,
    skin-on duck breasts, any excess
    fat removed

1 tablespoon kosher salt

1 teaspoon freshly ground
    black pepper

1 teaspoon chopped fresh thyme

1 teaspoon chopped fresh rosemary
    leaves

1 bay leaf, crumbled

FOR THE PEPPER GLAZE

½ cup prepared veal demi-glace
    (see sidebar, on the facing page)

½ cup water

¼ cup sherry vinegar

1 large shallot, finely chopped

2 tablespoons hot pepper jelly

1 tablespoon unsalted butter

Kosher salt

Susan Spicer, chef/owner of Bayona, a restaurant just on the fringes of the French Quarter in New Orleans, has been one of my favorite "flavorologists" for some 20 years. One of the first recipes of hers I ever tried was for pepper jelly–glazed duck breasts, and it has become one of my favorite recipes. Now, that first time I prepared the dish I did it the hard way, with a whole duck, cutting off the breasts, saving the legs for something else, and making a duck stock from the bones and then reducing the duck stock to a duck glace. It took all day, wore me out, but the end result was delicious and I vowed to figure out a few shortcuts. Here's my easier version of this chef-inspired dish that skips very few beats from the original recipe.

1. Lightly score the skin side of the duck breasts, but be careful not to go all the way to the meat. Mix together the salt, pepper, thyme, rosemary, and bay leaf in a small bowl and rub this mixture on the skin of the duck breasts. Refrigerate for 2 to 4 hours or let stand at room temperature for about 1 hour.

2. In the meantime, make the glaze. Combine the demi-glace, water, vinegar, and shallot in a small saucepan and bring to a boil. Lower the heat and simmer until the liquid has reduced by about a third. Remove from the heat and whisk in the pepper jelly and then the butter. Season to taste with salt. If you feel like the sauce is too sweet, add a hair more vinegar, or if it's too acidic a bit more jelly. Set aside at room temperature.

3. Oil the grill racks. Preheat your grill using all burners set on high and with the lid closed for 10 to 12 minutes.

4. Duck breasts tend to create flare-ups and a lot of smoke. Be prepared for the flare-ups by adjusting your heat and moving the duck breasts around on your grill. I have found that spritzing the flare-ups with water just seems to move fat to a different location. The smoke is inevitable, and it will drive your neighbors crazy.

5. Place the duck breasts, skin side down, on the grill. Close the lid and cook for 8 to 10 minutes. This will render much of the fat between the skin and the meat and also make the skin crispy. Turn and cook for about 3 more minutes. The duck breasts should yield easily to the touch. For me, duck is better rare or medium-rare, and these times should give you a medium-rare finish. Turn the breasts skin side up, cut off all your burners and your gas, and brush lightly with the pepper jelly glaze. Close the lid for about 2 minutes. Remove the duck breasts to a platter, drizzle with more of the pepper jelly glaze, and pass any additional at the table.

AT THE
MARKET

There are several companies now producing concentrated stocks. I particularly like D'Artagnan® veal demi-glace for this preparation, and the recipe here was based on using that product. More Than Gourmet® also makes an excellent product called Demi-Glace Gold®, which is a super-concentrated meat stock that you have to rehydrate before using.

When it comes to pepper jelly, if you live in the South, Braswell's is the brand. However, I've also experimented with Foster's Seven Pepper Jelly and two Dickinson's products, a Cherry Pepper Jelly and a Sweet 'n' Hot Pepper and Onion Relish, to make the glaze. All give excellent results.

ASIAN GRILLED QUAIL, SAVANNAH-STYLE

SERVES 8

DIRECT HEAT

¼ cup hoisin sauce

¼ cup chili sauce with garlic

¼ cup toasted sesame oil

¼ cup honey

2 tablespoons sesame seeds

1 teaspoon ground ginger

8 semi-boneless quail, butterflied

2 cups low-sodium chicken broth

2 teaspoons cornstarch

One of the top caterers in Savannah, Georgia, routinely uses this recipe for her Asian grilled quail. It's a beautiful dish that's just as appropriate for a sit-down dinner as it is for a buffet or heavy hors d'oeuvres. The ingredients are easy to find, and the lacquered little birds are heavenly to the tongue.

1. Take a large bowl and combine the hoisin sauce, chili sauce, sesame oil, honey, sesame seeds, and ginger. Add the quail, turning to coat all sides. Cover and refrigerate for 30 minutes.

2. Oil the grill racks. Preheat your grill using all burners set on high and with the lid closed for 10 to 12 minutes.

3. Remove the quail from the marinade, allowing as much of the marinade as possible to drip back into the bowl. Reserve the marinade. Place the quail on the grill and reduce the heat to medium. Close the lid and cook for about 10 minutes. Turn, cover again, and continue cooking for an additional 10 minutes. At this point the quail will be medium and still pink, which is okay with these little birds, or you can continue cooking for another 10 minutes, 5 minutes on each side, if you like your quail a little more well done.

4. Remove the quail from the grill to a platter and loosely cover with foil. Pour the reserved marinade into a medium saucepan. Reserve ¼ cup of the chicken broth and pour the remainder into the saucepan with the marinade. Place the saucepan over medium heat and bring to a boil. Whisk the cornstarch into the reserved broth until smooth, and then whisk this mixture into the marinade and continue to cook until the sauce is thickened, about 2 minutes.

5. Serve the quail with a little of the sauce drizzled over each bird, passing the rest of the sauce at the table.

OUT OF THE WATER AND ON TO THE FLAME

FISH AND SHELLFISH

Grilled **FISH WITH MINT VINAIGRETTE** *(Pesce alla Griglia con Salsa di Menta)* 163

FOOLPROOF Grilled Fish 164

Grilled **HALIBUT** with Balsamic-Tomato Vinaigrette 165

SIMPLE Grilled Fish 167

Whole Smoke-Grilled **MOUNTAIN TROUT** 169

HERB-MARINATED MONKFISH with Sherry Vinaigrette 170

Grilled **BARBECUED SALMON** 172

GRILL-ROASTED SALMON with Tomato Jam 173

Gene's Northern California **PLANKED SALMON** 174

Grilled **WILD KING SALMON,** Northwest-Style 176

CUBAN-STYLE Grilled Fish *(Pescados Asado)* 177

TUNA with Mango Relish 178

BACONIZED TUNA with Lemon Butter 179

GRILLED TUNA with Marinated Cucumbers 181

North African **GRILLED SHRIMP** 182

Spicy **GRILL-STEAMED CLAMS** 184

SEA SCALLOPS with Hot and Sweet Dipping Sauce 185

Grilled **SCALLOPS** with Rémoulade Sauce 186

The **OYSTER ROAST** 189

Simply Grilled **LOBSTER TAILS** 190

"COOKING FISH AND SHELLFISH ON THE GRILL scares

the bejesus out of otherwise competent grill enthusiasts." I wrote those words almost ten years ago, but they are still as true today as they were then. Wherever I go to teach a cooking class about grilling seafood, there will be an overflow crowd, and the two most common laments I hear are overcooking and sticking to the grill. We know the benefits of eating seafood, we go to restaurants and order grilled seafood that delights us, yet we seem to have difficulty or we're just plain afraid of putting fire to fish and shellfish.

Actually, it's pretty simple, as long as you follow two rules and forget two others. What you need to remember: Pick the right fish to grill, and—this is critical—keep your cooking grid impeccably clean. What do you need to forget? The old saw about cooking fish until it flakes. If fish flakes, it's overcooked. And unless you're cooking a whole fish, forget about cooking it for 10 minutes per inch of thickness. It's a good way to get fish to flake, which means it's overcooked. Eight minutes per inch is ideal for most fillets and steaks.

Another part of the problem might be the grill you use. I started my grilling career as a dyed-in-the-wool charcoal fan, but I always had difficulty cooking fish and shellfish because of my grill's temperature inconsistencies. When I got my first gas grill as a Father's Day present with a note that hinted that this might be quicker and thus I could spend more time with my daughter, I learned how easy grilling fish and shellfish could be. The gas grill allows for total control of temperature, and that makes grilling fish and seafood simple. It also allows me to grill fish more often because the preheat time is so short and there's so little preparation to get the grill ready. I don't think twice about firing it up, especially during the week, for some quickly seared salmon, tuna, or shrimp. Use these recipes and you, too, will overcome any fear that you might have about grilling these water dwellers, and you'll soon learn the grand flavor that seafood develops on a grill. You'll get ongoing tips on how to cook these sensuous items along with mouthwatering ideas for perfect seasoning.

IF FISH FLAKES, IT'S OVERCOOKED.

AT THE MARKET

When I wrote *The Big Book of Fish and Shellfish* I did extensive research to determine the most important things to look for when buying seafood. If your eyes are the most important tool for identifying quality beef, your nose is first for fish. It starts at the door to the market or as you enter the fish department of your supermarket. If you walk in and smell ammonia, chlorine, or that "fishy" smell, turn around and walk out. That store has more issues than you care to deal with. What you do want to smell is . . . nothing.

Once the market passes the initial smell test, your eyes come into play. What you want to see is *beaucoup de* ice, the gold standard in any fish market. Whole fish should be buried in ice and fillets should be in trays placed on top of ice. Look to see that shellfish and finfish are in separate cases. For various reasons, the two just don't play well together.

You should get to know your fishmonger, because you need to be politely demanding now: Ask to smell the fish. No, you don't need to put your nose into it—you will know if the fish is pristine or not when your nose is within a foot of its presence. Ask the fishmonger to press on the item. It should be springy and bounce back quickly. The flesh of older fish is not as elastic, and any fish whose flesh doesn't spring back was probably caught a while ago. Dark spots are also a sign of age, as is what I call the "halo rainbow" that you see on many tuna steaks. Shellfish like oysters, mussels, and clams should include a tag with the date of harvest and the waters they were taken from. Most will likely be from farms, which are regulated and where the waters are checked for weird stuff. All items in a seafood case should be labeled as farmed or wild caught, fresh or frozen.

Never turn your nose up at frozen seafood. The notion that a small boat goes off the shore, catches a few fish, throws them on ice, and brings them in daily is only a reality in top-flight restaurants. Many times a frozen fillet is much fresher than one labeled "fresh" in the case. In a normal supermarket I tend to buy more frozen than fresh because I will then know when it was thawed out.

I can't overemphasize the need to develop a relationship with your fishmonger. Once they know you're serious they will always make certain that you leave with the best in the case—whether it's what you went in to purchase or not. If you went in to buy tuna for a specific recipe but the tuna looks awful, substitute another meaty fish such as salmon or halibut. Always go with what's fresh—don't be driven by your recipe.

PICKING THE RIGHT SEAFOOD

FOR THE GRILL Notice: thin fillets need not apply.

MEATY, FIRM, AND THICK FILLETS AND STEAKS Direct Heat	MORE DELICATE BUT STILL FAIRLY MEATY FILLETS AND STEAKS Direct Heat	WHOLE FISH Indirect Heat	SHELLFISH Direct Heat
Grouper	Mahimahi	Mackerel	Shrimp
Salmon	Chilean sea bass	Bluefish	Scallops
Tuna	Halibut	Grouper	Lobster
Swordfish	Red snapper	Salmon	Oysters
Monkfish	Trout	Red snapper	Clams
Mackerel	Striped bass	Striped bass	
Catfish		Trout	

COOK IT RIGHT

You'll notice in the chart above that I say "thin fillets need not apply." You won't be happy if you grill a thin, delicate fish like flounder or sole, unless you invest in a grilling basket or a perforated grid. These tools make grilling delicate flat fillets possible, as well as smaller shrimp and scallops.

Most fish and shellfish are better cooked over direct heat. With few exceptions, the only times you'll want to grill a sea creature (or one from a lake or river) over indirect heat are when you're smoking them or if you're doing a whole one.

DON'T MAKE ME FLAKE

Timing is everything when you're cooking seafood, and you can definitely put more cook on, but you can't take cook off—that is, once a food is cooked, you can't uncook it. If you're accustomed to eating fish that's been cooked till it flakes, you may find the thought of fish cooked to medium-rare or medium a bit off-putting. But once you try it, you may enjoy it. Tuna, for instance, tastes best when it is cooked warm and caramelized on the outside and almost dead cold at the center, and it is the one exception to the rule about always cooking all foods with the grill covered. Tuna should always be cooked with the cover up, and it cooks quickly—just a couple of minutes on each side. Salmon is another fish that quite frankly is better when cooked to medium-rare to medium.

MAKING SEAFOOD NONSTICK

HERE ARE THE GUIDELINES and key things to remember to prevent seafood from sticking.

- Use high heat. The proteins from fish will release quicker and more easily if you place them over a super hot fire.

- Have a pristinely clean cooking grate. The proteins in the fish will stick to the protein deposits on the grill's grate. Remove those and you lessen the likelihood of sticking.

- Coat the fish with oil or an oil-based substance. Believe it or not, brushing a fillet with mayonnaise both prevents the fillet from sticking and helps seal in moisture, without imparting any mayonnaise flavor.

- There are two schools of thought as to whether you need to oil the fish and the cooking grate. Some people think that oiling the one or the other is enough, others oil both fish and grate. Experiment both ways and see what works best for you. Then put the fish or shellfish on the grill and let it stay in place until the proteins release, and turn the food only once. Another tip that I've learned when grilling fish fillets is to cook the first side just a bit longer than the second. This has partly to do with the proteins releasing, but since that first side down is going to be the presentation side, that's the side you really want to be beautiful.

WILD OR FARMED?

I WILL ADMIT THAT I HAVE A PREFERENCE FOR WILD or freshly caught sea-food, but the reason has to do as much with people as with fish. Fishermen, watermen, and other people who make their living from the waters are the last hunters and gatherers in this country. It's a hard life and I respect what they do and the way they go about it. Most good fishermen view the oceans as a bank. They only take out what they need to survive and they leave the rest.

Wild-caught fish does have a slight edge in the flavor department. Wild-caught is just that—fish from the open spaces of our waters. Farm-raised is a consistent source of protein, and Asian countries, for example, have used aqua-culture to sustain their well-being for many years. Does that piece of farm-raised salmon have the depth of flavor that wild Alaskan king salmon will have? No. All creatures are influenced by their habitat. Just as a Cabernet Sauvignon grape grown in the Napa Valley produces wine that tastes different from those of the Bordeaux region of France, so do the critters of the sea vary depending on where they live.

All seafood is now required to be labeled whether it was wild caught or farmed, the country where it was landed, and whether it was previously frozen. The best way to determine what you want to eat is to identify the most pristine product in the market that day. It may be farm raised one day and wild caught the next, but when we're talking about seafood, freshness is the only imperative.

GUIDELINES FOR GRILLING
PERFECT SEAFOOD

These are guidelines only; specific recipes may vary. Sometimes with thicker whole fish and when smoking fish, indirect heat is better. Check the recipe.

TYPE OF SEAFOOD	THICKNESS OR WEIGHT	TOTAL GRILLING TIME
FISH FILLETS AND STEAKS SUCH AS HALIBUT, SALMON, AND SEA BASS	1 in. thick	8–10 minutes
TUNA STEAKS	1 in. thick	4 minutes
WHOLE FISH	1 pound	20 minutes
WHOLE FISH	3 pounds	30–40 minutes
SHRIMP	21–24 count per pound	6 minutes
SEA SCALLOPS	11 per pound	About 5 minutes
OYSTERS	In shell	5–7 minutes
CLAMS	In shell	8 minutes
LOBSTER TAIL	6–8 ounces	7–9 minutes

The best way to test any fish fillet for doneness is to push a knife into the center, pull it out, and touch its tip to your tongue. The knife reflects how much heat has reached the center of the fish; most fish are done when warm at the center. You can also cut into a fish without losing moisture. Just use your knife to separate the flakes and take a quick peek inside to see if the flesh is translucent, which is about medium-rare, to just opaque, which is about medium, and which is absolutely perfect for 90 percent of your fish-grilling forays. Having done those two tests, press on the fish just as you would a steak or a chop to see how firm the fish feels. After a few times checking the inside and feeling the firmness, you'll figure out what doneness you like.

When grilling whole fish, cutting a small slit into the flesh is the best indicator. The touch test is somewhat reliable, but with the bones and the cavity of the fish, it's a little harder to learn that method. As I said earlier, forget cook until it flakes. Think in terms of separating instead of flaking. Eight minutes per inch is a better rule of thumb than ten minutes.

Shellfish such as shrimp and scallops should be barely cooked through or opaque at the center. Shrimp will take on their familiar pink color, and they should maintain a slight "C" shape. Anything tighter means it's overcooked. Scallops can be cooked to medium; again the touch test is your best indicator. If you enjoy rare tuna, try cooking scallops to a medium-rare, translucent-in-the-center stage.

GRILLED FISH WITH MINT VINAIGRETTE (PESCE ALLA GRIGLIA CON SALSA DI MENTA)

Most of my travels in Italy have been in the north-central regions of Umbria and Tuscany—places that celebrate wild boar. But one of the most breathtaking parts of Italy is the Amalfi Coast and the surrounding areas. In this region, "fish" means "it was in the water last night," so "fresh" takes on a whole new meaning. Most grilled fish is done whole and simply prepared, sometimes adorned with a sauce, but often with nothing more than lemon juice and olive oil. This mint sauce was inspired by the restaurant at the Hotel Delano, which hangs on the coast overlooking the isle of Capri. It'll take you to Italy with its taste sensation.

1. To make the mint vinaigrette, whisk the olive oil, garlic, vinegar, lemon juice, and salt to taste in a medium bowl. Stir in the mint. Make the sauce at least 1 hour ahead, but not more than 2 hours, and let stand at room temperature until ready to use.

2. Oil the grill racks. Preheat your grill using all burners set on high and with the lid closed for 10 to 12 minutes.

3. Rinse the fish under cold water and pat dry with paper towels. Season the cavity with salt. Combine the garlic, parsley, and mint. Rub the mixture into the cavity, then drizzle the cavity with 1 teaspoon of the olive oil.

4. Salt and dust one side of the fish with flour, then drizzle 1 teaspoon of the olive oil over that side of the fish. Place it on the grill, floured side down. Close the lid and grill for 8 to 10 minutes. Before turning the fish, sprinkle the other side with salt, dust again with flour, and drizzle with the remaining 1 teaspoon olive oil. Using a large metal spatula or two smaller ones, carefully lift the fish from the grill and turn it. Grill the fish for 8 to 10 minutes more, or until it is thoroughly cooked. Carefully transfer to a large serving platter and serve with the mint vinaigrette.

SERVES 4

DIRECT HEAT

FOR THE MINT VINAIGRETTE

¾ cup extra-virgin olive oil

1 small garlic clove,
    finely chopped or crushed

2 tablespoons white-wine vinegar

3 tablespoons fresh lemon juice

Sea salt or kosher salt

½ cup chopped fresh mint leaves

One 2½- to 3-pound whole
    striped bass or red snapper,
    scaled and gutted

Sea salt or kosher salt

1 medium garlic clove, chopped

1 teaspoon chopped fresh
    flat-leaf parsley

1 teaspoon chopped fresh
    mint leaves

3 teaspoons extra-virgin olive oil

2 teaspoons unbleached
    all-purpose flour

FOOLPROOF GRILLED FISH

½ teaspoon ground cumin

½ teaspoon ground coriander

½ teaspoon kosher salt

⅛ teaspoon freshly ground black
 pepper

Four 6-ounce halibut or
 sea bass fillets, cut 1 inch thick

4 tablespoons mayonnaise

Grilling fish can intimidate otherwise confident cooks, and it shouldn't. Grilling fish starts with listening to your mother: "Cleanliness is next to godliness." Your grill grate has to be as clean as you can get it. Without a clean grill, you are doomed from the start because the proteins in your fish will stick to the proteins on the grate. Next, a fat has to be involved. Using mayonnaise as that fat keeps the fish lubricated on the grill and also imparts moisture, without adding a flavor. This really is a foolproof way to grill most any thick, lean, white fish.

1. Oil the grill racks. Preheat your grill using all burners set on high and with the lid closed for 10 to 12 minutes.

2. Mix the cumin, coriander, salt, and pepper together in a small bowl. Sprinkle evenly over each fillet. With the back of a spoon, spread 1 tablespoon of mayonnaise over both sides of each fillet. It looks messy, but that's okay. Place the fish fillets on the grill, close the lid, and cook for 6 minutes. Turn the fillets and cook for 4 to 5 minutes longer, until they are opaque in the center. Serve at once.

GRILLED HALIBUT WITH BALSAMIC-TOMATO VINAIGRETTE

Halibut becomes regal when grilled—it takes on an "ocean-y" flavor that sometimes hides in this fish. Pair it with a great vinaigrette or a simple sauce of any kind and it's a meal that you'll get raves about. Always buy thicker cuts of halibut for grilling, and remember the first law of grilling fish: The grill must be pristinely clean. If not, disaster could loom when you go to turn the fish.

1. For the vinaigrette, combine the garlic, vinegar, ⅛ teaspoon of salt, and ⅛ teaspoon of pepper in a bowl or cup and whisk until nicely blended. Slowly whisk in the olive oil until the dressing becomes emulsified. Add the tomatoes and toss. Set aside.

2. Oil the grill racks. Preheat your grill using all burners set on high and with the lid closed for 10 to 12 minutes.

3. Season the fillets with salt and pepper and lightly brush with canola oil. Place the fish on the grill. Close the lid and grill for about 3 minutes, and then turn. Continue cooking for 3 minutes longer for medium doneness. Add a minute on both sides for a more medium-well result, but please don't overcook the fish. The fish will feel firm yet give slightly with pressure when it's done. Remove the fillets to a platter. Stir the herbs into the dressing and drizzle the dressing over the fillets. Pass any extra at the table.

SERVES 6
DIRECT HEAT

4 garlic cloves, crushed

2 tablespoons balsamic vinegar

Kosher salt

Freshly ground black pepper

5 tablespoons extra-virgin olive oil

2 large plum tomatoes, peeled, seeded, and diced, or 8 to 9 grape tomatoes, cut into quarters

Six 6- to 8-ounce halibut fillets, 1 inch thick

Canola oil

1 tablespoon finely chopped fresh tarragon (you can also use chives or basil when in season)

THE LAWS OF GRILLED FISH

IN GENERAL, GRILLING FISH REQUIRES MORE ATTENTION and care than grilling other forms of protein. You'll read this information throughout this chapter, but here are the four most important things to keep in mind when you're grilling fish and shellfish:

- Your grill grate must be impeccably, pristinely, absolutely clean, and it should be fully preheated.

- Coating the fish with fat, whether a drizzling of oil or a layer of mayonnaise, helps with heat transfer and with turning the fish. (Spraying it with vegetable oil cooking spray also works great—just do this *before* you put it on the grill!)

- Patience is a virtue. Give the fish time to release from the grill grate before trying to turn it.

- If you're grilling large fish fillets or whole fish, use two spatulas to turn.

SIMPLE GRILLED FISH

Grilling fish is not the challenge that some people believe it is. Just be sure your grill grate is clean and well oiled and that you are patient with your fish. Let the proteins cook enough to release themselves from the grate instead of forcing the issue and leaving a good portion of the fish seared to it. One other tip: Forget "flakes with a fork." By the time fish flakes it's overcooked and dry. Think in terms of about 8 minutes per inch and the flesh "separating" rather than flaking.

1. Combine the butter, lemon juice, garlic, paprika, Worcestershire, salt, cayenne, and hot sauce in a small saucepan over medium heat. Whisk until the butter is melted. Remove from the heat and let cool for several minutes.

2. Put the fish in a shallow dish and pour the butter sauce over the fillets. Let stand for about 30 minutes at room temperature.

3. Oil the grill racks. Preheat your grill using all burners set on high and with the lid closed for 10 to 12 minutes.

4. Adjust your burners to medium heat. Remove the fish from the marinade, reserving the marinade. Place the fish on the grill, close the lid, and cook for 5 to 8 minutes, depending on thickness. Carefully turn the fish and brush lightly with the reserved marinade. Cook for another 4 minutes, or until the fish is relatively firm to the touch and separates easily. Remove from the grill to a platter and serve immediately.

SERVES 4
DIRECT HEAT

6 tablespoons unsalted butter

3 tablespoons fresh lemon juice

1 small garlic clove, minced

½ teaspoon paprika

1 teaspoon Worcestershire sauce

¾ teaspoon kosher salt

¼ teaspoon cayenne

¼ teaspoon hot sauce

Four 6- to 8-ounce firm white fish fillets, such as trout or redfish

WHOLE SMOKE-GRILLED MOUNTAIN TROUT

The students in my fish-cooking classes rave over this dish. It will transport you to a mountain stream at sunset. The smoky, herbaceous flavors really make the trout jump, but without covering the gentleness of the fish. Anytime you see fresh whole trout at your market, buy some to give this recipe a whirl. They arrive at the store scaled and gutted but usually have the heads on. If the heads bug you, then have the fishmonger remove them.

1. Put the trout on a plate or in a baking dish. Coat the outside of each with the mayonnaise. Stuff 2 thyme sprigs, 2 oregano sprigs, 1 rosemary sprig, and 2 lemon slices into the body cavity of each trout. Add a little garlic if you like. Cover with plastic wrap and refrigerate until ready to grill, for up to 4 hours.

2. Oil the grill racks. Preheat your grill using all burners set on high and with the lid closed for 10 to 12 minutes. When the grill is almost ready, put the smoking chips in a foil pouch and punch lots of holes in it (see p. 16). Wait until a good head of smoke is obvious, then add the trout. Close the lid and cook for 5 to 6 minutes on each side, depending on the thickness of the trout. Because you are working with whole fish, use the 10-minute-per-inch rule as a guide. Remove the trout to a platter and let them rest for 5 minutes. Serve with a drizzle of first-rate extra-virgin olive oil.

SERVES 4

DIRECT HEAT

4 small whole rainbow, golden, or mountain trout, scaled and gutted

½ cup mayonnaise

8 sprigs fresh thyme

8 sprigs fresh oregano

4 sprigs fresh rosemary

8 lemon slices, ¼ inch thick

2 to 3 garlic cloves, minced (optional)

Apple wood chips, soaked in water for 30 minutes

Extra-virgin olive oil

HERB-MARINATED MONKFISH WITH SHERRY VINAIGRETTE

SERVES 4

DIRECT HEAT

Four 6-ounce monkfish fillets, all
   membranes removed
   (see drawings on facing page)

1½ tablespoons olive oil

⅓ cup coarsely chopped fresh chives,
   summer savory, parsley, tarragon,
   or a mix of your favorite herbs

1 teaspoon pure maple syrup
   (not pancake syrup)

¼ cup sherry vinegar

½ cup corn oil

¼ cup extra-virgin olive oil

2 to 3 medium shallots, finely
   chopped (about 3 tablespoons)

Kosher salt

Freshly ground black pepper

Monkfish may be the ugliest critter in the ocean. If you met one up close and personal, it would scare the living daylights out of you. Fortunately, monkfish tastes a whole lot better than it looks. Only the tail of the fish is used, and its texture is very similar to meat or to a cooked lobster tail. In fact, monkfish is sometimes called "poor man's lobster." When you cook monkfish at home, don't make the most common mistake of forgetting to remove the thin, purply membrane that is sometimes found on the fillets. It's much like silverskin on a pork or beef tenderloin—tough and not very appealing. It also causes the fish to twist and contort while cooking, which won't happen once the membrane is removed.

1. Place the monkfish fillets in a large mixing bowl and combine with the olive oil and the herbs you've chosen. Rub the fish well so that the herbs stick to the fish. Cover and marinate in the refrigerator for at least 2 hours but no longer than 4 hours.

2. In a medium mixing bowl, whisk the maple syrup and vinegar together. Slowly add the corn oil and olive oil to the mixture to create an emulsion. Whisk in the shallots, then taste and add salt and pepper if necessary. Refrigerate until needed. This can be made one day ahead, and if you remember to you should make it ahead because the flavor will improve. Bring to room temperature before serving.

3. Oil the grill racks. Preheat your grill using all burners set on high and with the lid closed for 10 to 12 minutes.

4. Sprinkle the fish with salt and pepper and place on the cooking grate. Close the lid and cook for about 3 minutes, then turn and cook for another 3 to 4 minutes. The fish should be just opaque in the center and relatively firm to the touch. Transfer to a platter and allow to rest for 2 to 3 minutes. To serve, slice the fillets diagonally and arrange on individual plates. Spoon the vinaigrette on top of and around the fish.

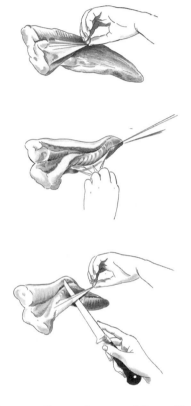

To remove the membranes, pull it up with your fingers, slide a fillet or boning knife under the membrane, and cut the length of the fillet. Repeat until all membrane is removed.

GRILLED BARBECUED SALMON

SERVES 4

DIRECT HEAT

Four 6-ounce center-cut skinless
   salmon fillets, pin bones removed

Vegetable oil cooking spray

1 tablespoon rib rub or any Cajun
   or blackened fish seasoning

½ cup barbecue sauce
   (use your favorite)

Salmon is probably the easiest fish to grill, thanks to its dense flesh and nice fat content. These days we even have a choice in the salmon we can buy. The three types that are most commonly available include Copper River, a sockeye salmon that is caught as it struggles to get upstream to mate. A lean and rich-flavored fish, Copper River salmon is capable of standing up to the essences of charcoal. But be quick if you find it—the season for Copper River is short. Wild king salmon is more and more available, and farm-raised salmon now has much more flavor and is easy to obtain. To grill salmon, choose thick fillets. Ask your fishmonger for 1-inch-thick, center-cut fillets. Stick to your guns here; accept no narrow tail flesh, which does not grill well. You might want to throw a couple of extra fillets on the grill for making salmon croquettes later.

1. Oil the grill racks. Preheat your grill using all burners set on high and with the lid closed for 10 to 12 minutes.

2. Lightly spray each fillet with the cooking spray. Sprinkle the top side of each fillet with the seasoning rub. Pat or rub the seasoning into the fillets.

3. Place the salmon, seasoned side down, on the grill. Close the lid and cook the fillets for about 5 minutes, allowing the seasoning to form a crust. Turn the fillets and quickly brush each one with barbecue sauce, then close the lid. Cook for an additional 4 to 5 minutes, or until they reach your preferred doneness. Please don't overcook. Leaving the fillets a little rare in the middle will add to your enjoyment. Serve immediately.

GRILL-ROASTED SALMON WITH TOMATO JAM

Tomato jam is a traditional southern condiment that is a perfect foil for the clean flavors of grilled salmon. This particular jam is a bit spicy and incorporates more southeastern Asian flavors than those of the Deep South. Don't let the term "jam" dissuade you—this all comes together very quickly. This would also be great with a simple grilled duck breast. If you've got a side burner on your grill, then I encourage you to make the jam on it, rather than on your stove. Serve this on a bed of Asian noodles for a cool presentation.

SERVES 4
DIRECT HEAT

4 tablespoons canola oil

1 tablespoon chopped fresh ginger

1 small yellow onion, finely chopped

One 14-ounce can petite diced tomatoes, drained

½ teaspoon crushed red chile flakes

2 tablespoons light brown sugar

2 tablespoons rice vinegar

Kosher salt

Freshly ground black pepper

Four 6-ounce center-cut skin-on salmon fillets, pin bones removed

1. To make the tomato jam, heat 2 tablespoons of the oil in a small saucepan. Add the ginger and onion and cook over medium heat until softened, about 4 minutes. Add the tomatoes, crushed red chile flakes, sugar, and vinegar. Cook over medium heat, mashing the tomatoes and stirring, until thick and preserve-like, about 10 minutes. Season the jam with salt and pepper to taste. Reserve. (You can make the jam up to a week ahead. Store it or any leftovers in the refrigerator, covered.)

2. Oil the grill racks. Preheat your grill using all burners set on high and with the lid closed for 10 to 12 minutes.

3. Brush each salmon fillet with the remaining 2 tablespoons oil, then season with salt and pepper. Place the salmon, skin side up, on the grill. Close the lid and cook for about 3 minutes, then turn the salmon, close the lid, and cook for about 5 minutes more. The salmon should be at a medium doneness and should give slightly when pressed. Remove to a platter and serve with the tomato jam.

GENE'S NORTHERN CALIFORNIA PLANKED SALMON

SERVES 6

DIRECT HEAT

½ cup snipped fresh dill

½ cup chopped shallots

2 garlic cloves, minced

1 scallion, chopped
    (white and green parts)

2 tablespoons freshly ground
    black pepper

2 tablespoons olive oil

1 tablespoon pure maple syrup
    (not pancake syrup)

Juice of 1 lemon

Six 6- to 8-ounce center-cut skin-on
    salmon fillets, pin bones removed

6 cedar planks, soaked in water for
    about 4 hours (see sidebar, p. 191)

Kosher salt

Lemon wedges, for serving

I don't think I could write a cookbook without a Gene Mattiuzzo recipe somewhere within its pages. Gene and his wife, Sue Ann, have been good friends since I first met them seven years ago. Gene is the unofficial "mayor" of Noyo Harbor in Fort Bragg, California, and has taught me a great deal about seafood from the north coast of California up through British Columbia. Here's his take on what is trendy for the rest of us and old hat to folks along that coastal area.

1. Combine the dill, shallots, garlic, scallion, pepper, oil, maple syrup, and lemon juice in a medium bowl. Use your hands to mix it thoroughly.

2. Generously spread this mixture over the flesh side of each fillet. Let the fillets sit at room temperature until your grill is ready.

3. Oil the grill racks. Preheat your grill using all burners set on high and with the lid closed for 10 to 12 minutes.

4. Take the cedar planks from the water and season them with salt. Place them on the grill, close the lid, and let them heat until they start to smoke and crackle, usually about 5 minutes. Keep a close eye on the cedar planks while they are heating. Sometimes they tend to catch on fire, and you might want to have a spray bottle filled with water handy to control this. Turn the heat down to medium and place the salmon on the planks, skin side down. Close the lid and cook without turning the fillets for about 12 minutes. This will give you a medium doneness; the fish will still yield to the touch. When the salmon is done, remove the planks from the grill and transfer the salmon to a platter. Serve immediately with the lemon wedges.

GRILLED WILD KING SALMON, NORTHWEST-STYLE

SERVES 6

DIRECT HEAT

6 ounces frozen limeade concentrate, thawed

¾ cup extra-virgin olive oil

¾ cup tamari

4 to 6 large garlic cloves, minced (about 2 tablespoons)

2 tablespoons chopped fresh rosemary

Six 6- to 8-ounce center-cut skin-on king salmon fillets, pin bones removed

Katrina Moore, my Seattle-based food buddy and blogger, shared this recipe with me. The limeade struck me as unreal and out of place till I tried it. The acidity is wonderful and brightens the salmon.

1. Combine the limeade, olive oil, tamari, garlic, and rosemary in a baking dish or gallon-size zip-top plastic bag.

2. Place the salmon in the marinade, squishing the bag or turning the fish in the baking dish several times to coat. Seal the bag or cover the dish and refrigerate for 1 hour.

3. Oil the grill racks. Preheat your grill using all burners set on high and with the lid closed for 10 to 12 minutes.

4. Remove the salmon from the marinade and place on the grill. Close the lid and cook for 4 to 5 minutes, then turn the fish and cook for another 4 minutes, or until the fish is barely opaque throughout and yields slightly to the touch. Serve immediately.

CUBAN-STYLE GRILLED FISH (PESCADOS ASADO)

Many Cuban expatriates have settled in the Little Havana area of Miami, and we should be thankful that they brought most of their food customs with them. This is a vibrant recipe for grilled fish that was inspired by Lorenzo Monteagudo and his wife, Tracy, who left the Cuban communities in Florida for the mountains of east Tennessee. Use this when you're grilling fish for a crowd. The marinade makes a lot but it just doesn't work if you try to cut it in half. Use the leftovers with chicken breasts.

1. Mix the olive oil, lime juice, lemon juice, garlic, cilantro, oregano, scallions, salt, pepper, and crushed red chile flakes in a large glass or plastic bowl. Whisk to combine well.

2. You need to marinate the fish in a nonreactive container, such as a 9x13-inch glass baking dish. (Most metals will react with the acids in the marinade, producing "off" flavors.) You probably will need two dishes. Place the fish in the baking dishes in a single layer and evenly divide the marinade between them. Cover with plastic wrap and refrigerate for no longer than 2 hours.

3. Oil the grill racks. Preheat your grill using all burners set on high and with the lid closed for 10 to 12 minutes.

4. When the grill is hot, adjust the heat to medium-high.

5. Remove the fish from the marinade and pat dry. Discard the marinade. Brush each piece with oil. Place on the grill, close the lid, and cook for about 4 minutes (do not close the lid if you are cooking tuna). Carefully turn the fish and cook for an additional 4 to 5 minutes for medium doneness. Depending on which fish you use, you may want to adapt the cooking time. For tuna you might want to cut the time in half; for swordfish you should probably add a couple of minutes. The fish will be done when it's firm to the touch and separates slightly. Remove to a platter and serve.

SERVES 8

DIRECT HEAT

½ cup olive oil, plus more for the fish

Juice of 1 lime

Juice of 1 lemon

6 garlic cloves, crushed

¼ cup chopped fresh cilantro

1 tablespoon chopped fresh oregano

4 scallions, chopped

1 teaspoon kosher salt

½ teaspoon freshly ground black pepper

1 teaspoon crushed red chile flakes

Eight 6- to 8-ounce swordfish steaks, salmon fillets, or tuna steaks, 1 inch thick

TUNA WITH MANGO RELISH

SERVES 4
DIRECT HEAT

Four 6-ounce tuna steaks,
    1 inch thick

1 garlic clove, minced

¼ teaspoon kosher salt

1 fresh jalapeño chile, seeded and
    finely chopped (wear gloves to
    prevent irritation)

1 mango, peeled, seeded and
    chopped (about 1 cup)

1 tablespoon honey

1 tablespoon finely chopped
    fresh ginger

IN THE KITCHEN

Jalapeños, serranos, and other hot chiles contain oils and compounds that can be very irritating. Wearing something like latex surgical gloves is a good way to keep these compounds from your hands. If you don't have gloves around, be sure to wash your hands thoroughly, including under your fingernails, and keep your hands away from your lips, nose, eyes, or other delicate areas until you are certain that all of the oils and residue have dissipated.

A good grilled tuna steak plays nicely with a wide variety of seasonings, but sweet heat is one of its favorites. Mango relish might seem a bit dated, but it's still just as good today as it was a decade ago, when fruit relishes and salsas became the rage on the restaurant scene. If you prefer a more salsa-like condiment, add some lime juice and finely chopped red onion. The first time you grill tuna steaks, cook them to the doneness that you feel is your favorite. Then each time after that, cut off a minute until you discover the pure wonder of a tuna steak cooked medium-rare. The hot exterior against the cool interior, the spices, and the caramelization from the grill will stimulate your taste buds completely.

1. Rinse the fish and pat dry with paper towels. Combine the garlic and salt and rub over the fish.

2. For the relish, combine the jalapeño, mango, honey, and ginger in a small bowl. The relish can be made up to 3 days in advance and stored, covered, in the refrigerator.

3. Oil the grill racks. Preheat your grill using all burners set on high and with the lid closed for 10 to 12 minutes.

4. Place the fish on the grill and cook with the lid open for 3 to 4 minutes, then turn and cook for an additional 3 to 4 minutes. The tuna should be firm yet give readily to the touch. What you want is a medium-rare to medium doneness.

5. Remove the tuna from the grill and spoon the relish over each steak. Serve immediately.

BACONIZED TUNA WITH LEMON BUTTER

There's some perverse pleasure in taking a low-in-fat, good-for-you protein like tuna and surrounding it with bacon fat and butter. You're still going to get the health benefits of eating the tuna, but you'll also experience the pure joy of having the fat.

1. Bring a medium saucepan of water to a boil. Poach the bacon slices in the boiling water for 3 minutes, then drain them. Wrap each tuna steak with 2 slices of bacon and secure with a wooden skewer or toothpick.

2. Melt the butter in a small saucepan over medium heat. Stir in the garlic, lemon juice, and parsley. Set aside, keeping warm.

3. Oil the grill racks. Preheat your grill using all burners set on high and with the lid closed for 10 to 12 minutes.

4. Lightly oil the wrapped tuna steaks on both sides. Place on the grill. Cook the steaks with the lid open, brushing with the lemon-butter sauce frequently but turning only once, to your desired doneness. Discard any sauce you don't use. Tuna typically is best when served rare to medium-rare, which should take a total of 5 to 6 minutes. Remove to a platter, sprinkle with salt and pepper, and serve.

SERVES 6
DIRECT HEAT

12 slices bacon, preferably peppered or apple-wood smoked

Six 8-ounce tuna steaks, 1 inch thick

½ cup (1 stick) unsalted butter

1 medium garlic clove, minced

¼ cup fresh lemon juice

2 tablespoons chopped fresh flat-leaf parsley

Canola oil

Kosher salt

Freshly ground black pepper

GRILLED TUNA WITH MARINATED CUCUMBERS

This is a takeoff of a recipe that Debra Ponzek did during her stint as executive chef at New York City's Montrachet. All the flavors are reminiscent of Southeast Asia, and they delight in being paired with a fresh tuna steak. Please don't skip the marinated cucumbers. They are an integral part of the yin and yang of this dish.

1. Make the marinated cucumbers by slicing the cucumbers very thinly lengthwise. (If you have a mandoline, use it; otherwise use a sharp knife or even a vegetable peeler.) Add to a medium bowl. In a small saucepan set over low heat, combine ¾ cup of the vinegar and the sugar, stirring until the sugar is dissolved. Cool the mixture slightly, then pour over the cucumbers and toss. Cover and marinate at room temperature for at least 1 hour.

2. In a small bowl, whisk together the chili oil and the remaining 1 tablespoon vinegar. Set aside.

3. Oil the grill racks. Preheat your grill using all burners set on high and with the lid closed for 10 to 12 minutes.

4. Mix together the cumin seeds, black pepper, salt, and crushed red chile flakes in a small bowl. Brush each tuna steak with the canola oil. Sprinkle each steak with the spice mixture, gently pressing the spices into the fish. Place the tuna on the hot grill and cook with the lid open for about 2 minutes per side. We're looking for a sear with a very cool middle. Remove the tuna to a cutting board and let cool slightly. Divide the marinated cucumbers among 4 plates. Put a tuna steak on top of the cucumbers and drizzle the hot chili oil vinaigrette over the top. Serve immediately.

SERVES 4
DIRECT HEAT

2 English cucumbers, peeled

¾ cup plus 1 tablespoon champagne vinegar

¼ cup sugar

3 tablespoons hot chili oil (in the Asian section of most large grocery stores)

1 tablespoon crushed cumin seeds

1 tablespoon freshly cracked black peppercorns (see sidebar, p. 111)

2 teaspoons kosher salt

1 tablespoon crushed red chile flakes

Four 6-ounce tuna steaks, about 1 inch thick

1 to 2 tablespoons canola oil

AT THE MARKET

What the heck are English cucumbers? They're the long, thin ones, usually wrapped in plastic. They have fewer seeds than regular cucumbers and they're meatier, so they don't add unnecessary liquid to a recipe.

NORTH AFRICAN GRILLED SHRIMP

2½ pounds 20- to 24-count shrimp,
   peeled and deveined

½ cup extra-virgin olive oil

2 large garlic cloves, thinly sliced

4 sprigs fresh rosemary

2 cups pine nuts

3 slices whole-wheat bread, crusts
   removed and torn into pieces

½ cup fresh lemon juice

2 garlic cloves, peeled

¾ teaspoon kosher salt

½ teaspoon freshly ground
   black pepper

⅓ cup water

6 or 10 skewers (if using bamboo,
   soak in water for 30 minutes)

So what makes grilled shrimp North African? Well, thanks to my New York City neighbor Mohamed, a native of Morocco, I learned this twist on shrimp cocktail. The *tarator* sauce is used throughout the Middle East, North Africa, and some parts of Eastern Europe. It is usually sesame based, but Mohamed uses pine nuts in his. This sauce would also be welcome over most any grilled fish or lamb. Surprise your family and friends with this recipe the next time you cook shrimp.

1. Place the shrimp in a single layer in a large shallow baking dish. Pour the olive oil over them, sprinkle with the sliced garlic, and break the rosemary sprigs and tuck them down among the shrimp. Cover and refrigerate for about 4 hours.

2. Meanwhile, make the sauce. Place the pine nuts, bread, lemon juice, peeled garlic, salt, pepper, and water in the bowl of a food processor. Pulse 5 or 6 times to combine, then process for 30 seconds. Scrape down the sides of the bowl and process for another 30 seconds or until smooth. Remove to another container, cover, and refrigerate until ready to serve.

3. Remove the shrimp from the refrigerator. Thread about 5 shrimp onto each of 10 skewers for a first course, or about 8 shrimp onto each of 6 skewers for a main course.

4. Oil the grill racks. Preheat your grill using all burners set on high and with the lid closed for 10 to 12 minutes.

5. Place the shrimp on the grill and close the lid. Cook for about 2 minutes, turn, and cook for another 2 minutes. The shrimp should have a gentle "C" shape to them. Remove from the grill and either place the skewers on a platter or slide the shrimp off the skewers onto the platter. Serve hot or at room temperature, with the sauce.

SPICY GRILL-STEAMED CLAMS

SERVES 6
DIRECT HEAT

¾ cup dry sake or beer

1½ teaspoons minced fresh ginger

2 to 3 garlic cloves, minced

1 teaspoon crushed red chile flakes

3 scallions, sliced on the diagonal

3 pounds (about 54) Manila clams,
    washed thoroughly

3 tablespoons unsalted butter

½ cup olive oil

2 tablespoons hot paprika

1 loaf crusty bread,
    cut into ½-inch-thick slices

3 tablespoons chopped fresh cilantro

1½ limes, quartered

Here's another cool way to use your gas grill. We can employ two cooking methods quickly and conveniently on clams, which results in a unique new take on an old favorite.

1. In a large measuring cup, combine the sake, ginger, garlic, crushed red chile flakes, and scallions. Divide the liquid equally among 3 disposable aluminum pie plates or similar-size disposable pans, then divide the clams among them. Place 1 tablespoon of butter atop each. Seal each with foil.

2. Oil the grill racks. Preheat your grill using all burners set on high and with the lid closed for 10 to 12 minutes.

3. Place the sealed pie plates on the grill and steam the clams for 10 to 12 minutes. Remove from the heat.

4. Meanwhile, make the toast. Whisk together the oil and paprika and brush this mixture on both sides of the bread. Place on the grill and cook until toasted, 1 to 2 minutes.

5. Remove the foil from the pie plates carefully, as steam will escape, then sprinkle with the cilantro. Divide the clams and their juice between 6 bowls and serve immediately with lime wedges and the grilled toast. Discard any clams that do not open.

SEA SCALLOPS WITH HOT AND SWEET DIPPING SAUCE

This recipe can serve double duty, as an entrée or as a wonderful appetizer for the beginning of a grilled fish meal. The dipping sauce is magnificent with any grilled fish or shellfish, and believe me, it will surprise you even with a grilled or roasted chicken. When serving as an appetizer put one scallop on a skewer and serve, but make sure that your really good friends are at this cocktail party.

1. For the dipping sauce, mix together the garlic, tamari, vinegar, fish sauce, sugar, and crushed red chile flakes in a small saucepan. Place over medium heat and bring to a simmer. Remove the pan from the heat and add the lime juice. You can hold the sauce at room temperature for a couple of hours or refrigerate longer, but bring back to room temperature before serving.

2. Completely brush each scallop on all sides with canola oil and season with salt and pepper. If you like, thread two scallops each through doubled skewers. (This helps in the cooking and turning process. By all means you can skip this step, because your scallops should be big enough not to fall through the grill grate when cooking.)

3. Oil the grill racks. Preheat your grill using all burners set on high and with the lid closed for 10 to 12 minutes.

4. Place the scallops over direct heat and cook for 2 to 3 minutes on one side, and then turn and cook for an additional 2 to 3 minutes. The scallops should be barely opaque in the center and should feel firm to the touch but with some give. There is nothing worse than an overcooked scallop. Trust your skill here and take them off before you overcook them.

5. Add the cilantro leaves to the sauce and serve alongside the scallops.

SERVES 4 AS A MAIN COURSE,
OR 6 AS A FIRST COURSE
DIRECT HEAT

4 garlic cloves, crushed or minced

2 tablespoons tamari or
    light soy sauce

2 tablespoons seasoned rice vinegar

½ to 1 tablespoon Thai fish sauce

1 tablespoon sugar

½ teaspoon crushed red chile flakes

1 tablespoon fresh lime juice

20 to 24 large sea scallops (1½ to
    1¾ pounds), all about the same
    thickness, side muscle removed

Canola oil

Kosher salt

Freshly ground black pepper

40 to 48 skewers (optional; if
    using bamboo, soak in water
    for 30 minutes)

1 tablespoon finely chopped
    fresh cilantro leaves

GRILLED SCALLOPS WITH RÉMOULADE SAUCE

FOR THE RÉMOULADE SAUCE

½ cup good-quality mayonnaise, such as Duke's or another brand without a lot of sugar

1 tablespoon capers, drained and minced

1 tablespoon sweet pickle relish

1 tablespoon finely chopped fresh tarragon

1 tablespoon finely minced shallot

1 teaspoon tarragon or Champagne vinegar

1 to 2 garlic cloves, minced

½ teaspoon Dijon mustard

Kosher salt

A good sprinkle of paprika

20 to 24 large sea scallops (1½ to 1¾ pounds), all about the same thickness, side muscle removed

Canola oil

Kosher salt

Freshly ground black pepper

40 to 48 skewers (optional; if using bamboo, soak in water for 30 minutes)

This is a take on the more-familiar shrimp rémoulade. However, in this case we want the bold grilled flavor to come through, so we use the rémoulade sauce as a dipping sauce, much like you would a cocktail sauce. If you prefer, you could toss everything together and serve it over shredded lettuce in the style of a New Orleans lunch.

1. For the rémoulade sauce, put the mayonnaise, capers, pickle relish, tarragon, shallot, vinegar, garlic, mustard, salt, and paprika into a blender. Pulse several times, until well combined. You can make this up to 24 hours in advance. Cover and refrigerate until ready to serve.

2. Brush each scallop on all sides with the canola oil and season with salt and pepper. If you like, thread two scallops each through doubled skewers. (This helps in the cooking and turning process. By all means you can skip this step, because your scallops should be big enough not to fall through the grill grate when cooking.)

3. Oil the grill racks. Preheat your grill using all burners set on high and with the lid closed for 10 to 12 minutes.

4. Place the scallops over direct heat and cook for 2 to 3 minutes on one side, and then turn and cook for an additional 2 to 3 minutes. The scallops should be barely opaque in the center and should feel firm to the touch but with some give. Please don't overcook the scallops, or they become hockey pucks. Serve the rémoulade sauce along with the scallops.

THE OYSTER ROAST

Along the coastal areas, an oyster roast can mean feeding two or two thousand. Most large oyster roasts are done by professionals who can handle huge amounts of folks just like the Brunswick stew masters of Virginia, the Texas barbecue caterers, or the crab-feed cooks of the West Coast. But having an oyster roast at home is not difficult. "Roast" is a bit of a misnomer. The oysters are really steam-roasted over an open fire. The old-fashioned way to do this was to dig pits and start oak-wood fires, then cover the fires with pieces of sheet metal. When the sheet metal got hot, oysters were poured on top and covered with wet burlap bags. It's a little simpler now. Your gas grill is the perfect tool for having an easy and frustration-free oyster roast. It's a sloppy way to eat, but it's so much fun on a crisp fall day that the butter and juices dripping off your chin don't seem to matter at all. Your pleasure will be enhanced even further by large amounts of corn on the cob and cole slaw, not to mention plenty of cold beer and a bottle of fine bourbon. This recipe can be doubled or tripled easily.

SERVES 8

DIRECT HEAT

1 bushel oysters,
   rinsed and scrubbed

Your favorite cocktail sauce

Melted butter

Lemon wedges

8 leather garden gloves

8 oyster knives

Lots of paper towels

1. Oil the grill racks. Preheat your grill using all burners set on high and with the lid closed for 10 to 12 minutes.

2. Place as many of the oysters in a single layer as you can over your grill grate. Get your condiments close to the grill on another table and make sure everyone has put on their gloves. Have 8 aluminum pie pans available, if you like, to use as plates. As the oysters start to open, usually after about 15 minutes, encourage everybody to dig in, start opening their oysters, and topping them with their favorite condiments. Continue cooking the oysters in batches until they're gone. Any oysters that don't open should be discarded.

FISH AND SHELLFISH

SIMPLY GRILLED LOBSTER TAILS

SERVES 4

DIRECT HEAT

Four 7- to 8-ounce lobster tails

Canola oil

Kosher salt

Freshly ground black pepper

4 skewers (if using bamboo, soak in water for 30 minutes)

4 tablespoons (½ stick) unsalted butter, melted

Juice of ½ lemon

1 tablespoon finely chopped fresh flat-leaf parsley

Grilling a whole lobster is an exercise fraught with peril. You have to dispatch the lobster, and the most effective method is with the point of a knife while it's alive and wiggling. Why bother when the best part of the lobster is the tail? Lobster tails are easy to find (they're often frozen) and they make an elegant treat. How cool is it to do surf and turf right there on that big beautiful gas grill?

1. Place the lobster tails, shell side down, on a cutting board. Take a pair of kitchen shears and cut down the middle of the underside membrane and slightly pull apart. (Some people like to cut the tail in half lengthwise to expose more meat, but I like using this method because it gives me a little fudge factor so I won't overcook the lobster.) Brush each lobster tail with oil and sprinkle with salt and pepper. Run a skewer through each lobster tail. This will prevent the tail from curling as it cooks and will promote even cooking.

2. Oil the grill racks. Preheat your grill using all burners set on high and with the lid closed for 10 to 12 minutes.

3. Place the tails on the grill, shell side up, close the lid, and cook for about 4 minutes. Turn and continue cooking for another 6 minutes, or until the shells have turned bright red and the meat is opaque throughout. Remove to a platter and again using kitchen shears, release the meat from the shells. Stir together the melted butter, lemon juice, ¼ teaspoon salt, and the parsley. Divide among 4 small containers and serve immediately with the lobster tails.

PLANKING FISH

PLANKING FISH HAS BECOME WILDLY POPULAR IN THE PAST FEW YEARS. It's actually the original "barbecue" of the Northwest. This method has been widely used since the nineteenth century for meats and poultry as well. It adds a special flavor and a subtle smoke, just as if you had a large smoker with a whole pig and some oak and hickory wood. Start with cedar but then try other woods like cherry, maple, and especially alder. Large supermarkets and fish-mongers as well as kitchenware stores now carry a ready supply of the planks. If you buy planks at a home-improvement store, get them from the grilling section of the store, not from the roofing or lumber section, and make sure they are not treated with pesticides or other chemicals. Planks can be washed and reused, but three uses is probably the max you'll get out of one plank. All kinds of fish and shellfish are great on a plank. Salmon is the most common, but try halibut, sea bass, and tuna as well. I've even tried oysters on planks with neat results. Shrimp and large sea scallops work nicely, too.

BIG, THI'CK, JUICY, AND FUN

BURGERS, DOGS, SAUSAGES, AND PIZZA

FOOD CRAVINGS ARE A FUNNY THING. They are intense, they demand attention, and no matter how hard you try to avoid them, they're only satisfied when they're met. How many hamburger cravings have you had in your life? What about that uncontrollable desire for a pizza? For many of us the search for the perfect hot dog is a never-ending adventure. I can't claim that this chapter will cure all your ills, but I can guarantee you some exceptional eating. The foods in this chapter aren't necessarily indigenous to the USA, but we Americans have adopted them with passion and have made them our own.

BURGERS

A burger is a thing of beauty and ingenuity. From its humble beginnings as poor immigrant food, the hamburger has become part of our culinary heritage. Unfortunately, thanks to fast food, burgers are often mistreated. Few things come close to the delightfully intense beef flavor of a hamburger cooked on a grill. No matter how we top it, the taste always transports us to a great memory or a great taste experience. It's comfort food on a bun.

An outstanding hamburger starts with the meat, but beef is not the only thing that makes a great burger. Some chefs stuff foie gras and truffles in the center of their burgers to separate them from the masses. Ground pork, lamb, tuna, turkey, and veal can be used to

make exceptional burgers as well, and you'll find recipes for them in this chapter. That said, beef is the most popular meat for burgers. Many of the new upscale hamburger joints are very secretive about their meat combinations. Jeffrey Steingarten, the food writer for *Vogue*, tells a story of Danny Meyer, owner of the Shake Shack in New York City's Madison Square Park as well as other superior restaurants, going ballistic when he thought that his secret recipe for the superb hamburger patty had become part of Internet legend.

I prefer to use a combination of about 1½ pounds of ground chuck to ½ pound of ground sirloin. If you want a slightly leaner burger then 1 to 1 is a good ratio. Chuck is usually 80 to 85 percent lean and sirloin is around 90 percent lean. Most good supermarkets label some of their ground beef by the cut it's from, but if it just says "ground beef" and the fat content then it can be ground from any cut of beef. You might have to go to the meat counter to request beef ground from chuck or sirloin. A trick to help very lean burgers stay moist is to add 3 to 4 tablespoons of ice-cold water to the meat as you season and shape it. The principle is the same as using ice water when making a pie crust: The cold water helps to keep the fat, whether in the pie crust or the burger, cool while you're working with it.

Once you've got the meat home, keep it simple, keep it tender, and keep it cold. Simple seasonings are best, although I like to get exotic with putting flavorings on a hamburger. Salt and pepper should be the base for all your hamburger attempts. Salt of course also brings up controversy—do you mix it in with the meat or do you sprinkle on the outside? I think both work, although I'm fonder of sprinkling the salt on the outside and letting it become part of the crust that forms when you cook a burger.

The less you handle ground beef, or any ground meat for that matter, the juicier it will be. A light touch in making the patties is important. I like to use an 8-ounce plastic deli container that's about 3½ inches across as a mold to form my burgers. It accomplishes two things—it makes a slight bevel in the patty, and, since most deli containers have a concave bottom, it also makes a small indentation on the burger that helps to keep it from puffing as it cooks. Let me explain that a little. When a hamburger cooks, it shrinks from the outside in and the middle puffs up, which leads to uneven cooking, makes a bad presentation, and makes it difficult for toppings to stay on top of the burger. One of my grilling friends calls this phenomenon the "swollen belly syndrome." Whether you use a deli container or not, always make a thumbprint in the middle of one side of each patty to ensure even and level cooking.

I believe the minimum size for a good burger is a raw weight of about 6 ounces, with

...BEEF IS NOT THE ONLY THING THAT MAKES A GREAT BURGER.

GUIDELINES
FOR GROUND MEAT These are guidelines only; specific recipes may vary.

THE CUT	RAW WEIGHT	TIME PER SIDE	INTERNAL TEMPERATURE
GROUND BEEF	5–8 ounces	8–10 minutes	160°F
GROUND PORK	5–8 ounces	8–10 minutes	160°F
GROUND TURKEY	5–8 ounces	10–12 minutes	165°F
GROUND CHICKEN	5–8 ounces	10–12 minutes	165°F
GROUND LAMB	5–8 ounces	8–10 minutes	160°F
GROUND VEAL	5–8 ounces	8–10 minutes	160°F

a patty 4½ to 5 inches in diameter and ½ to ¾ inch thick. If you want a thin burger you might as well go to a fast-food joint. Burgers should be slightly larger than the buns you plan to use because they'll shrink about 30 percent during cooking. Shape the burgers gently with your hands; I have found that rinsing your hands in cold water makes forming them easier.

Once the patties have been made, keep them cold. The chill helps to keep the fat coagulated, and the fat acts as a binder when you first put the burgers on the grill. Go back to that tender thing again. You don't want those burgers firmly packed, so the cold actuality helps to keep them together until the heat from the grill starts pulling at the proteins and binding the meat.

Another key to a great hamburger is making sure that your cooking grate is very clean and very hot before you place the burgers on it. That means a full-bore, all-burners-on pre-

heat and patience until the temperature reaches 500°F. Then slightly reduce your temperature and put the burgers on to cook. A *few* flare-ups on a burger are a good thing, and the new design of most gas grills makes flare-ups short-lived. Try not to turn your burger but once, and for heaven's sake, don't press down on it with a spatula. You might as well be putting a tap in the burger to drain out all the juice.

Doneness is a personal decision. The USDA would have us cook all of our burgers to 160°F, which leaves no pink inside. Sure, there are burgers that you should fully cook, including East Tennessee's Famous Pig Burger (p. 207), A Turkey Burger Worth Eating (p. 211), or any burger made with poultry. But for a beef burger, 160°F kills a lot of the juice and flavor and tenderness. I personally feel comfortable with a burger that's cooked to medium, or 145°F to 150°F internally, and I occasionally will even cook it slightly less. But it's my stom-

ICE IS
NICE

Okay, USDA be damned and you want a rare burger. They're difficult to cook because you still need time to develop the outside crust, but cooking too long may take the inside past rare. Here's a trick. Take a small ice cube and place it in the center of the patty, then shape it exactly as you normally would. The ice cube slows down the cooking in the center of the burger, helping you to develop that wonderful char that is so important to the taste of a great hamburger. Please sign the liability waiver on your way out the door.

own meat at home, which is a fairly easy process. KitchenAid® stand mixers have an attachment that makes short work of this process. Generally with burgers the size that I have described, 8 to 10 minutes per side will give you a medium doneness and 160°F internal temperature.

No matter what you make your burger from, the handling instructions here fairly well marry to all these options. But refer to the chart at left for more specifics on their cooking.

When you test your burgers for doneness, the touch method is the best option (see p. 13). Gauging doneness with an instant-read thermometer can be difficult because you need to insert it horizontally all the way to the middle of the burger to check it.

HOT DOGS
AND SAUSAGES

ach that I'm putting at risk, and I'm willing to accept the consequences for myself. Of course, if you are feeding children, elderly people, pregnant or breast-feeding women, or anyone with a compromised immune system, that 160°F temperature is mandatory. Determining your comfort level comes in part from knowing your butcher and the quality of the meat that the store sells. I stay away from those tubes of ground beef and would rather have beef ground at the store (which is usually sold at the butcher counter). If foodborne bacteria are a concern then you might want to grind your

Nothing beats a great grilled sausage, whether it's a brat, kielbasa, or good old hot dog. A little extra char just puts one more flavor element into the mix. I have a friend who taught me how to make "porcupine" dogs, when you cut vertical slits through the length of the dog. Once it hits the grill the heat lets the little slits separate slightly and you get a larger surface for tasty char. (You can try this with other cooked sausages, but I find it takes best to hot dogs.) Other than that, there's really not a whole lot to tell you about cooking these foods, except that a quickly grilled bun adds to the sublime pleasure.

But hot dogs shouldn't be the only cylinder of meat you grill. Try cooked sausages, which many times have already been smoked and are full of flavor and work great with grilled onions and peppers. They can be made from a variety of meats and seasoned in countless ways, and include kielbasa, bratwurst, knockwurst, and even bologna. They are quick cooking and delicious. Don't overlook the range of flavored sausages either, such as chicken-apple or mushroom-stuffed turkey. You probably will find some delight there as well. Fresh sausages, those that have not been cooked or cured, are also an enviable treat when exposed to fire. Southern-style country sausages, Mexican chorizo, fresh bratwurst, and sweet and hot Italian sausages are excellent choices to hit the grill top.

Make sure you know whether you have purchased cooked or fresh (raw) sausage. If you don't know what you've bought, ask the butcher; while most labels are clearly understandable now, it can still be tricky because some sausages (like bratwurst and kielbasa) are available both ways. Raw sausage is usually best prepared slowly over indirect heat for 20 to 25 minutes, turning occasionally. They will be browned and plump when done. Cooked sausage is best over direct heat and normally takes only 5 to 7 minutes, turning occasionally.

ROLL WITH IT

When you're buying hot dog or burger buns, don't skimp on quality. You'll be happier with a flavorful, sturdy piece of bread holding your grilled food. Potato buns are terrific, but a national brand like Pepperidge Farm® is fine. Consider looking in the bakery section of your store for kaiser rolls or other rolls, or even try your burger on an English muffin.

PIZZA

Grilling pizza is not only fun but also adds volumes of flavor and can be a perfect appetizer for a crowd or a meal for the kids when they don't like the lamb chops you're making. Also consider pizza as part of a tapas-like meal. Combining lots of little items on your grill is a fun way to host a gathering.

Good pizza starts with the crust. When pizza was first "imported" to this country, coal-fired ovens were the cooking medium of choice. They produced thin, crackly, and slightly charred pizza crusts and added a smoky nuance to the toppings. Your gas grill generates enough heat to do the exact same thing, and it's a whole lot less stressful than

TO BRAT OR NOT TO BRAT

People get as cantankerous about discussing the "right" way to cook bratwurst as they do discussing the "right" way to cook barbecue. Some "experts" think that bratwurst should be poached in liquid before grilling, while others believe grill first, poach later. I can't tell much difference. So my suggestion is do what's easiest for you unless you happen to have someone from Wisconsin dining with you that night—then follow their advice to the letter. Oh, and never put ketchup on a bratwurst. You'll be shunned for life.

flying to New York City, standing in line at Lombardi's on Spring Street, and wishing you had tried grilling pizza at home.

I've included a recipe for pizza dough in this chapter that was developed specifically for grilling, but you also have other options. Some pizzerias sell dough; frozen pizza dough found in grocery stores and specialty shops can be used. Prebaked pizza shells and even pita bread are good substitutes. In a pinch I've even used refrigerated dough, either from the case near the packaged biscuits and pie crust or in bags from the deli case.

Once the dough decision has been made, successful pizza cooking is all about getting your grill *hot*. You need enough heat to char one side of the dough, and then it's just a matter of flipping the dough over and topping it as you desire while cooking the other side. I've used a couple of different methods. If you do this entirely over direct heat, you have to be organized, work fast, and have little hair on your arms. Another way involves a little less pressure and lends itself to the abilities of your gas grill—cook one side of the pizza dough over direct heat, then flip it to the indirect section of your grill. You still need to be organized, but the heat is not as intense and you have a little more time to get your toppings on.

When cooking pizzas, consider doing more than one. Divide your dough into several balls, roll them out, lightly oil one side, and place a piece of parchment on the other side. This way you can stack your doughs, take them out to the grill, and use the parchment paper to help get them on the grill. Most gas grills today are big enough to give you plenty of room to cook three 10-inch pizzas at a time. If you're doing this, try to get your guests and family to add the toppings. It gets them involved, which is fun, they have a voice in the flavor of the pizza, and you get to relax.

Whether you choose burgers, dogs, sausages, or pizza, these are the foods of traditional American backyard cookouts (okay, maybe pizza is a stretch), and as you cook your way through this chapter you are continuing some great American traditions.

CLASSIC ULTIMATE HAMBURGER

SERVES 6
DIRECT HEAT

1½ pounds 80% lean ground chuck

8 ounces 90% lean ground sirloin

Kosher salt

Freshly ground black pepper

3 tablespoons unsalted butter,
   at room temperature

6 good-quality hamburger buns

6 slices dead-ripe tomato

6 iceberg or romaine lettuce leaves

Condiments of your choice

AT THE GRILL

If you feel your burger is not complete without cheese, then have 6 slices of your favorite cheese ready and add them during the last 2 minutes of the cooking time. The cheese should melt nicely but not turn to liquid, and will continue to melt even after you take the burger off the grill.

From the beginnings of backyard barbecue in the 1950s, with the rickety old charcoal-fired brazier-style grills, to today's newfangled easy-to-use gas grills, the hamburger has always been one of America's favorite cookout items. It's also probably one of the most disappointing items that we cook at home. I know for years it seemed that I could cook nothing but hockey pucks, but then I discovered a few truths about dealing with a burger.

The meat is super-important. In New York City, for example, where burger and barbecue world wars are topics of daily conversation, the better burgers are always made with a mixture of meat. There's a reason for that. You need a certain amount of fat to make a good burger. And you need a certain amount of flavor, and using different cuts of beef gives you the best combination.

To prevent burgers from falling apart, turn them only once, and for heaven's sake don't press on a burger with a spatula. All you're doing is pushing all the juice out of the burger. Another trick to getting an evenly cooked burger is to put a depression in the center of each patty before you put it on the grill. Some people take an index finger and literally put a hole through the middle. I take my thumb and put a fairly good indentation in the middle of one side, about a third of the thickness of the patty. As the individual fibers of the meat begin to expand over the heat, the patty will stay flat. You'll wind up with a nice-looking hamburger that's much more evenly cooked.

1. Oil the grill racks. Preheat your grill using all burners set on high and with the lid closed for 10 to 12 minutes.

2. Put the meat in a medium bowl and season with salt and pepper; go light on the salt here because we're going to add more. Carefully, being as tender as you possibly can, use your hands to mix the seasonings into the meat and then form it into 6 patties that are ¼ to ½ inch thick and slightly wider than the buns you intend to use. Take your thumb and make a good depression in the middle of each burger. Season the patties with salt and pepper. Slather some butter on the cut side of your hamburger buns.

3. Place the burgers on the grill, close the lid, and cook for 4 to 6 minutes. Turn the burgers and cook for an additional 4 minutes for a medium-pink doneness. If you want a well-done burger, cook for 12 to 15 minutes. They should start to feel firm when pressed. If you want to use an instant-read thermometer, do like the health inspectors do and go in through the side, not the top. During the last minute of the cooking time, add your buns to the grill, cut side down, and grill until lightly toasted.

4. Hamburgers are best served straight off the grill, into the bun, into your mouth. If the burgers are going to have to sit for a few minutes, place them on one platter and the buns on another instead of inserting the burger between the buns. Top each burger with tomato and lettuce, and dress with the condiments of your choice.

THE ULTIMATE ONION LOVER'S BURGER

SERVES 6 TO 8

DIRECT HEAT

2 pounds 80% lean ground chuck

1 medium onion, finely chopped

1 teaspoon freshly ground
   black pepper

1 teaspoon granulated garlic

1 teaspoon chopped fresh cilantro

Kosher salt

Canola oil

8 good-quality hamburger buns

8 slices cheese (use your
   favorite; optional)

8 slices ripe tomato

Condiments of your choice

Beef and onions are like two best friends: They always enjoy being in each other's company, and for many, a burger just wouldn't be complete without some sort of onion adornment. Here, we're going to take the onion and put it right in with the ground beef. Add a few other little spices and grill up what should be an onion lover's perfect burger.

1. At least 2 hours before cooking, but preferably 4 and even 8 hours if you can manage, combine the chuck, onion, pepper, garlic, and cilantro. Mix gently, using your hands to combine the ingredients. Cover with plastic wrap and refrigerate until ready to use.

2. Oil the grill racks. Preheat your grill using all burners set on high and with the lid closed for 10 to 12 minutes.

3. Remove the meat mixture from the refrigerator and form into 8 patties. Make a small depression in the center of each patty. Sprinkle each burger with salt. Brush with oil and place on the grill.

4. Cook for 7 to 8 minutes, then turn and cook for another 7 minutes. When you turn the burgers, place the hamburger buns cut side down on the grill. Cook until nicely toasted, usually 1 to 2 minutes. If you want cheese, place slices of cheese on the burgers about 2 minutes before they are done. Check the burgers for doneness. They should be relatively firm with a little give, which should yield a medium to medium-well doneness. Continue to cook until your preferred doneness has been reached. Remove the buns to a platter with the bottom halves ready for the hamburgers. When the hamburgers are done, place one on each bottom bun, top with a tomato slice, and serve with your choice of condiments.

SLIDERS ARE KING

It seems as if mini burgers have taken America by storm. They're everywhere—at cocktail parties and on restaurant menus. Of course, the fun thing about mini burgers is that if you eat three of them, which is about equivalent to one regular burger, you can have three different toppings, three different cheeses, three different anythings. These are great for a kid's birthday party or for an appetizer at a party where you're making longer-cooking grilled meats. So just for fun, pretend you're White Castle® and make some mini burgers.

1. Place the ground beef in a medium bowl and sprinkle liberally with salt and pepper. Using your hands, gently mix the seasonings with the meat. Brush a baking sheet with oil or spray with cooking spray. Using a 2-inch biscuit cutter as your form, make 12 mini burgers. Make sure that you put a thumbprint indention in the center of each one. Cover with plastic wrap and refrigerate for about 1 hour.

2. Meanwhile, combine the butter, shallots, Worcestershire, and granulated onion in a small bowl. Season with salt and pepper. Refrigerate if it's going to be longer than an hour before you grill, but you want this butter to be soft and at room temperature when using.

3. Oil the grill racks. Preheat your grill using all burners set on high and with the lid closed for 10 to 12 minutes.

4. Split your party rolls in half and put them, cut side down, on the grill. Toast for about 2 minutes. As you take them off, smear them with the butter on the insides. Place on a platter and tent with foil. Place the burgers on the grill and grill for about 3 minutes. Turn and continue grilling for an additional 2 to 3 minutes. Remove to a platter. Add one burger to each roll and serve with your favorite condiments.

SERVES 4 AS A MAIN COURSE, OR 6 TO 12 AS APPETIZERS; MAKES 12 MINI BURGERS
DIRECT HEAT

2 pounds 80% lean ground chuck, or 1½ pounds 80% lean ground chuck plus 8 ounces 90% lean ground sirloin

Kosher salt

Freshly ground black pepper

Vegetable oil cooking spray

½ cup (1 stick) unsalted butter, at room temperature

2 medium shallots, finely chopped

1 tablespoon Worcestershire sauce

½ teaspoon granulated onion

1 package soft white party rolls (I like using potato rolls for these burgers)

Condiments of your choice

AT THE TABLE

Need some party ideas? You can goose these sliders up a bit more if you like. Instead of the butter, use blue cheese or boursin as a taste addition. Top with fried or caramelized onions, guacamole, taco sauce, Asian barbecue sauces (try hoisin or teriyaki), or spreadable port wine cheese.

FRED'S TWO-HANDED ULTRA BURGER

I fancy myself a connoisseur of great burgers. When visiting any new city I hit what the locals consider the best burger joints. This burger is the melting pot of those adventures. This is a guy's burger, but I know plenty of women who will belly up to the burger bar for this one.

1. Melt the butter in a large skillet and add the onions. Cut the heat to medium-low and cook the onions, stirring occasionally, until caramelized, about 20 minutes. Remove from the heat and keep warm. Refrigerate if making ahead (they will keep for 1 day), but warm the onions before serving.

2. In a large bowl, using your hands, gently blend the meats, garlic, salt, and pepper together. Still being gentle, form the meat into 6 patties large enough to cover the size of your bun. Don't forget to put a thumbprint in the middle of each patty. This is especially important with this burger because of all the stuff you're going to put on top. Refrigerate until ready to cook, up to 4 hours.

3. Oil the grill racks. Preheat your grill using all burners set on high and with the lid closed for 10 to 12 minutes.

4. Place the patties on the grill and cook for 4 to 5 minutes, then turn and cook for an additional 5 to 6 minutes, or until they give slightly to the touch. When you turn the burgers, place the ham on the grill. About 2 minutes before the burgers are done, turn the slices of ham over, slide the rolls on the grill to toast, and place a slice of cheese on each burger.

5. When the burgers are done, remove them, the buns, and the ham from the grill. To build the burgers, place them on the bottom half of each roll. Top with a couple slices of grilled ham, a tablespoon of the barbecue sauce, and caramelized onions. Add tomato, lettuce, and any other condiments you think you might need. Get lots of napkins, hold over your plate, smush the burger down, and enjoy.

SERVES 6

DIRECT HEAT

2 tablespoons unsalted butter

2 large sweet onions, thinly sliced

1½ pounds 80% lean ground chuck

8 ounces 90% lean ground sirloin

4 garlic cloves, minced

Kosher salt

Freshly ground black pepper

12 slices Black Forest ham

6 kaiser or onion rolls

6 slices provolone cheese

6 tablespoons barbecue sauce (use your favorite)

6 tomato slices

6 lettuce leaves

Condiments of your choice

SOUTH-OF-THE-BORDER BURGERS

SERVES 6

DIRECT HEAT

1 large egg

2 pounds 80% lean ground chuck, or 1½ pounds 80% lean ground chuck plus 8 ounces 90% lean ground sirloin

One 4-ounce can diced green chiles, drained and rinsed

2 tablespoons chunky salsa (use your favorite)

2 tablespoons finely chopped onion

¼ cup crushed plain tortilla chips

2 garlic cloves, minced

1 teaspoon chili powder

Kosher salt

Freshly ground black pepper

6 hamburger buns

1 cup shredded Mexican blend cheese or *queso fresco*

Shredded lettuce

Taco sauce (optional)

A little salsa, a little chili powder, and some taco sauce make for a really interesting hamburger, and it's also one that kids seem to really like. If you sense boredom in the burger department, give this one a whirl.

1. Beat the egg in a large bowl. Add the meat, chiles, salsa, onion, tortilla chips, garlic, and chili powder. Use your hands to mix gently until just barely combined. Remember, overworking the ground beef makes for a tough burger.

2. Divide the ground beef into 6 equal portions and shape into patties about ¾ inch thick. Remember to put a slight indentation into the center of each patty. Season both sides of the burgers liberally with salt and pepper.

3. Oil the grill racks. Preheat your grill using all burners set on high and with the lid closed for 10 to 12 minutes.

4. Adjust the heat to medium. Place the burgers on the grill and cook somewhere between 8 and 12 minutes total, turning only once halfway through the grilling time. The burgers will have a small amount of give when touched and the internal temperature should be about 160°F for medium-well.

5. Just before your burgers are done, place the hamburger buns on the grill, cut side down. Divide the shredded cheese evenly over the hamburgers. When the buns are toasty and the cheese is melted, remove the buns to a platter and place a hamburger on each of the bottom buns. Serve immediately, topped with shredded lettuce and taco sauce, if desired.

EAST TENNESSEE'S FAMOUS PIG BURGER

If you're heading toward the Smoky Mountains in east Tennessee up from Gatlinburg, you might pass the Townsend Grill. It's one of those perfect dives where you know the food is going to be great. Burgers are their passion, and they are most renowned for their pig burger, which is a blend of country sausage and beef. Getting the recipe wasn't easy, and they may have left out an ingredient or two, but quite frankly, I can't tell much difference between this one and the one at the Grill.

1. In a large bowl, blend the beef and the sausage together gently; your hands are best for this. Add the onion, hot sauce, sage, seasoned salt, and pepper. Again, mix together until just combined.

2. Divide the ground meat into 8 equal portions and shape into patties about ¾ inch thick. Remember to put a slight indentation into the center of each patty. Season both sides of the burgers liberally with salt and more pepper. Place the burgers on a baking sheet, cover with plastic wrap, and refrigerate for an hour to allow the flavors to blend.

3. Oil the grill racks. Preheat your grill using all burners set on high and with the lid closed for 10 to 12 minutes.

4. Remove the pig burgers from the refrigerator and place on the grill. Cook for about 8 minutes per side. You want these burgers to be completely cooked through because of the pork. The internal temperature should be 150°F to 160°F. Use an instant-read thermometer to test, going in through the side of the burger. During the last 2 minutes, place your buns, cut side down, on the grill until nice and toasty. Remove the buns and burgers to a platter and dress as desired with tomato, lettuce, and your favorite condiments.

SERVES 8
DIRECT HEAT

2 pounds 80% lean ground chuck, or 1½ pounds 80% lean ground chuck plus 8 ounces 90% lean ground sirloin

12 ounces country sausage, hot or mild, casings removed if necessary

1 small onion, chopped (about ½ cup)

1 tablespoon hot sauce

1½ teaspoons dried sage, crushed between your fingers

¼ teaspoon seasoned salt, such as Lawry's

¼ teaspoon freshly ground black pepper

Salt

8 hamburger buns

Tomato slices

Lettuce leaves

Condiments of your choice

PIMIENTO CHEESEBURGERS

SERVES 6
DIRECT HEAT

1 small white onion, grated

8 ounces sharp Cheddar cheese, grated

4 ounces mild Cheddar cheese, grated

½ cup good-quality mayonnaise (I prefer Duke's or JFG®)

One 2-ounce jar diced pimientos, drained

Freshly ground black pepper

2 pounds 80% lean ground chuck, or 1½ pounds 80% lean ground chuck plus 8 ounces 90% lean ground sirloin

Kosher salt

6 hamburger buns, preferably onion flavored

Pickled jalapeño chile slices

IN THE KITCHEN

This homemade pimiento cheese can be used not only with this burger but also as a dip or a spread for just about anything you want. It will keep for about a week in the refrigerator.

Even folks in the South, where pimiento cheese is lovingly called the "pâté of the South," will give you a quizzical look when you mention this burger. I always thought its true home was around Columbia, South Carolina, and the lower upstate area. But then I saw a pimiento cheeseburger on the menu in a wonderful burger joint and restaurant called Litton's, in Knoxville, Tennessee, so I guess a good idea can cross state lines. So here's how to do it, complete with a little pimiento cheese recipe, but the burger's not bad even if you have to use a good-quality store-bought pimiento cheese.

1. In a medium bowl, mix together the onion, both cheeses, mayonnaise, and pimientos. If you need additional mayonnaise to make it creamy, add a little bit at a time. Grind copious amounts of black pepper and stir that into the cheese mixture.

2. Divide the ground beef into 6 equal portions and shape into patties about ¾ inch thick. Remember to put a slight indentation into the center of each patty. Season both sides of the burgers liberally with salt and pepper.

3. Oil the grill racks. Preheat your grill using all burners set on high and with the lid closed for 10 to 12 minutes.

4. Place the burgers on the grill and lower the heat to medium. Grill for about 5 minutes. Turn the patties and continue grilling until they reach your desired doneness, about 4 additional minutes for medium, 6 minutes for medium-well. During the last 2 minutes of cooking time, add the buns, cut side down. At the last minute before taking the hamburgers off the grill, put a generous spoonful of pimiento cheese on each. Take the buns from the grill, place on a platter, set a burger on each bun bottom, add pickled jalapeños on top of the pimiento cheese, and serve.

ASTORIA LAMB BURGERS

SERVES 6

DIRECT HEAT

2 tablespoons pitted minced
    kalamata or other black olives

2 tablespoons finely chopped
    fresh flat-leaf parsley

1 tablespoon finely chopped
    fresh mint

1 tablespoon Dijon mustard

2 teaspoons dried rosemary,
    crushed between your fingers

1 garlic clove, minced

1½ pounds ground lamb

8 ounces 80% lean ground chuck

2 tablespoons ice water

Kosher salt

Freshly ground black pepper

6 hamburger buns or pita breads

6 tablespoons Tzatziki Sauce
    (p. 295)

AT THE GRILL

To make this burger a lamb cheeseburger, sprinkle each patty with about a tablespoon of feta cheese about 2 minutes before the burgers are done. Just one more indulgent trip into Greek foodways.

One of the most intoxicating food smells can be found on Greek Orthodox Easter as you ride through Astoria, Queens. This traditionally Greek neighborhood of New York City is filled with the aroma of lambs being spit-roasted over coals, gas, and wood fires. If you don't get hungry riding through that area, something is wrong. These lamb burgers are an attempt to recreate that memory in a more streamlined form. Feel free to use pita bread or hamburger buns. They're delicious in either. The addition of a little hamburger and some water helps to give you a bit of fudge factor so that you don't dry out the lamb burgers. Please do not overcook these morsels.

1. Take a large bowl and combine the olives, parsley, mint, mustard, rosemary, and garlic. Using your hands, gently work in the lamb and the ground beef. Add the ice water and again gently blend.

2. Divide the ground meat into 6 equal portions and shape into patties about ¾ inch thick. Remember to put a slight indentation into the center of each patty. Season both sides of the burgers liberally with salt and pepper.

3. Oil the grill racks. Preheat your grill using all burners set on high and with the lid closed for 10 to 12 minutes.

4. Place the burgers on the grill and adjust the temperature to medium. Grill for 8 to 10 minutes total for a medium doneness, turning once during the cooking process. The internal temperature should be between 150°F and 160°F and the patties should give slightly when pressed. During the last minute of the cooking time, place the buns or pitas on the grill and toast. Remove the buns to a platter and place a lamb burger on each bun bottom. Top with a spoonful of the Tzatziki Sauce.

A TURKEY BURGER WORTH EATING

Turkey burgers get a bad rap. They tend to be dry and overcooked, tasteless to some extent. But we think that by eating turkey burgers we're eating something healthy. Of course, if we don't eat something that's healthy because there's no taste, then we've defeated the purpose. Turkey burgers are good. This one takes a few cues from your Thanksgiving bird for abundant flavor and extra moisture from some added milk.

1. Grab a large bowl and combine the ground turkey, breadcrumbs, onion, parsley, sage, ginger, salt, and pepper; lightly wet your hands and combine these ingredients together gently. Start with 2 tablespoons of milk and gently work that in to the burger mixture. You want this mixture to feel wet but not soppy, so if necessary add more milk, a little at a time.

2. Divide the ground meat into 6 equal portions and shape into patties about ¾ inch thick. Remember to put a slight indentation into the center of each patty. Season both sides of the burgers liberally with salt and pepper.

3. Oil the grill racks. Preheat your grill using all burners set on high and with the lid closed for 10 to 12 minutes.

4. Place the burgers on the grill and lower the heat to medium. Cook for about 15 minutes total, turning halfway through, or until an instant-read thermometer registers 160°F to 165°F. The burgers should be firm to the touch, and until you get used to cooking turkey burgers, make a small incision with a knife to make sure that no pink remains.

5. During the last minute of cooking, place the buns on the grill, cut side down, and cook until lightly toasted. Remove the buns to a platter, spread each bottom with mustard, and place burger on each. Add cranberry sauce and serve.

SERVES 6

DIRECT HEAT

2 pounds ground turkey, preferably not all white meat

¼ cup fine dry breadcrumbs

1 red onion, finely chopped

2 tablespoons chopped fresh flat-leaf parsley

1 teaspoon dried sage, preferably Dalmatian

¼ teaspoon ground ginger

2 teaspoons kosher salt

½ teaspoon freshly ground black pepper

2 to 4 tablespoons milk, cream, or fat-free half-and-half

6 hamburger buns

Stone-ground mustard

Prepared cranberry sauce

AT THE MARKET

Dalmatian sage is stronger in flavor than regular sage, which helps with this burger.

KATRINA'S SEATTLE SALMON BURGERS

Katrina Moore is a friend of mine who lives in Seattle. We worked out this salmon burger recipe together. The biggest thing we had to overcome was keeping the burger together on the grill without compacting it to the point of making it dry. I think we did a pretty good job.

1. Remove the skin from the salmon or have your fishmonger do it for you. Check the fillet over for pin bones and remove any you find with tweezers or needle-nose pliers. Cut the salmon into 2-inch chunks. Put the salmon, scallions, garlic, ginger, tamari, and sesame oil in the bowl of a food processor. Pulse until combined. This may take 5 to 6 pulses, but do *not* let the machine run. Pour this mixture into a medium bowl and add the breadcrumbs and sesame seeds. Use your hands to gently combine.

2. Divide the salmon mixture into 4 equal portions and shape into patties about ¾ inch thick. Remember to put a slight indentation into the center of each patty. Season both sides of the burgers liberally with salt and pepper. Refrigerate for at least 1 hour. This will help the burgers hold together on the grill.

3. Oil the grill racks well, and make sure that they are impeccably clean. Preheat your grill using all burners set on high and with the lid closed for 10 to 12 minutes.

4. Remove the burgers from the refrigerator and spray both sides of each with the cooking spray. Place on the grill and cook for 5 minutes. Turn and cook for 4 minutes longer, so the burgers are just cooked through. Use a spatula to turn your burgers, but loosen them from the grill before you make the attempt. During the last minute or two, place the buns on the grill, cut side down, so they get warm and toasty. Remove all from the grill to a platter, and top with lettuce and either the Peanut Sauce or the sweet chili sauce.

SERVES 4
DIRECT HEAT

1 pound salmon fillet
   (use tail or belly)

4 scallions (green parts only),
   cut into 1-inch pieces

4 garlic cloves, minced

2 tablespoons grated fresh ginger

2 tablespoons tamari

1 tablespoon toasted sesame oil

¼ cup fine dry breadcrumbs

2 tablespoons sesame seeds

Kosher salt

Freshly ground black pepper

Vegetable oil cooking spray

4 hamburger buns

Lettuce leaves

Peanut Sauce (p. 295) or
   Asian sweet chili sauce

AT THE TABLE

You might want to try mixing ¼ cup good-quality mayonnaise with ¼ cup of the sweet chili sauce and then spreading the buns with it as you would with mayonnaise. Any left over can be kept in the refrigerator for several weeks and is also good as a little dip for grilled tuna.

YELLOWFIN TUNA BURGERS WITH GINGER-MUSTARD GLAZE

SERVES 4

DIRECT HEAT

FOR THE GINGER-MUSTARD GLAZE

⅓ cup lower-sodium teriyaki sauce

2 teaspoons finely grated
   fresh ginger

1 small garlic clove, finely minced
   (about ½ teaspoon)

1 tablespoon honey

1 tablespoon Dijon mustard

½ teaspoon rice vinegar or
   white-wine vinegar

1½ pounds yellowfin tuna

2 garlic cloves, minced

3 tablespoons Dijon mustard

½ teaspoon cayenne

1 teaspoon kosher salt

¼ teaspoon freshly ground
   black pepper

Canola oil

4 good-quality hamburger buns,
   preferably with sesame seeds

¼ cup Japanese pickled ginger,
   drained (available in most large
   supermarkets in the Asian
   section)

Thank you, Michael Romano and Danny Meyer of the Union Square Café in New York City, for having the inventiveness to put a tuna burger on the restaurant's menu and make the concept famous. They are quick to credit the great French chef Pierre Franey with actually suggesting the dish as a way to use tuna loin that was too small to be cut into steaks. This is my version of that great Union Square burger.

1. Make the glaze first. In a 1-quart saucepan, combine the teriyaki, ginger, garlic, honey, mustard, and vinegar. Bring to a boil, lower the heat to a simmer, and cook until the glaze coats the back of a spoon, 4 to 5 minutes. Strain through a sieve. This can be prepared 2 days in advance and stored, covered, in the refrigerator. Bring to room temperature or warm slightly in a microwave before serving.

2. Take the tuna and use a large, sharp knife to chop it until it has the texture of hamburger meat. (Using a food processor shreds tuna.) Place the tuna in a bowl and combine it with the garlic, mustard, cayenne, salt, and pepper. Divide the tuna mixture into 4 equal portions. Using your hands, form into patties.

3. Oil the grill racks. Preheat your grill using all burners set on high and with the lid closed for 10 to 12 minutes.

4. Brush both sides of each tuna burger with canola oil. Make certain that your cooking grid is very hot. Place the burgers on the grill and cook for about 4 minutes. Turn and cook for 3 minutes longer, or until the burger feels slightly firm to the touch. When you turn the burgers, place your hamburger buns, cut side down, on the grill. To serve, place each burger on a bun bottom. Spread a tablespoon of the glaze over each burger and divide the pickled ginger slices equally on top. Cover with the top half of the bun and dig in.

PORTABELLA MUSHROOM BURGERS

SERVES 4

DIRECT HEAT

4 large portabella mushrooms, stems removed

¼ cup fresh lemon juice

¼ cup extra-virgin olive oil

2 teaspoons herbes de Provence

Kosher salt

Freshly ground black pepper

4 whole-wheat hamburger buns or pitas

1 cup arugula leaves

4 tomato slices

4 onion slices

Condiments of your choice

Need a great meaty flavor without the saturated fat? Let me introduce you to a portabella mushroom. Almost steak-like in flavor, it's the perfect replacement for ground beef in a hamburger-like preparation. Portabellas even cook like a piece of beef, and you should handle them exactly that way. Even the most avid hamburger advocate would be happy to have this burger on more than one occasion.

1. Take the portabellas and, with a teaspoon, gently rub around the inside of each one to clean out the dark brown gills. (There's nothing wrong with them, they just don't add much to this dish.) Drizzle the lemon juice over each mushroom, then brush each with the olive oil. Sprinkle evenly with the herbs de Provence, salt, and pepper. Let sit at room temperature while the grill preheats.

2. Oil the grill racks. Preheat your grill using all burners set on high and with the lid closed for 10 to 12 minutes.

3. When the grill is hot, cut the temperature on all burners to medium. Place the mushrooms on the grill, close the lid, and cook for about 5 minutes. Turn and cook for about 5 minutes longer. During the last 2 minutes of cooking, put the hamburger buns or pitas on the grill, cut side down. The mushrooms are done when they can be easily pierced with the tip of a knife and feel soft to the touch. Place each mushroom between the buns or in a pita and serve with arugula, tomato, onion, and condiments.

SMOKED TURKEY SAUSAGE WITH GRILLED ONIONS AND SAUERKRAUT

Smoked sausage and sauerkraut are just made for each other. But when you add nicely caramelized onions off the grill a fabulous transition takes place. Instead of tasting the components, you taste the whole as they intermingle into a wonderful and simple supper. You can put this in buns if you like, or just serve it up on a plate. Have a little spicy mustard to the side for dipping.

1. Oil the grill racks. Preheat your grill using all burners set on high and with the lid closed for 10 to 12 minutes.

2. Brush the onion slices on both sides with the oil.

3. Lower the heat to medium and place the onions on the grill. Close the lid and cook slowly, turning every so often, until the onions are very soft and nicely browned, about 10 minutes.

4. Meanwhile, combine the sauerkraut, caraway seeds, and water in a small saucepan. Place over medium heat and cover. Cook until warmed through, and hold over low heat until the onions are done.

5. When the onions are done, toss them in the pan with the sauerkraut. Using a fork, break the slices into rings and combine well with the kraut. Add the balsamic vinegar, cover, and keep warm.

6. Place the sausage pieces on your grill and cook, turning every 2 to 3 minutes, until all sides have picked up some color and the sausage is hot to the middle. Remember, these sausages are cooked when you buy them. Remove from the grill, put on a platter, and pour the onion-kraut mixture over the top. Serve with the mustard on the side.

SERVES 4
DIRECT HEAT

2 large red onions, cut into ½-inch slices, skewered if desired (if using bamboo, soak in water for 30 minutes)

1 tablespoon canola oil

One 1-pound bag refrigerated sauerkraut, drained

½ teaspoon caraway seeds

2 tablespoons water

1 tablespoon balsamic vinegar

2 pounds smoked turkey sausage, cut into 8-ounce pieces

Spicy grainy mustard

THE HOG DOG—AMERICA'S PASTIME

6 fully cooked hot dogs
(use your favorite)

4 tablespoons unsalted butter,
at room temperature

6 hot dog buns

Chili

Cole slaw

Sauerkraut

Cooked onions

Raw onions

Shredded lettuce

Pickle relish

Sport peppers

Mustard

Ketchup

Celery seeds

There aren't many of us who don't love hot dogs. We may fight over the type, whether it's a bright red southern-style Carolina Pride dog, or the garlic-infused Sabrett® of New York City, or the equally delightful Vienna® of Chicago. What goes on that dog is a source of discussion as well. In some ways, a hot dog is like barbecue: What's "best" is subject to intense debate, and your favorite is typically the one you grew up with. I've listed some of the most common ones below, and you and your guests should feel free to pick and choose, or to add your own favorites.

A sad reality goes on today, where the hot dog winds up in the microwave for a quick nuking. Let's stop that. Your gas grill will only take about 10 minutes to get hot, and think about how much better the dogs will taste and look with those charred grill marks adding another dimension. A trick I've learned is to make shallow diagonal cuts over the length of the dog, and you especially need to try this if you like crispy bits that form on a grilled dog. As the hot dog expands, these slits open up and increase the surface area for a little charring and caramelization to take place. Looks a little funny but adds a great deal of flavor.

1. Oil the grill racks. Preheat your grill using all burners set on high and with the lid closed for 10 to 12 minutes.

2. Place the hot dogs on the grill and lower your heat to medium. Cover and grill for 6 to 8 minutes, turning occasionally, until the hot dogs have developed some color and bits of char and are nicely plump.

3. Butter your hot dog buns and place them on the grill during the last minute to toast lightly.

4. Remove the hot dogs and the buns from the grill and take your pick from that lengthy list of condiments.

THE REAL DEAL CHILI

DON'T BUY CANNED CHILI. HOT DOG CHILI IS EASY TO MAKE, and when I make a batch I divide it into smaller amounts and freeze them for later use. It's infinitely better than anything you'll find in a can. Brown 1½ pounds ground round over medium heat, using a spatula to break up any clumps. Drain out the fat. Add a chopped medium onion and cook until soft. Stir in two 6-ounce cans tomato paste, 1 cup water, 1½ tablespoons sugar, 1 tablespoon chili powder, ½ teaspoon dried oregano, kosher salt, and freshly ground black pepper to taste. Let the mixture come to a boil, cover, reduce the heat, and let simmer for about 1½ hours.

Those cooked red onions at every hot dog vendor's cart in New York City are easy to make as well. Take 2 or 3 sweet onions and slice them thinly. Add a little oil to a large skillet and cook the onions until they have softened. Add a 14.5-ounce can of tomato sauce, 2 whole cloves, and 4 minced garlic cloves. Bring to a boil, then reduce the heat to a simmer. Let cook for about 30 minutes. You may need to add some water to keep the consistency the way you want it, and you may want to fish out the cloves, but I don't bother. This will keep for a couple of weeks, covered, in the refrigerator. And by the way, it's just as good on a hamburger as it is on a hot dog. And—if you're from Wisconsin, stop reading here—I think it's pretty darned good on a brat, too.

"CHEESEHEAD" BRATS

If you're a Green Bay Packers fan, you know the importance of a bratwurst prior to game time. I guess if you prepare brats in this manner it helps you to endure the cold of Lambeau Field and prepares your head for that wedge-of-cheese hat that those football fanatics seem to love. Whatever, it works for their football team, which never seems to be far from the top. This is the method that I was taught by tailgaters when I was researching *Barbecue Nation*. If you're anywhere near Green Bay, I highly suggest that you use this method. Packer fans would never use a precooked brat. You might need to make a trip to a butcher shop to find them.

1. Oil the grill racks. Preheat your grill using all burners set on high and with the lid closed for 10 to 12 minutes.

2. Combine the beer, onions, and brats in a large saucepan. If your grill has a side burner, feel free to do this process there. Otherwise, place over medium-high heat and bring to a boil. Reduce the heat to low and simmer until the brats are just cooked through, usually about 8 minutes. Remember, we're going to continue cooking these brats on the grill.

3. Remove the brats from the pot and place them on the grill. Grill the brats for 8 to 10 minutes, turning them frequently to brown them evenly on all sides. When they are done, slide them into your buns and top with mustard and sauerkraut. Do not, under any circumstances, even think about putting ketchup on brats unless you are not in the state of Wisconsin. Even then, I think they would hunt you down.

SERVES 6
DIRECT HEAT

Two 12-ounce cans beer, preferably the cheap stuff

2 large onions, thinly sliced

6 uncooked bratwursts (if you have big eaters, you might want to double this number)

6 good-quality hot dog buns or small submarine rolls (again, for big eaters, see above)

Brown mustard

One 1-pound bag refrigerated sauerkraut, drained

BELINDA'S FOOLPROOF PIZZA DOUGH

MAKES 4 CRUSTS
DIRECT HEAT

1 envelope active dry yeast

½ teaspoon sugar

⅔ cup warm water (105°F to 115°F)

2 cups bread flour, plus more
    to roll out the dough

1 teaspoon kosher salt

½ teaspoon freshly ground
    black pepper

2 tablespoons extra-virgin olive oil,
    plus more for brushing the crust

Cornmeal

My "all things with flour" pro, Belinda Ellis, developed this pizza dough for me that's especially designed to work on a grill. And that it does. Whether you grill directly on the grates or heat up a pizza stone, this pizza dough will work like a dream.

1. In a medium bowl, combine the yeast, sugar, and water. Stir briefly and let stand until the mixture is foaming, about 5 minutes. Add the flour, salt, pepper, and olive oil. Stir until the dough pulls away from the side of the bowl and is soft. Flour your hands and lightly flour a work surface. Pull the dough out onto the work surface. Knead the dough once or twice and form into a ball. Grease another medium bowl, and place the ball in the bowl, turning to coat. Cover with plastic wrap and set aside in a warm, draft-free area until the dough doubles in size, 1 to 1½ hours.

2. Punch the dough down. Roll it out of the bowl onto a lightly floured surface and, using a pastry cutter or chef's knife, cut into 4 equal pieces. The dough may be used immediately or wrapped in plastic wrap and refrigerated for up to 24 hours. If using refrigerated dough, allow it to sit at room temperature for 30 minutes before trying to roll it out. The dough also can be frozen; thaw completely in the refrigerator, then let it sit for 30 minutes at room temperature.

3. Dust two baking sheets with cornmeal. Dust a rolling pin with flour and roll each piece of dough into an 8-inch round that's about ⅛ inch thick. Lightly brush both sides of the crusts with olive oil, and then carefully move them to baking sheets. The easiest way to do this is to push a rimless cookie sheet under the dough.

IN THE KITCHEN

Having frozen pizza dough is a godsend if you enjoy grilling pizza. Double or triple this recipe and divide it up in individual freezer bags; be sure to date the bags. It usually takes less than four hours to thaw.

4. Oil the grill racks. Preheat your grill using all burners set on high and with the lid closed for 10 to 12 minutes.

5. Carefully slide the crusts from the baking sheets onto the grill and cook until the underside is well marked, about 2 minutes. The crust may bubble, but that's okay, so don't panic. Transfer the crusts back to your baking sheets with the grilled side up.

6. From this point, it's all up to you and your creativity. Assemble your ingredients—cheeses, whatever you desire—on the grilled side of the crust (see p. 224 for some ideas). Then gently slide the pizzas, uncooked side down, back onto the grill, close the lid, and cook for 4 to 5 minutes, or until nice and crispy. Remove from the grill, cut into wedges, and serve warm.

PIZZA MAGIC

A gas grill makes for one fine pizza oven. The temperature gets high enough to closely replicate many commercial units. A beautiful char develops on the crust, and that adds volumes of flavor to the entire event. Grilling pizzas is a perfect way to start a party, whether the rest of the meal is going to be on the grill or not. I like to do three or four different types of pizza so that everybody gets a little bit of their favorite. What follows will give you starting points, and then let your imagination run. Make one recipe of Belinda's Foolproof Pizza Dough (p. 222), and then pick your favorite additions from these suggestions.

THE CLASSIC— PIZZA MARGHERITA

First conceived to impress Queen Margherita as she visited Naples, you know the story, red, white, green, color of the Italian flag, tomatoes, mozzarella, basil. Over 100 years later it's still one of the best and most classic of pizzas. You'll need ½ cup marinara sauce or 8 to 10 plum tomatoes, cored and thinly sliced; 8 ounces mozzarella cheese, shredded, or 8 ounces fresh mozzarella, thinly sliced; ½ cup basil leaves torn into small pieces; 2 garlic cloves, minced; kosher salt; and freshly ground black pepper. After toasting the first sides of the crusts, build your pizza thusly. Swirl some of the sauce on each crust (or place the tomato slices if using), sprinkle with the garlic, top each pizza with cheese, sprinkle with salt and pepper, and place back on the grill for 4 to 6 minutes. Remove and throw the basil over the top. Cut into wedges and serve.

UPSCALE URBAN

Another thought is a pesto, mozzarella, and ricotta pizza. Use a good-quality pesto sauce, 8 ounces fresh mozzarella, thinly sliced, and 2 cups of the best ricotta cheese you can find. Spread the pesto over the crusts, top with the mozzarella, and spoon dollops of the ricotta cheese all around.

CALIFORNIA DREAMING

Get rid of any leftover roast chicken by making a barbecue pizza. Use any thick barbecue sauce brushed over the crusts, and add the leftover chicken and some diced pineapple. Cover with 8 ounces of shredded mozzarella cheese and you've got a two-for-one deal.

FRED'S FAVORITE

One more thought that's a bit upscale. Take 4 pears, core them and slice into ½-inch slices lengthwise, brush each pear with a little olive oil, and place on the grill over medium-low heat for about 3 minutes per side. You could do this the day before if needed. Just keep the pear slices refrigerated. When ready to do a killer pizza, divide the pear slices equally on the crusts and top with 4 slices prosciutto for each pizza. Sprinkle crumbled blue cheese or goat cheese or both over the top and slide onto the grill. When the pizza is done, throw torn basil leaves over the top and drizzle with a fruity extra-virgin olive oil.

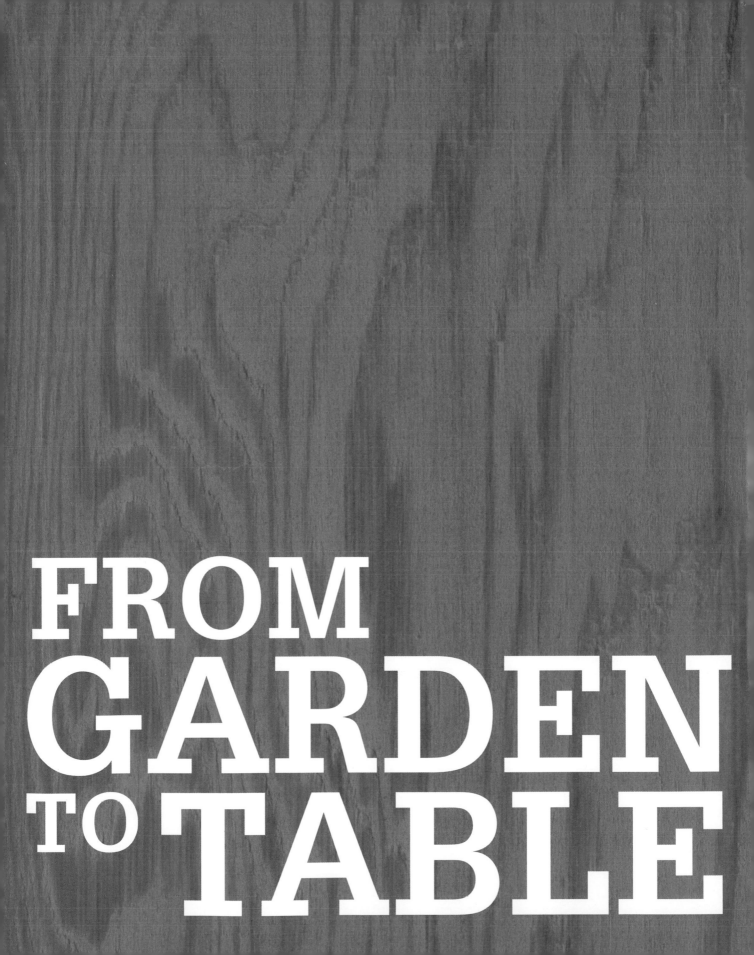

FROM GARDEN TO TABLE

VEGETABLES, SIDES, AND VEGETARIAN ENTRÉES

MOST OF US ARE FAMILIAR with grilled asparagus or corn on the cob, but it may be surprising to learn that practically all vegetables—even lettuce—can be grilled. The opportunity to do a whole meal on the grill is more than a possibility, it's a boon. Once you're comfortable with juggling multiple items on the grill, you'll find this is much more relaxing than the mad dash between the grill and the kitchen to deal with your sides.

A few of these recipes are entrées. Most are side dishes, but they also can be served together for a vegetarian meal. And a few are not cooked on the grill at all, but are included because they go so well with grilled foods.

VEGETABLES

There is magic in what the grill does to vegetables, pure magic that even the most ardent vegetable-hater will love. Grilling brings out the natural sweetness of vegetables and adds a smoky depth of flavor that to my mind is irresistible.

Grilling vegetables can be a bit tricky. Vegetables vary from day to day as to their available moisture. If you're fortunate, a good farmers' market can help with this by providing consistently fresh vegetables. You can help yourself by trying to grill what's in season, because these vegetables will be at the peak of their flavor and moisture content.

The key is to minimize the loss of natural moisture that most vegetables contain. One way to do this is to cut your veggies just prior to cooking, and a drizzle of oil and a quick toss to coat will also help. If you're doing an assortment of vegetables, try to cut them as close to the same size as possible. This will also help with even cooking. Also cut them as large as you can. It maximizes the contact with the grill and—I know this has never happened to you—it keeps them from falling through the grill grates and into the burners.

For most vegetables, direct heat is typically the best way to go. Dense vegetables like potatoes and winter squash, if left whole, need to be cooked over indirect heat (they also benefit from a quick blanching to start the cooking process). I have also had barbecued cabbage that had been cooked over indirect heat, but for the most part contact with the direct heat of the grill is priceless. That also means you need to pay attention, because most vegetables

APPROXIMATE GRILLING TIMES
FOR VEGETABLES USING DIRECT HEAT
These are guidelines only; specific recipes may vary.

TYPE	SIZE	ROUGH ESTIMATE OF TIME
ASPARAGUS	Whole	6–7 minutes
BELL PEPPER	Whole	10–15 minutes
BELL PEPPER	Halved or quartered	6–8 minutes
BELL PEPPER	¼-in. slices	6–8 minutes
MOST CHILES	Whole	7–8 minutes
CORN	Husked	10–15 minutes
CORN	In husk	25 minutes
EGGPLANT	½-in. slices	8–10 minutes
JAPANESE EGGPLANT	Halved lengthwise	10–12 minutes
FENNEL	¼-in. slices	10–12 minutes
LEEKS	Halved lengthwise	8–10 minutes
ROMAINE LETTUCE	Halved lengthwise	6–8 minutes
PORTABELLA MUSHROOMS	Whole caps	8–10 minutes
ONIONS	½-in. slices	8–10 minutes
POTATOES	½-in. slices	14–16 minutes
POTATOES (SMALL, RED, FINGERLING, ETC.)	Halved	15–20 minutes
SCALLIONS	Whole	3–4 minutes
YELLOW SQUASH	½-in. slices	6–8 minutes
SWEET POTATOES	¼-in. slices	6–8 minutes
GREEN TOMATOES	½-in. slices	6–8 minutes
RED TOMATOES	½-in. slices	4 minutes
RED TOMATOES	Halved lengthwise	6–8 minutes
ZUCCHINI	½-in. slices	6–8 minutes
ZUCCHINI	Sliced lengthwise	6–10 minutes

APPROXIMATE GRILLING TIMES

FOR VEGETABLES USING DIRECT HEAT These are guidelines only; specific recipes may vary.

TYPE	SIZE	ROUGH ESTIMATE OF TIME
BEETS	Whole	1–1½ hours
CABBAGE	Whole or halved	2 hours
PUMPKIN	3 pounds cut in half lengthwise	1–1½ hours
ACORN SQUASH	Halved	40–45 minutes
BUTTERNUT SQUASH	Halved	50–55 minutes
RUSSET POTATO	Whole	45–60 minutes
SWEET POTATO	Whole	50–60 minutes
GARLIC	Whole head	45–50 minutes

cook quickly. Keep your heat in the medium range, but don't be afraid to turn that knob even lower. Just like a good steak, most vegetables are best if turned only once. If some begin to burn or cook too quickly, the beauty of a gas grill is the ability to reach over and completely turn off a burner and continue to cook those items more gently.

Many of the recipes in this chapter goose up vegetables pretty well, but sometimes simplicity is the best. Put your cut veggies in a large zip-top bag, drizzle in a couple of tablespoons of oil and add a sprinkling of salt and pepper, close the bag, and squish everything together. It's simple but effective. Heck, one of my grilling buddies just sprays his vegetables with vegetable oil cooking spray, sprinkles some salt over them, and throws them on the grill.

If you're looking for true, individual vegetable and fruit flavor, simple is always the best.

Doneness is really a matter of personal preference, and the touch test is usually the best indicator. It's hard to have cooking times that are written in stone for vegetables, since they do change from day to day and season to season. The chart on p. 229 is a guide only and lists some of the more popular ones to grill. Don't let this be your limiting factor. If it grows, you can probably grill it.

SIDES

My friend, the James Beard award–winning chef Ben Barker, once told me that it's often what's served with the protein that makes the

THERE IS MAGIC IN WHAT THE GRILL DOES TO VEGETABLES...

meal. No truer words were ever spoken. Go to any family reunion in any region of this country and you'll see the importance of sides. I would never think of serving Jean Lynn's brisket without her incredible potato salad. A pure heresy would be committed to have Lexington style barbecue without the famous red slaw. The most perfect platter of ribs is kind of lonely without decadent baked beans. During my travels researching *Barbecue Nation*, it quickly became apparent that while I might have been at somebody's house for their ribs, steak, or chicken, what they served with that was as important to them as the key element of the meal.

VEGETARIAN ENTRÉES

Not all vegetarians are absolute purists. Many laugh and admit to being what I call "vege-mostlies," which usually means they will eat fish or dairy or eggs, but some people truly want to avoid flesh in favor of plants. Vegans, on the other hand, eat no animal products at all, including honey—there are no "vegan-mostlies." Make sure you understand what category a guest might fall into and respect that. That stuff that's stuck to the grill is more than likely an animal protein, and to throw a piece of tofu in that same area is a no-no. Take your brush and clean the area where you will be cooking a vegetarian's or vegan's food.

Also think about the drips and splatters. If you're cooking meat on one part of a grill and tofu on another, take care as you move and turn the meat around that you don't contaminate the non-meat-eater's meal. Be considerate, but relax. The gas grill, with its infinite number of heating combinations, comes to your rescue when you need to grill two separate menus. And, oh, by the way, be sure to taste what you cook for the vegetarian. I'll bet you'll like it.

SUMMER'S BOUNTY GRILLED VEGETABLE SOUP

SERVES 4 TO 6

DIRECT HEAT

3 ribs celery, cut into 2-inch lengths

One 32-ounce bottle V8® juice

2 cups tomato juice

3 tablespoons fresh lemon juice

1 tablespoon Worcestershire sauce

1 large garlic clove, minced

2 teaspoons fresh thyme leaves

1 medium yellow summer squash,
    halved lengthwise

1 medium zucchini,
    halved lengthwise

1 red bell pepper, seeded and
    cut into 1-inch strips

1 yellow bell pepper, seeded and cut
    into 1-inch strips

1 fresh poblano chile, halved
    lengthwise and seeded
    (wear gloves to prevent irritation)

½ cup olive oil

1 teaspoon kosher salt
    (or less to taste)

½ teaspoon freshly ground
    black pepper

1 medium red onion,
    cut into ½-inch-thick slices

2 ripe, meaty tomatoes,
    halved lengthwise and seeded

This soup has a delicate, deliciously smoky flavor that will make even those who aren't too fond of vegetables ask for more. When a trip to the farmers' market results in some serious overbuying or your garden throws out more stuff than you can possibly eat, make grilled vegetable soup. It also keeps well in the refrigerator for about a week, and it freezes beautifully.

1. Combine the celery, V8, tomato juice, lemon juice, Worcestershire, garlic, and thyme in a food processor and puree until smooth. Pass the puree through a fine sieve to remove any fibers and set aside.

2. Oil the grill racks. Preheat your grill using all burners set on high and with the lid closed for 10 to 12 minutes.

3. Add the vegetables and olive oil to a gallon-size zip-top plastic bag. Squish to coat. Remove the veggies and season with the salt and pepper. Place the onion slices on the grill, close the lid, and cook for about 3 minutes, then add the squash, zucchini, peppers, and chile. Close the lid and cook for an additional 3 minutes. Turn the vegetables after the onions have cooked for about 6 minutes and the other vegetables for 3 to 4. Add the tomatoes, skin side down, and cook for 3 minutes. The vegetables should be close to being done. Look for a nice char and softness to the touch as your signal to remove them from the grill.

4. Place half of the vegetables in the food processor, add the reserved vegetable puree, and process until smooth. Transfer to a soup pot. Cut the remaining vegetables into small dice and stir into the puree. Taste and season with salt and pepper. Bring slowly to a boil over medium heat, then reduce the heat to low and simmer until heated through, 5 to 7 minutes. Serve at room temperature or chilled. It will keep refrigerated for several days or frozen for several months.

PENNE PASTA WITH GRILLED VEGETABLES AND FETA

This may be the most versatile recipe in this book: The vegetables can be anything to your liking, the pasta shape can be your favorite, and the cheese could easily be replaced with goat or boursin or Parmesan or Brie. Go to your local farmers' market and buy the freshest vegetables you can find. Look for unusual local cheeses. Take this recipe and play with it to make this dish become your specialty.

1. Oil the grill racks. Preheat your grill using all burners set on high and with the lid closed for 10 to 12 minutes.

2. Pour the dressing into a large bowl and add the bell pepper strips, onion wedges, and cherry tomatoes. Toss with your hands to coat thoroughly. Thread the cherry tomatoes on skewers and then add all of the vegetables to the grill. Close the lid and cook until nicely charred but still tender. Usually the onion will take about 15 minutes, the peppers about 10 minutes, and the cherry tomatoes about 5 minutes, turn all the vegetables about halfway through their respective cooking times. As the vegetables are done, add them back to the bowl with the dressing. When all the vegetables are in the bowl, sprinkle in the oregano and toss again.

3. Meanwhile, bring a large pot of salted water to a boil and cook the pasta until tender but still firm to the bite. Drain. Pour the pasta into the bowl with the grilled vegetables. Crumble the feta over the pasta and vegetables. Season with salt and pepper. Toss, pour into a nice serving bowl, and serve.

SERVES 6
DIRECT HEAT

½ cup Italian dressing
(use your favorite)

3 bell peppers (use different colors
for better plate appeal), seeded
and cut into ¾-inch strips

1 large red onion, cut into 6 wedges
(keep some of the root attached to
each wedge)

One 12-ounce package cherry or
grape tomatoes

Skewers (if using bamboo,
soak in water for 30 minutes)

2 tablespoons chopped fresh oregano

One 1-pound box penne pasta,
preferably whole wheat or
multigrain

4 ounces feta cheese

Kosher salt

Freshly ground black pepper

SUMMER VEGETABLE KEBABS WITH HARISSA AND YOGURT SAUCE

2 eggplants, peeled and cut into
   1-inch chunks (I like to use the
   smaller Italian ones)

2 zucchini, cut into 1-inch chunks

3 green bell peppers, seeded and
   cut into 1-inch pieces

16 grape tomatoes

4 small red onions,
   peeled and quartered

¼ cup olive oil

Juice of ½ lemon

1 garlic clove, minced

1 teaspoon ground coriander

1 teaspoon ground cinnamon

2 teaspoons honey

Kosher salt

Skewers (if using bamboo,
   soak in water for 30 minutes)

2 cups plain whole-milk yogurt,
   strained

2 to 4 tablespoons harissa (available
   in the Middle Eastern or Indian
   section of your grocery store)

½ cup chopped fresh cilantro leaves

¼ cup chopped fresh mint leaves

Freshly ground black pepper

2 cups cooked couscous

Harissa is a condiment made of ground hot peppers that's common in North Africa and the Middle East. It is sold usually in cans and is pretty hot by itself. The yogurt helps to cool it down. If you can find Greek yogurt (FAGE® is a common brand), use it. It is thicker and has a stronger flavor than most supermarket brands.

1. Place all the vegetables in a large mixing bowl. In a small bowl, whisk together the olive oil, lemon juice, garlic, coriander, cinnamon, honey, and 1 teaspoon salt. Pour this mixture over the vegetables and toss gently with your hands to fully coat the veggies.

2. Thread the vegetables onto skewers, mixing them up so that each one is next to a different type.

3. Oil the grill racks. Preheat your grill using all burners set on high and with the lid closed for 10 to 12 minutes.

4. While the grill is heating, mix the yogurt and harissa together in a small bowl. Start with the smaller amount of harissa and taste, adding more depending on how hot you like things. Reserve a bit of the cilantro and mint for garnish, then add the rest to the yogurt mixture. Season to taste with salt and pepper.

5. Place the kebabs on the grill and reduce the heat to medium-high. Close the lid and cook for about 2 minutes per side, or until the vegetables are nicely browned, give to the touch, and appear to be cooked through, 8 to 10 minutes usually. Remove from the grill and slide the vegetables off the skewers onto a platter covered with the couscous. Sprinkle with the reserved herbs and serve with the yogurt sauce.

GRILLED EGGPLANT "PARMESAN"

Bring the vegetarians to your table with this hearty take on a classic Italian dish, but don't reserve it for just an entrée. It's also an awesome side dish for grilled or roasted chicken. If you need to make this in advance, feel free. Just reheat it gently before serving.

1. Place the tomato and eggplant slices on a baking sheet in a single layer. Blend the olive oil, garlic, vinegar, and about half the basil in a bowl until combined. Liberally brush the eggplant and tomatoes on all sides with this mixture.

2. Oil the grill racks. Preheat your grill using all burners set on high and with the lid closed for 10 to 12 minutes.

3. Place the eggplant on the grill, close the lid, and cook until tender and slightly charred, 4 to 5 minutes per side. A couple of minutes into cooking the eggplant, add the tomato slices. Close the lid and cook the tomatoes for about 2 minutes per side. Use a spatula and a fork to turn them, and be very gentle so that they don't fall apart. Remove the vegetables to a baking sheet.

4. Spoon 1 to 2 tablespoons of the marinara onto each of 6 salad plates. Begin to make stacks: Using the largest slices first, start with an eggplant on top of the marinara, then add a slice of tomato, sprinkle with Parmesan, then add a slice of mozzarella, another slice of tomato, a slice of eggplant, several slices of the red pepper, and one additional slice of mozzarella. Finish the stack with a slice of tomato and another couple of tablespoons of marinara sauce. Garnish with additional red pepper, more Parmesan cheese, and the remaining basil. Season to taste with salt and pepper. Serve at room temperature or slightly warm.

SERVES 6

DIRECT HEAT

4 large tomatoes, cored and
    cut into ½-inch slices

2 eggplants, sliced into
    ½-inch rounds

½ cup extra-virgin olive oil

2 garlic cloves, minced

2 tablespoons balsamic vinegar

4 medium fresh basil leaves,
    stacked, rolled into a cigar,
    and thinly sliced

2½ to 3 cups marinara sauce
    (use your favorite)

1 cup freshly grated
    Parmesan cheese

8 ounces fresh mozzarella cheese,
    sliced into ¼-inch-thick rounds

2 roasted red peppers, sliced into
    thin strips (about ¾ cup;
    see sidebar, below)

Kosher salt

Freshly ground black pepper

AT THE GRILL

To grill-roast red bell peppers cook them over direct heat until well charred. Place in a zip-top bag, seal, and let steam for 20 minutes. Peel off the skins under cool running water.

GRILLED BREAD
AND TOMATO SALAD

SERVES 6 TO 8
DIRECT HEAT

½ cup (1 stick) unsalted butter

2 garlic cloves, minced

8 ounces day-old Italian bread,
    cut into ¾-inch-thick slices

6 dead-ripe meaty tomatoes, cored,
    seeded, and cut into quarters

¼ cup minced red onion

⅓ cup fruity extra-virgin olive oil

2 tablespoons balsamic vinegar

2 tablespoons chopped fresh basil

1 tablespoon chopped fresh tarragon

½ teaspoon kosher salt

7 or 8 grindings black pepper

The Italian classic *panzanella* gets a new spin when you grill the bread. This added dimension, I think, further brings out the summer sweetness of dead-ripe beefsteak tomatoes. The juxtaposition of the caramelized, toasted bread against the sweet-tart tomatoes makes for plenty of contrast in flavor and texture. You can also try this without grilling the tomatoes, if you prefer. Just don't make this salad too far in advance. You want the bread to have a little structure and crispness.

1. Place a small saucepan over medium heat and add the butter. When it's about half melted, throw in the garlic and cook for 3 to 4 minutes, allowing the garlic to take on a little bit of color. Remove from the heat and brush this mixture on both sides of each slice of bread.

2. Oil the grill racks. Preheat your grill using all burners set on high and with the lid closed for 10 to 12 minutes.

3. Place the bread on the grill, close the lid, and cook, turning once, until well marked. Careful here; depending on the moisture content of the bread, this could happen as quickly as 2 minutes (or about 1 minute on each side), but it usually takes about 4 minutes. Place the tomatoes on the grill, close the lid, and cook for a few minutes per side.

4. Remove the bread to a cutting board, cut into ¾-inch cubes, and place in a large mixing bowl. Add the tomatoes, onion, olive oil, vinegar, herbs, salt, and pepper. Toss gently with your hands to combine. Taste and adjust the seasonings if you desire. Serve at room temperature.

GRILLED CORN ON THE COB IN ITS HUSK

SERVES 6
DIRECT HEAT

6 ears corn, in their husks

Butter

Kosher salt

Freshly ground black pepper

At street fairs and state fairs across the country, you'll find at least one booth selling grilled corn. No matter where you are, the grilled corn vendors always have the longest lines. Folks just seem to love grilled corn on the cob, and nothing could be simpler to do on your gas grill.

1. Use a pair of scissors or a knife to trim the silk ends of the corn. Fill your sink or a bucket with cold water and soak the corn, husk and all, for 45 minutes.

2. Oil the grill racks. Preheat your grill using all burners set on high and with the lid closed for 10 to 12 minutes.

3. Remove the corn from the water, shaking off as much excess liquid as you can. Place the corn on the grill and cook, turning occasionally, until the outside is slightly charred and the inside kernels are tender. To test, peek between the husks and push on a kernel with your thumbnail. Here's the dilemma. The fresher the corn, the less time it takes to cook. Farm-fresh, picked-that-day corn, especially small-kernel corn like Silver Queen or bicolor, might take as little as 5 minutes, but usually no more than 10 minutes. If the corn came from the grocery store, it more than likely will take at least 10 minutes, and big-kernel corn could go even closer to 15 minutes. Be vigilant, because overcooked corn becomes dry and tasteless.

4. Remove the corn from the grill and pull back part of the husk on each piece. Serve with butter, salt, and pepper and let everyone finish shucking their own corn and seasoning it as desired.

AT THE TABLE

Here's something that will add a little zip to your basic grilled corn. Stir together 1 teaspoon paprika (or even better, smoked paprika), $1/2$ teaspoon granulated onion, $1/2$ teaspoon kosher salt, $1/4$ teaspoon dried thyme, and $1/4$ teaspoon dried oregano. Take this mixture and sprinkle it directly on your corn, or make a little Cajun butter by blending it with half a stick of room-temperature butter.

FABULOUS BAKED BEANS

My neighbors had been after this recipe for years, and when I finally gave it up, it took on a life of its own. The recipe has been passed to friends and relatives in North Carolina, South Carolina, Maryland, Tennessee, Indiana, and even Houston, Texas. When I found out about Houston, I laughed. Here was a recipe that has come full circle, literally. I wish I could claim this recipe as my own creation, but alas, I can't. In my recipe files, they are called "Martha's Baked Beans," after Martha Sanderson. She, her husband David, and their family had moved to North Carolina from Houston.

One warning about this recipe, or any you have that everybody loves. Once you part with the recipe, find something else to bring to the party, 'cause the rest of the crowd will be calling dibs, especially on these beans. After I published it in my newspaper column, it became the second-most-requested recipe, after my ribs.

1. Preheat your oven to 350°F.

2. Pour the pork and beans into a 9x13-inch baking dish. Add the sausage and drippings and the onions and stir to mix. Pour in the corn syrup, brown sugar, both mustards, and the Worcestershire. Stir to blend throughout the beans.

3. Cover the beans and bake for at least an hour; 1½ hours is better. Cooking the beans the day before and reheating them for about 30 minutes before serving is the best way to get great flavor.

SERVES 8 TO 10 OR MORE

Three 32-ounce cans pork and beans, drained (preferably VanCamp's®)

2 pounds country sausage, browned and crumbled, drippings reserved

2 medium onions, sliced

1 cup dark corn syrup

1 cup packed brown sugar

3 teaspoons dry mustard

¼ cup yellow mustard

2 teaspoons Worcestershire sauce

IN THE KITCHEN

You can mix up these beans in a disposable 9x13-inch pan and set them on the indirect section of your grill to cook as well. This works better with a grill that has four or more burners, and it is nice to cook alongside your protein if that is also an indirect item that will cook for at least 1½ hours.

SHELL BEANS VINAIGRETTE

SERVES 4 TO 6

1 tablespoon olive oil

1 small sweet onion, such as Vidalia, finely chopped

4 garlic cloves, minced

1 bay leaf

¼ teaspoon crushed red chile flakes

2 pints shelled purple hull or other peas (or two 10-ounce bags frozen crowder or field peas)

2 cups low-sodium chicken broth

Kosher salt

Freshly ground black pepper

¼ cup balsamic vinegar

¼ cup fruity extra-virgin olive oil

1 tablespoon chopped fresh thyme leaves

3 or 4 medium fresh basil leaves, stacked, rolled like a cigar, and thinly sliced

This side dish is good both warm and at room temperature and eats fairly well straight out of the refrigerator. It will make a lot of the dishes in this book happy by saddling up on the same plate. It's especially good with the Cauliflower "Steaks" on p. 242 and with simply grilled fish and shellfish—try them with Whole Smoke-Grilled Mountain Trout (p. 169) or Grilled Scallops with Rémoulade Sauce (p. 186). Use any bean that's available to you, even black-eyed peas. And when you can't get fresh, don't hesitate to use frozen—but don't use canned. The texture won't be right.

1. Take a medium saucepan and place over medium heat. Add the olive oil, and when it begins to shimmer throw in the onion. Cook until soft and with just a tiny bit of color, about 5 minutes. Add the garlic, bay leaf, and crushed red chile flakes. Cook, stirring, for 2 minutes. Pour in the peas and broth and bring the mixture to a simmer. Cook until the peas are tender but still maintain their shape, about 20 minutes. A lot of the liquid will have been absorbed, so watch carefully so that you don't burn the peas on the bottom. Season with salt and pepper.

2. Drain the peas if desired (most of the liquid will evaporate) and add to a large bowl. Whisk together the vinegar and olive oil. Pour this over the warm peas and toss to thoroughly combine. Add the herbs and toss again. Serve immediately, or cover and refrigerate. The peas can be served warm, at room temperature, or chilled.

GRILLED ROMAINE

When my friend and traveling buddy Robin Kline first told me about grilling romaine, I thought she had lost her mind. But Robin is known for combining improbable ingredients with delicious results (see her Surprising Pork Tenderloin on p. 89), so I knew better than to dismiss what sounded like a nutty idea. This actually has become one of my favorite side dishes for a host of grilled foods, especially a good porterhouse steak. Don't hesitate to change the vinegar or the oil to your liking. I occasionally will use walnut oil or rosemary-infused vinegar and substitute blue cheese for the Parmesan. In other words, make this salad your own.

SERVES 8
DIRECT HEAT

4 hearts of romaine lettuce, halved lengthwise

¼ cup balsamic vinegar

Fruity extra-virgin olive oil

Kosher salt

Freshly ground black pepper

1 cup freshly shaved Parmesan cheese (use a vegetable peeler)

1. Oil the grill racks. Preheat your grill using all burners set on high and with the lid closed for 10 to 12 minutes.

2. Toss the lettuce with the vinegar in a large bowl. Place the lettuce, cut side down, on the grill. Close the lid and cook for 4 to 6 minutes, or until you have some char and the lettuce has wilted slightly.

3. Remove the lettuce from the grill to individual salad plates. Drizzle liberally with olive oil and season well with salt and pepper. Divide the cheese shavings among the greens and get this salad to the table.

CAULIFLOWER "STEAKS"

2 heads cauliflower, stalky parts
    and leaves pulled off

Olive oil

1 teaspoon ground cumin

1 teaspoon ground coriander

½ teaspoon curry powder

Shell Beans Vinaigrette (p. 240)

I first saw a recipe for roasted cauliflower steaks in *Bon Appétit* magazine, and it intrigued me. If you can roast them, I thought, why can't you grill them? So as part of an upscale southern dinner, I did just that. Cauliflower is one of those vegetables that we need to eat more of, and this recipe will definitely make you look at this cruciferous vegetable differently. Remember Mark Twain's words on the vegetable: "It's nothing but cabbage with a college education." Kind of simplifies this, doesn't it?

1. Taking care to keep the core intact, slice each cauliflower lengthwise into four to six 1-inch-thick "steaks." Reserve the remaining cauliflower (the rounded end slices) for another use.

2. Oil the grill racks. Preheat your grill using all burners set on high and with the lid closed for 10 to 12 minutes.

3. Brush the cauliflower steaks liberally with olive oil. Mix together the cumin, coriander, and curry powder, and sprinkle evenly over each.

4. Carefully lay the cauliflower steaks on your grill, close the lid, and cook for 4 to 5 minutes per side, using a large spatula to turn. The steaks may try to come apart on you a little bit. Don't worry, just try to shove the florets all back into place. Press the cauliflower near the core, and if it gives easily, it's done. You want it to be a little soft but still fairly crisp. Remove each steak to an individual plate and garnish with some of the shell beans vinaigrette. Serve.

GRILLED FENNEL AND RADICCHIO WITH ORANGE VINAIGRETTE

SERVES 8

DIRECT HEAT

4 medium bulbs fennel
(about 1 pound), fronds removed

3 heads radicchio

½ cup fresh orange juice

2 garlic cloves, minced

2 teaspoons honey

½ teaspoon freshly ground
black pepper

¾ teaspoon kosher salt

½ cup fruity extra-virgin olive oil

These two vegetables aren't exactly what you'd call common, but fennel and radicchio seem to benefit from an outdoor fire more dramatically than just about any other vegetable. Put the two together with a bright and fresh vinaigrette and you have a side dish or salad that will complement the most humble or extravagant of grilled foods.

1. Cut the fennel bulbs lengthwise into ½-inch-thick slices, keeping the root end intact. Cut each head of radicchio into 8 wedges, again keeping the roots intact. Place the fennel and radicchio in a single layer on a baking sheet.

2. In a medium bowl, whisk together the orange juice, garlic, honey, pepper, and ½ teaspoon of the salt. Going slowly, whisk in the olive oil until the dressing is well blended and emulsified. Set aside half of the vinaigrette. Drizzle the remaining half over the fennel and radicchio and sprinkle with the remaining ¼ teaspoon of salt. Let stand for 5 to 10 minutes.

3. Oil the grill racks. Preheat your grill using all burners set on high and with the lid closed for 10 to 12 minutes.

4. Place the fennel on the grill, close the lid, and cook for about 7 minutes on each side. Add the radicchio about 2 minutes after you turn the fennel over. Turn the radicchio after 2 minutes. When the radicchio is slightly wilted and has taken a bit of color and the fennel is soft to the touch, remove to a platter and toss with the reserved vinaigrette. Serve immediately.

CREAMED TURNIP GREENS

Don't miss this southern spin on a steakhouse favorite. Serve these sumptuous greens with any grilled steak, lamb chops, or any highly seasoned pork. Thanks to Chef Frank Stitt, chef/owner of Highlands Bar and Grill in Birmingham, Alabama, for putting this thought in my head. Use fresh greens if they look good in your market, and substitute any bitter green you like for the turnip greens. To lighten this dish, use 2 percent milk and one-third-less-fat cream cheese.

1. Melt the butter in a large nonstick skillet over medium-high heat. Stir in the onion and garlic and sauté for 3 minutes, or until tender. Stir in the turnip greens, chicken broth, and red chile flakes, if desired. Cook for 4 to 5 minutes or until the liquid evaporates.

2. Sprinkle the turnip green mixture with the flour and sauté for 2 minutes. Gradually stir in the milk and cook, stirring occasionally, for 3 minutes. Add the cream cheese and stir until melted. Season with salt to taste. Transfer to a serving bowl and garnish with the Parmesan cheese.

SERVES 4

1 tablespoon unsalted butter

1 small yellow onion, chopped

2 garlic cloves, minced

One 16-ounce bag frozen turnip greens, thawed

½ cup chicken broth

½ teaspoon crushed red chile flakes (optional)

2 tablespoons all-purpose flour

1 cup milk

5 ounces cream cheese, cut into pieces

Kosher salt

Freshly shaved Parmesan cheese

THE LAWS OF SLAWS

I resent people who consider cole slaw a plate filler. Slaw deserves respect. It can be the ideal foil to so many foods and is especially handy as a side for many grilled and barbecued foods. I think there are four distinct types of slaw—mustard-based Memphis-style, which is phenomenal with ribs and beef brisket; a mayonnaise-and-black pepper slaw that's popular in the South and Midwest that plays well with grilled fish and shrimp; eastern North Carolina barbecue slaw, which is a sweet mustard-and-mayonnaise mixture that works well with any food that has been coated with a vinegar-based sauce; and finally the ubiquitous and, to some, odd red slaw that's tossed with a thin barbecue sauce and that's found with the purveyors of Lexington-style 'cue.

Now, yes, granted there are Asians slaws and there are tricolored pepper slaws, probably hundreds of versions, but if you use these four slaws as a base, then you can add your own touches and personalize them to fit the foods you love to eat and to your region.

All of the following variations serve 8 to 10 and start with half a head of green cabbage, 4 to 5 cups shredded.

MEMPHIS-STYLE MUSTARD SLAW

Blend ¼ cup yellow mustard, ¼ cup mayonnaise, ¼ cup sugar, ¼ cup distilled white vinegar, ½ teaspoon celery seeds, ½ teaspoon freshly ground black pepper, kosher salt to taste, and 2 tablespoons diced red bell pepper. Toss with the cabbage and chill.

CLASSIC EASTERN NORTH CAROLINA SLAW

This slaw also makes its way through most of Georgia and Mississippi. Blend together ½ cup Miracle Whip®, ¼ cup sweet pickle relish, 2 tablespoons yellow mustard, 1 tablespoon sugar, 1 teaspoon kosher salt, ¼ teaspoon celery seeds, and freshly ground black pepper to taste. Toss with the cabbage. Finely grated carrots are a good addition to this slaw.

THE PERFECT SLAW FOR FISH

Try this one: ¾ cup mayonnaise, 2 tablespoons apple-cider vinegar, 1 teaspoon kosher salt, 1 teaspoon sugar, and at least ¼ teaspoon freshly ground black pepper (more is better). Blend together and toss with the cabbage. Let it sit in the refrigerator for at least 2 hours or overnight before serving. Besides grilled fish, it's also endearing to fried chicken and burgers, and if you're in North Carolina you'd put this on a hot dog for a Slaw Dog.

RED SLAW

Blend ½ cup apple-cider vinegar, ½ cup ketchup, ¼ cup sugar, ½ teaspoon kosher salt, some freshly ground black pepper, and at least 1 teaspoon hot sauce. Stir until the sugar dissolves. Chop your cabbage as finely as possible—don't shred or grate it—so it's almost the size of BBs. Toss everything together and let sit for at least 2 hours, refrigerated, before serving.

PORTABELLA MUSHROOM "PIZZAS"

The woodsy flavor and meaty texture of portabella mushrooms make them a natural for the grill, and treating them like a "crust" and loading them with typical pizza toppings yields a wonderful first course or vegetarian entrée. If you want to get fancy, try the alternative preparation in the sidebar (below). It's a little "cheffy," but for a party or a special vegetarian in your life, it's pretty impressive.

1. Brush both sides of the mushrooms with the oil. Place on a baking sheet, stem side up, and season with salt and pepper. Top each with a slice of mozzarella and a slice of tomato. (The mushrooms can be assembled several hours in advance. Cover with plastic wrap and refrigerate. Bring to room temperature before grilling.)

2. Oil the grill racks. Preheat your grill using all burners set on high and with the lid closed for 10 to 12 minutes.

3. Place the mushrooms on the grill and close the lid. Adjust the heat to medium and cook the mushrooms for 6 to 8 minutes. The mozzarella should have begun to melt and the tomato slice wilted into the cheese. Remove the mushroom caps to individual plates. Drizzle with the pesto and serve.

SERVES 6 AS A FIRST COURSE, OR 2 TO 3 AS A MAIN COURSE

DIRECT HEAT

6 large portabella mushroom caps, gills removed

¼ cup fruity extra-virgin olive oil

Kosher salt

Freshly ground black pepper

8 ounces mozzarella cheese, cut into 6 slices

6 ripe beefsteak tomato slices, about ¼ inch thick

½ cup pesto (use your favorite)

IN THE KITCHEN

Slice each mushroom cap in half horizontally so you can make a sandwich. On the bottom half, put the mozzarella and tomato, and then put the top half over it. Grill for 3 to 4 minutes, turn, and grill for 3 to 4 minutes more.

GRILLED SWEET POTATO SALAD WITH CITRUS DRESSING

SERVES 6

DIRECT HEAT

3 large sweet potatoes
   (1½ to 2 pounds)

1 tablespoon canola oil

Kosher salt

Freshly ground black pepper

½ cup fresh orange juice

¼ cup rice vinegar

1 tablespoon pure maple syrup
   (not pancake syrup)

1 fresh jalapeño chile, seeded and
   finely chopped (wear gloves to
   prevent irritation)

2 scallions, thinly sliced
   (white and green parts)

1 teaspoon grated fresh ginger

¾ cup extra-virgin olive oil

3 to 4 cups mixed salad greens

If you're looking for a way to get sweet potatoes in your diet because of the health benefits that lurk in their flesh, consider this recipe. Okay, that's the responsible reason for having it. The real reason you should eat it is that this is an awesome side, whether you serve it with ribs, barbecued chicken, or pulled pork. The grill emphasizes the natural sweetness of this vegetable, and the dressing has just enough tartness for a sumptuous treat.

1. Place the sweet potatoes in a large pot and add water to cover them by 1 inch. Bring to a simmer over medium-high heat and cook until a knife can be easily inserted about ¼ inch into the potato but the center is still very firm, about 15 minutes. Drain the potatoes and let cool completely, then peel and cut into ¾-inch-thick slices. Brush with the canola oil and season well with salt and pepper.

2. Oil the grill racks. Preheat your grill using all burners set on high and with the lid closed for 10 to 12 minutes.

3. Place the sweet potatoes on the grill, close the lid, and cook for about 3 minutes but no longer than 5 minutes per side. They should still be firm but have softened a bit. Remove from the grill to a plate.

4. In a medium bowl, whisk together the orange juice, vinegar, maple syrup, jalapeño, scallions, and ginger. Whisking very slowly, drizzle in the olive oil until the dressing is nicely emulsified. Taste and season with salt and pepper. If the flavor is too oily, add additional salt. If too acidic, add a bit more oil.

5. Divide the greens among 6 plates. Arrange the sweet potato slices on top of the greens. Drizzle the vinaigrette over the salad and serve immediately.

ULTIMATE POTATO SALAD

Stop buying that store-bought stuff and make this recipe. It's so incredibly delicious, you'll be tempted to forget that it's a side dish and just sit down with the bowl and a spoon and fill yourself to oblivion. It's one of my most requested recipes from my columns, and I have to thank Jean Lynn of Memphis, Tennessee, as my teacher on all things potato salad. It's great with all the barbecued foods in this book and many of the more simply prepared recipes. Just two caveats, and one bit of advice: Do not think about making this with mayonnaise, because it just won't taste right. Do not make this with pickle relish or salad cube pickles, as they both diminish the overall flavor. And try using your food processor to chop the pickles—just pulse it to chop.

1. Place the potatoes in a large saucepan or Dutch oven and cover generously with water. Add the salt. Place over medium heat and bring to a slow boil. Cook, uncovered, until the potatoes are very soft when tested with a fork, 20 to 25 minutes. Drain and mash the potatoes slightly (it's okay to do this still in the pot). Stir in the eggs, onion, and pickles.

2. In a large bowl, whisk the Miracle Whip, sugar, vinegar, and mustard until blended. Taste—you want a sweet-tart flavor—and adjust if necessary with additional sugar or vinegar, or pickle juice. Add the warm potato mixture to the dressing and stir to combine. Serve warm or cold. Leftovers will keep for up to a week in the refrigerator.

SERVES 12 TO 14

5 pounds russet Burbank potatoes, peeled and cut into large cubes

1 tablespoon kosher salt

5 large eggs, hard-cooked and chopped

1 Vidalia or other sweet onion, chopped

Two 12-ounce jars sweet gherkins or midget pickles, drained, juice reserved, and chopped

2 cups Miracle Whip salad dressing (do not use mayonnaise)

½ cup sugar

1 tablespoon distilled white vinegar

½ teaspoon yellow mustard

ROASTED POTATO SALAD WITH ROSEMARY AND ASIAGO CHEESE

SERVES 6

3 pounds red-skinned new potatoes

3 tablespoons olive oil

Kosher salt

Freshly ground black pepper

**1 tablespoon finely chopped
fresh rosemary**

⅓ cup grated Asiago cheese

Here is the ideal picnic potato salad. Because it doesn't have any mayonnaise, it doesn't need to be chilled (in fact, it's actually best at room temperature), and because it's better made ahead, you have one less side dish to mess with when you need to pay attention to the ribs on your grill. And if you need another reason, it's just a doggoned good recipe.

1. Preheat your oven to 400°F.

2. Quarter the large potatoes and cut the smaller ones in half. Place the potatoes in a large bowl. Drizzle with the olive oil and a good sprinkle of salt. Be generous with the black pepper. Use your hands to toss the potatoes, oil, and seasonings together.

3. Transfer the potatoes to a large rimmed baking sheet that will hold them in a single layer. Roast the potatoes, stirring occasionally, until they are crispy and brown on the outside and tender when tested with a knife, about 1 hour.

4. Remove the potatoes from the oven and let cool slightly. Transfer them to a large bowl, add the rosemary, and toss. Let the potatoes cool completely. Add the cheese just before serving and toss again. Serve at room temperature.

CREAMY GRUYÈRE GRITS

South of the Mason-Dixon Line, it's all about grits. If you live north of that line, just think of it as coarsely ground polenta, but no matter where you live, try this recipe. It's a perfect match with many grilled foods and a nice change of pace from mashed potatoes or rice. Feel free to use any cheese you like; I just like the nutty flavor that Gruyère brings to the grits.

Pour the water and salt into a medium saucepan. Place over medium-high heat and bring to a boil. Slowly whisk in the grits and return to a boil. Reduce the heat to medium-low and simmer, whisking occasionally, for 12 to 15 minutes or until the grits have thickened. Whisk in the cheese, half-and-half, and butter, and continue whisking until the cheese is melted and the mixture is blended. Season with pepper and serve.

SERVES 8

5¼ cups water

1 teaspoon kosher salt

1½ cups uncooked
   quick-cooking grits

8 ounces Gruyère cheese, shredded

½ cup half-and-half

1 tablespoon unsalted butter

Freshly ground black pepper

IN THE KITCHEN

Even if you're only serving four, make this whole recipe of grits so you can use the leftovers for grits cakes: Spray a casserole dish that is just large enough to hold the leftover grits in a layer about 1 inch thick with vegetable oil cooking spray. Pour the grits into the casserole dish and let cool to room temperature, then cover and refrigerate. Within the next day or so, dump the grits onto a cutting board and cut into blocks. Brush with olive oil and grill for 3 to 4 minutes per side. These grits cakes play happily together with grilled fish, chicken, and especially a good, thick, juicy pork chop.

VEGETABLES, SIDES, AND VEGETARIAN ENTRÉES

BELINDA'S ULTIMATE GARLIC-CHEESE BISCUITS

MAKES 12

Vegetable oil cooking spray

2½ cups soft-wheat self-rising flour

¼ cup cold vegetable shortening

1 cup shredded Cheddar cheese, preferably sharp

¾ cup buttermilk

3 tablespoons butter, softened

½ teaspoon granulated garlic

Belinda Ellis comes to my rescue again with this perfectly tender, garlicky biscuit that sits on the side of any plate of grilled food with honor. I like to grill sausage patties and put them in these biscuits for the ultimate sausage-biscuit breakfast. If you have trouble finding the flour in your local stores, you may find it online from the White Lily® website.

1. Preheat your oven to 450°F. Line a baking sheet with parchment paper or foil. Spray lightly with cooking spray.

2. Measure the flour into a large bowl. Divide your shortening into small pieces and scatter them on top of the flour. Work the pieces into the flour with a pastry cutter, two knives, or your fingertips if you have cold hands until the mixture resembles large peas. Gradually stir in the cheese and buttermilk, stirring only enough to moisten the flour and hold the dough together. Drop by rounded tablespoons onto the baking sheet. Bake for 8 to 10 minutes or until the tops are golden.

3. Meanwhile, combine the softened butter and the granulated garlic in a small bowl.

4. When the biscuits are done, remove them from the oven and quickly brush the tops with the garlic butter. Remove the biscuits from the baking sheet and serve hot or at room temperature.

CORNBREAD TO DIE FOR

In my opinion, all cornbread is to die for if it's done right—and by that I mean baked in a cast-iron skillet. Here's the proper way to perfect cornbread that is a tasty addition to a plate of ribs.

1. Preheat your oven to 425°F. Spray an 8- or 10-inch heavy skillet, like cast iron (use an 8-inch metal pan in a pinch), with cooking spray. Place the skillet in the oven to heat.

2. In a large bowl, combine the cornmeal mix, buttermilk, oil, egg, and sugar, if desired.

3. Open your oven and slide out the rack that the skillet is on. Pour the batter into the heated skillet. Slide the rack back in the oven and bake for 20 to 25 minutes for a 10-inch skillet or 25 to 30 minutes for an 8-inch skillet or the 8-inch pan. Remove from the oven, let cool a little if you like, and cut into 8 wedges or squares. Serve hot.

SERVES 8

Vegetable oil cooking spray

2 cups self-rising cornmeal mix

1⅓ cups buttermilk

¼ cup corn oil

1 large egg, lightly beaten

1 to 2 tablespoons sugar (optional, unless you were born north of the Mason-Dixon Line)

GRILLED MARINATED TOFU

SERVES 4

DIRECT HEAT

½ cup lower-sodium teriyaki sauce

¼ cup toasted sesame oil

¼ cup rice vinegar

1½ to 2 pounds firm or
    extra-firm tofu, drained

Black and white sesame seeds
    (optional)

Japanese pepper (optional; available
    in Asian markets and some
    specialty food stores and larger
    supermarkets)

You need to be careful nowadays, because somebody on your guest list is probably a vegetarian or perhaps even vegan. Keeping a block of firm or extra-firm tofu on hand is smart entertaining. With a little teriyaki sauce and toasted sesame oil, you have a quick marinade that even the most ardent carnivore will enjoy.

1. Mix the teriyaki sauce, sesame oil, and vinegar together in a small bowl.

2. Slice the tofu in half lengthwise. Place the sliced tofu in a shallow dish and pour the marinade over it. Let stand for at least 30 minutes at room temperature.

3. Oil the grill racks well—tofu can stick. Preheat your grill using all burners set on high and with the lid closed for 10 to 12 minutes.

4. Once the grill is hot, turn all burners to medium and let the grill stay open for just a minute or two before placing the tofu on the grill. Reserve the marinade. Close the lid and cook until lightly seared, about 5 minutes per side. Remove, which is best accomplished with a metal spatula, to a platter. Quickly brush some of the marinade over the top. Sprinkle with the sesame seeds and Japanese pepper, if desired.

TANDOORI TOFU KEBABS

Here's another fun take on tofu, but because of the marinating process here the tofu should be pressed rather than frozen. Serve this dish, with its intense Indian flavors, alongside some spinach sautéed with feta cheese and basmati rice for an exotic and intriguing meal.

1. Press the tofu for 30 minutes. Cut the blocks of tofu into 1-inch cubes and arrange on a baking sheet.

2. In a small bowl, combine the saffron and warm water and let bloom for about 5 minutes. In a larger bowl, combine the yogurt, garlic, ginger, cream, lemon juice, salt, coriander, cumin, turmeric, black pepper, and cayenne. Add the saffron-infused water and stir well to combine. Pour the marinade over the tofu cubes and roll the tofu around so that each piece is well coated. Cover the baking sheet with plastic wrap and refrigerate for 2 to 4 hours.

3. Oil the grill racks. Preheat your grill using all burners set on high and with the lid closed for 10 to 12 minutes.

4. Remove the tofu from the refrigerator and assemble the skewers. Thread a piece of tofu, then a tomato, in an alternate pattern, on each skewer ending with a cube of tofu. Place the skewers on the grill, close the lid, and cook for about 2 minutes per side, or a total of 8 minutes. Each side should be nicely browned and the tomatoes should have picked up some char. Remove the skewers to a platter, sprinkle with cilantro, and serve.

SERVES 4
DIRECT HEAT

1½ to 2 pounds extra-firm tofu, drained

½ teaspoon saffron threads

1 tablespoon warm water

1 cup plain whole-milk yogurt

6 garlic cloves, smashed and rubbed into a paste

One 1-inch piece fresh ginger, grated

¼ cup heavy cream

¼ cup fresh lemon juice

1 teaspoon kosher salt

1 teaspoon ground coriander

½ teaspoon ground cumin

½ teaspoon ground turmeric

¼ teaspoon freshly ground black pepper

Pinch cayenne

12 cherry tomatoes

¼ cup chopped fresh cilantro

8 skewers (if using bamboo, soak in water for 30 minutes)

WHAT TO SERVE BEFORE, DURING, AND AFTER

GRILLED FRUITS, DESSERTS, AND BEVERAGES

Grilled **FIGS** with American "Prosciutto" 260

Warm **CANTALOUPE** with Prosciutto 261

Grilled **APPLES** with Cheddar Cheese 262

Grilled **BROWN SUGAR PEACHES** with Dark Chocolate 263

Don Fry's **FANTASY GRILLED PANINI** 264

Grilled **BANANA SPLITS** 265

German **CHOCOLATE PIE** 266

Sue Anne's **OATMEAL CHOCOLATE CHIP COOKIE CAKE** 267

Beach **BOURBON SLUSH** 268

Barbecue **BLOODY MARY** 269

GRILLED FRUIT? YES INDEED. While I've grilled asparagus for years, the first time I had a grilled peach was a revelation that catapulted me into another realm. Fruit, already rich with natural sugars, becomes something surreal as those sugars caramelize on a hot grill. Grill your favorites and grill them often, but don't think of grilled fruit only as a dessert—this chapter includes a few recipes that work as appetizers and side dishes, too.

That said, there's something about a meal that's been prepared on the grill that demands dessert. Maybe it's that intoxicating smoke wafting around that insists on a sugar fix to finish the evening. A libation or two while we're watching the grill is, for many of us, as much an accessory as our tongs. In this chapter are recipes for sweet and savory sides, some incredible desserts, and a couple of beverages that will keep you happy all through the grilling season. Don't stop here, however. Whatever your combinations of the recipes in this book, your tongue will thank you.

DESSERT FROM THE GRILL—WHY NOT.

FRUIT

Grilled fruit makes a great appetizer, snack, side dish, or dessert. As with most vegetables, fruit is better with direct heat. And just as with vegetables, you need to watch fruit as it cooks, since most only needs a few minutes on the grill to reach perfection, and you don't

want to overcook it. If necessary, turn down or turn off the heat to keep those sugars from going from caramelized to charred.

Gauging doneness with fruit is best done by touch. Because fruits vary in the amount of moisture they contain, it can be tricky to give hard-and-fast cooking times. The chart on the facing page is a guide only and a list of some of the more popular fruits to grill. Don't let this be your limiting factor. If it grows, you can probably grill it.

APPROXIMATE GRILLING TIMES
FOR FRUIT These are guidelines only; specific recipes may vary.

TYPE	SIZE	ROUGH ESTIMATE OF TIME
APPLES	½-in. slices	4–6 minutes
BANANAS	Halved lengthwise	6–8 minutes
CANTALOUPE	Wedges	8–11 minutes
NECTARINES	Halved lengthwise and pitted	8–10 minutes
ORANGES	Halved	4–6 minutes
PEACHES	Halved lengthwise and pitted	6–8 minutes
PEARS	Halved lengthwise	10–15 minutes
PINEAPPLE	½-in. rings	5–8 minutes
PINEAPPLE	1-in. wedges	5–10 minutes
STRAWBERRIES	Whole	4–5 minutes
FIGS	Halved	3–5 minutes

For dessert, serve grilled fruit simply with just a scoop of ice cream or as a base for cake. I love to end a meal that's been cooked entirely on the grill with grilled fruit. This allows you to appreciate the special nuances that the fire has given to each portion of that meal. Plus, it's just real easy to do.

There is so much fun to preparing grilled-fruit desserts—everyone can get into the act. They are also surprising and delicious and interesting to the eye. Put your thinking cap on for your personal creations.

BEVERAGES

Beer, wine, and libations like mojitos and margaritas are fairly standard at cookouts, and I won't add to that list. But I have included two drinks that are a bit different and have gotten raves at my parties. Start the Beach Bourbon Slush at least the night before you plan to consume the icy nectar.

GRILLED FIGS WITH AMERICAN "PROSCIUTTO"

SERVES 10 TO 12 AS AN
APPETIZER

DIRECT HEAT

16 fresh Mission or
    Brown Turkey figs

4 ounces blue cheese,
    at room temperature

4 ounces mascarpone,
    at room temperature

Freshly ground black pepper

¾ cup balsamic vinegar

6 ounces thinly sliced
    country ham or prosciutto

Any time you see fresh figs, pick up a container and make this recipe. I have yet to find a living soul who doesn't covet this taste combination. I even had a vegetarian go nuts over these, and now she blames this recipe for making her a meat-eater again. I credit Ben Barker, chef/owner of Magnolia Grill, in Durham, North Carolina, and Frank Stitt, chef/owner of Highlands Restaurant, in Birmingham, Alabama, for leading me down this path. American "prosciutto" is nothing more than a thinly sliced country ham that has been cured but not cooked. It has the same genetic makeup as Italy's famous prosciutto. I like Point Reyes blue cheese for its mild flavor, but if you prefer a bolder statement, use Maytag.

1. Slice the figs in half lengthwise. Using a grapefruit spoon, scoop out a bit of the flesh, taking care not to break the skin, and put into a bowl. Add the blue cheese and mascarpone and mix well; a fork works well. Season generously with black pepper and stir to combine.

2. In a small saucepan over medium heat, simmer the vinegar until it is reduced to about 6 tablespoons and nice and syrupy. Let cool, but keep at room temperature.

3. Take each fig half and stuff with about a tablespoon of the fig mixture. Wrap a piece of ham around the fig and stuffing. Place on a baking sheet and cover with plastic wrap. Refrigerate for at least 1 hour or up to 4 hours.

4. Oil the grill racks. Preheat your grill using all burners set on high and with the lid closed for 10 to 12 minutes.

5. Remove the figs from the refrigerator and place each fig on the grill, cut side up. Close the lid and cook them until the ham is a bit crispy and the figs are warm, about 5 minutes. Remove to a platter and drizzle with the reserved balsamic syrup. Serve immediately.

AT THE MARKET

If you can't find country ham in your area, I highly recommend you call Benton's Ham Shop, in Madisonville, Tennessee, for what most chefs in this country believe is the best country ham available. Although Allan Benton's pork products are served in some of the finest restaurants from New York City to San Francisco, expect an "aw shucks" kind of attitude and prices far too cheap.

WARM CANTALOUPE WITH PROSCIUTTO

I regularly teach grilling classes at Southern Seasons cooking school, in Chapel Hill, North Carolina. Before one class, we were prepped and ready to go with plenty of time left before the students arrived. We kind of needed something to nibble on but we couldn't get into the food we had done for class. There was some leftover cantaloupe and prosciutto, and someone suggested that classic combination. Well, the grill was hot and I thought, hmm, I wonder how this would do. So we wrapped the melon, drizzled it with a little olive oil, and put it on the grill. The test was a success, so here's a fun new way with an old standby.

1. Oil the grill racks. Preheat your grill using all burners set on high and with the lid closed for 10 to 12 minutes.

2. Cut the cantaloupe in half. Scoop out all the seeds and cut each half in half, then cut those pieces in half. You now should have 8 wedges. Peel the cantaloupe by carefully running your knife between the melon flesh and its skin. Wrap each wedge with 2 slices of prosciutto. Brush each with olive oil.

3. Place the melon on the grill and lower the heat to medium-low. Close the lid and cook for about 6 minutes, then turn. Cook for another 5 minutes or so, until slight charring has occurred and the melon appears to be warmed through. Remove the melon wedges from the grill to a platter. Drizzle with extra-virgin olive oil and sprinkle with salt. Serve immediately.

SERVES 8
DIRECT HEAT

1 ripe cantaloupe

16 slices prosciutto

Olive oil

Fruity extra-virgin olive oil

Hawaiian sea salt or coarse gray sea salt

IN THE KITCHEN

Don't waste your money cooking with extra-virgin olive oil—this is like cooking with estate-bottled reserve wine. Regular olive oil has a sturdiness that's better for cooking. Extra-virgin olive oil's delicate flavor is destroyed by (or at least lost in) cooking, so save it for salad dressings or for dipping.

GRILLED APPLES WITH CHEDDAR CHEESE

SERVES 6
DIRECT HEAT

4 firm cooking apples, on the large
side, such as Granny Smith

Canola oil

1 teaspoon ground cinnamon

½ teaspoon chipotle chile powder

Twelve 2-inch-square slices
extra-sharp Cheddar cheese

While you don't see it much any more, apple pie used to be served regularly with a slab of melted Cheddar on top. The sweet-versus-sharp flavor contrast was always interesting to me, so I've tried to replicate it on the gas grill. Don't think of this just as a dessert—it's also wonderful with a plate of your favorite barbecued ribs or any other pork that you've laid up against the fire. For a more traditional dessert version, see the sidebar below.

1. Slice about ¼ inch off the top and bottom of each apple. Then cut each apple horizontally into 3 thick slices (if you're doing this ahead, you need to sprinkle these apple slices with lemon juice to keep them from browning). Brush each apple slice with a little oil. Then mix together the cinnamon and chile powder and sprinkle evenly on one side of each apple slice.

2. Oil the grill racks. Preheat your grill using all burners set on high and with the lid closed for 10 to 12 minutes.

3. Place the apple slices on the grill, spice side down. Close the lid and cook for about 3 minutes. Turn the apples and cook for an additional 3 to 4 minutes, or until they begin to give when touched. Place a cheese square on each slice and cook for another 2 minutes, or until the cheese melts and becomes gooey. Remove to a platter and serve.

IN THE KITCHEN

For Twisted Apple Pie, leave out the chile powder and instead mix about a teaspoon of brown sugar with the cinnamon. Grill as directed above, leaving off the cheese. When done, place 2 apple slices in each of 6 small bowls and serve with a scoop of vanilla ice cream.

GRILLED BROWN SUGAR PEACHES WITH DARK CHOCOLATE

We're told to eat more fruit and indulge in dark chocolate occasionally. That makes this recipe perfect. Fresh peaches that have picked up extra caramelization from the grill, been stuffed with dark chocolate seductively melting, and been finished with a textural foil of pistachios—you could add ice cream, but why? Don't use chocolate chips here—they don't melt as readily.

1. In a large bowl, whisk together the butter, sugar, and cinnamon. Add the peach halves and toss to coat well.

2. Oil the grill racks. Preheat your grill using all burners set on high and with the lid closed for 10 to 12 minutes.

3. Place the peaches, cut side down, on the grill, reserving any remaining butter in the bowl. Grill until slightly charred, 1 to 2 minutes. Using tongs, turn the peaches over. Divide the chocolate evenly among the peach cavities and drizzle any remaining butter mixture over the chocolate. Grill until the chocolate just begins to melt and the peaches are charred, about 2 minutes.

4. Remove from the grill and divide the peach halves among bowls. Sprinkle with the pistachios and serve.

SERVES 4

DIRECT HEAT

¼ cup (½ stick) unsalted butter, melted

2 tablespoons packed dark brown sugar

½ teaspoon ground cinnamon

4 ripe unpeeled peaches, halved and pitted

⅓ cup finely chopped dark chocolate

3 tablespoons coarsely chopped toasted salted pistachios

DON FRY'S FANTASY GRILLED PANINI

SERVES 4
DIRECT HEAT

2 to 3 ripe bananas

8 slices crusty European-style bread

1 cup Nutella

12 tablespoons (1½ sticks) unsalted butter, softened

2 to 3 tablespoons Sugar in the Raw or confectioners' sugar (optional)

Don Fry is a friend and a writing coach whom I see too infrequently. He salivates over the thought of that chocolate-hazelnut spread Nutella®. I've stolen a page from Elvis to make Don the ultimate grilled sandwich.

1. Slice the bananas into a medium bowl, then coarsely mash them with a fork. Place the slices of bread on your counter and spread each slice with some of the Nutella. Equally divide the bananas over 4 slices of bread and top with the remaining slices. Spread one side of each sandwich with some of the butter.

2. Oil the grill racks. Preheat your grill using all burners set on high and with the lid closed for 10 to 12 minutes.

3. Place the sandwiches on the grill, butter side down, close the lid, and cook until the first side is golden brown, 3 to 5 minutes. Spread the top of each sandwich with some more of the butter, then turn and continue to grill until the second side is golden brown, 5 to 10 minutes total. Remove from the grill and sprinkle with the sugar, if desired. Serve immediately.

AT THE TABLE

Your panini menu is only as short as your imagination. Try this technique with your favorite meat and cheese, roasted veggies, or even tuna fish. Prosciutto, brie, and tomatoes is one of my favorite combinations, or use a pesto mayonnaise on a turkey panini. Tapenade makes a great spread with a variety of Italian meats. A Cuban sandwich takes on a whole new meaning when cooked on the grill. If you want a flatter, more compressed grilled sandwich, place a cast-iron skillet on top of the sandwich with a brick or other heavy object in the skillet. Use an oven mitt when moving the skillet.

GRILLED BANANA SPLITS

Surprise your guests with this whimsical take on a classic banana split. Like most anything, the bananas get an extra oomph of flavor when grilled. I like to microwave a little Marshmallow Fluff® to pour over the splits as well. The caveat to this recipe is making sure the fruit is ripe but not mushy. I err on the side of firm versus overripe.

1. In a small saucepan over medium-high heat, bring the cream to a simmer. Remove the pan from the heat and stir in the chocolate. Stir until smooth and dark.

2. In a small skillet, melt the butter over medium heat. Add the cinnamon, sugar, ginger, and cloves. Continue to heat, stirring occasionally, until the sugar has dissolved. Remove from the heat.

3. Leaving the peels on, slice the bananas in half, then cut each half lengthwise in half. Brush the bananas on the cut sides with the butter mixture. Let sit until the grill is ready.

4. Oil the grill racks. Preheat your grill using all burners set on high and with the lid closed for 10 to 12 minutes.

5. Brush the cut sides of the bananas once more with the butter mixture and place, cut side down, on the grill. Close the lid and cook without turning until warm, with nice grill marks, about 3 minutes total. Remove the bananas to a cutting board and carefully remove the peel. Cut each banana piece into ½-inch-thick slices and divide them equally between 4 bowls. Put one scoop of vanilla ice cream in each bowl and drizzle with the chocolate sauce. Microwave the Marshmallow Fluff until fluid. (The time will depend on your microwave's wattage. Start with 20 seconds and, if necessary, add 10-second increments.) Drizzle over the banana splits. Sprinkle 1 tablespoon of nuts over each banana split and serve immediately.

SERVES 4
DIRECT HEAT

½ cup heavy cream

3 ounces semisweet chocolate, chopped

4 tablespoons (½ stick) unsalted butter

½ teaspoon ground cinnamon

½ teaspoon sugar

¼ teaspoon ground ginger

Pinch ground cloves

4 ripe but firm bananas

1 pint vanilla ice cream

½ cup Marshmallow Fluff

4 tablespoons chopped wet walnuts (walnuts in syrup) or dry-roasted peanuts

GERMAN CHOCOLATE PIE

SERVES 8

4 ounces Baker's® German sweet chocolate, chopped

¼ cup (½ stick) unsalted butter

One 12-ounce can evaporated milk

1½ cups sugar

3 tablespoons cornstarch

⅛ teaspoon kosher salt

2 large eggs, lightly beaten

1 teaspoon pure vanilla extract

One 9-inch unbaked prepared deep-dish pie shell

1½ cups sweetened flaked coconut

1 cup chopped pecans

Whipped cream (optional)

This is a killer pie. Simple to make, with flavors that everybody loves. Not only does this pie work with grilled foods, but you'll be a hero if you take it to a potluck or family-reunion dinner.

1. Preheat your oven to 375°F.

2. Melt the chocolate and butter in a saucepan over low heat. Stir until smooth. Remove from the heat and blend in the milk.

3. Mix the sugar, cornstarch, and salt together in a medium bowl. Beat in the eggs and the vanilla. Fold in the chocolate mixture. Pour the filling into the unbaked pie shell. Combine the coconut and pecans and sprinkle them evenly on top of the filling. Place the pie in the oven and bake for 45 minutes or until the coconut is toasted and the filling is set at the sides but the center is still a bit jiggly. Cool completely at room temperature before serving. Serve with whipped cream, if desired.

SUE ANNE'S OATMEAL CHOCOLATE CHIP COOKIE CAKE

Sue Anne is a chocoholic buddy who lives outside Richmond, Virginia. Knowing how much I love oatmeal chocolate chip cookies, she found this cake recipe that fits the bill.

1. Preheat your oven to 350°F. Arrange the oven racks so that one is in the center.

2. Brush a 9x13-inch baking pan with 1½ teaspoons of the butter, then dust the pan with 1 tablespoon of the flour, shaking to coat completely. Shake out any excess.

3. Sift together the remaining 1¾ cups flour, the cocoa, baking soda, and salt. Pour onto a large piece of parchment or waxed paper.

4. Place the oats in a large heatproof bowl. Pour the boiling water over the oats and let stand for 10 minutes. Add both sugars, the eggs, and the remaining ½ cup butter. Fold until the ingredients are well combined. Add the dry ingredients and again fold until the mixture is well blended. Add 1 cup of the chocolate chips and stir to distribute evenly. Pour the batter into the prepared baking pan.

5. Combine the remaining chocolate chips with the pecans in a small bowl. Sprinkle this mixture on top of the batter.

6. Place the pan on the center rack of your oven and bake 40 minutes, rotating the pan a half-turn after 20 minutes, or until a toothpick inserted in the center comes out clean.

7. Remove the cake from the oven and cool in the pan for 20 minutes. Carefully turn the cake out onto a cutting board, then turn the cake so that the chocolate chip–nut side is up. Use two wide spatulas to pull off this maneuver. Cool for an additional 10 minutes before serving. Use a serrated knife that you've run under hot water to cut the cake into 12 equal pieces. Serve with ice cream or whipped cream.

SERVES 12

½ cup (1 stick) plus 1½ teaspoons unsalted butter, melted

1¾ cups plus 1 tablespoon all-purpose flour

1 tablespoon unsweetened natural cocoa powder

1 teaspoon baking soda

½ teaspoon salt

1 cup quick-cooking oats

1¾ cups boiling water

1 cup granulated sugar

1 cup packed light brown sugar

3 large eggs, beaten

2 cups semisweet chocolate chips

¾ cup pecans, toasted and coarsely chopped

Ice cream or whipped cream, for serving

BEACH BOURBON SLUSH

SERVES USUALLY 6 TO 8,
DEPENDING ON WHO IS
DRINKING

2 cups unsweetened brewed black tea

5 cups water

2 cups Jack Daniel's Black Label

¼ cup sugar

One 12-ounce can frozen lemonade concentrate, thawed

One 6-ounce can frozen orange juice concentrate, thawed

Chilled ginger ale, as needed

My sister likes to call this drink an adult Slurpee®. And in some ways she is right. It's really almost like a whiskey sour that's been frozen and stirred so that it crystallizes like a granita. It may be the ultimate hot summer day libation. But be warned, once you fix this for your friends and neighbors, they'll expect it all through the summer heat. You can either brew the tea and let it cool, or use bottled or canned.

1. Combine the tea, water, Jack Daniel's, sugar, and the two juice concentrates in a 9x13-inch metal baking pan. Place in the freezer. About every 45 minutes, stir the blend with a fork. Continue this for a couple of hours, until the mixture has the consistency of a granita: icy, slushy, and granular.

2. To serve, use an ice-cream scoop or large heavy spoon and fill a glass two-thirds full with the frozen tea. Top with a bit of ginger ale, but don't stir. Let the ginger ale coagulate with the frozen tea, then enjoy.

BARBECUE BLOODY MARY

Ed Mitchell, one of the finest pit masters in the South, turned me on to making Bloody Marys with a barbecue twist. Normally, I'm not very fond of this typical brunch beverage, but this concoction I thoroughly enjoy. It's a great drink to serve the adults when several families are over for a hamburger cookout.

Pour the vodka, V8, Worcestershire, and barbecue sauce into a 32-ounce pitcher. Stir until well blended. Add ice to 6 glasses and put a celery stick in each. Fill with the Barbecue Bloody Mary. Cheers.

1 cup good-quality vodka

4 cups Spicy Hot V8 juice

1 teaspoon Jason Smith's House-Made Worcestershire Sauce (p. 300)

About ½ cup Lexington-Style Barbecue Sauce (p. 294), or for a sweeter taste the Slow-Cooked Memphis-Style Barbecue Sauce (p. 297) or the Surprising Kansas City–Style Sauce (p. 295)

6 celery sticks

THE
FLAVOR
FACTORS

RUBS, MARINADES, AND SAUCES

THERE ARE MANY FACTORS IN PLAY when you're grilling.
First and foremost is the quality of the food that you're placing on the grill—a bad
steak will be a bad steak no matter what you do to it. Whether your grill is properly
heated and whether you're using the right method for your food will also play a
major role in how your meal will eventually taste. But without good seasoning
there won't be much good eating. Salt and pepper can elevate the blandest of
items, but the real flavor tools are sauces, rubs, and marinades. With them, you can
personalize your food to the preferences and palates of your friends and family.

I don't know how many secret sauces, rub blends, and marinades I've tried to cajole from people and only gotten in return a sly smile or a shuffle of the feet or that age-old cliché, "If I told you I'd have to kill you." This is part of what makes the experience and the community of outdoor cookers fun. This chapter is in large part based on the volumes of grilled food that I've eaten across the country and the conversations I've had with the cooks who fed me.

Through the next pages you'll find a variety of good, solid, basic rubs, marinades, and sauces. These recipes have not been tied to a specific protein or vegetable because they are so versatile and can be used in so many different ways. Use them as a springboard to develop your own special blend. And don't stop with this chapter. Throughout the book there are many more recipes embedded in

individual recipes that are versatile enough to try with a large number of items that you might grill.

So let's talk about what each one does and how to use it.

RUBS

Rubs come in two forms, dry and wet (wet rubs are sometimes called pastes). The former are, quite simply, blends of dried or fresh herbs and spices, salt, pepper, and, in more cases than not, some type of sweetener like sugar. Don't think that sugar and meat don't go together. In a rub, sugar is the equalizer for the other spices, almost making sure that one spice is not too dominant. Sugars also act as browning agents for the protein, assisting in

NOT ALL SUGAR IS EQUAL

The legendary Mike Mills, who has been a grand champion at Memphis in May and holds the distinction of having security clearance for Air Force One (it seems Bill Clinton just loved Mike's ribs), gave me a piece of advice about rubs. "Always use white sugar rather than brown. Brown burns too quickly, while white sugar holds a bit longer in the rub and adds sweetness without the burn." For the most part I agree, but the molasses flavor of brown sugar is sometimes hard to beat. More times than not, I use a blend of white and brown sugars in different ratios for different foods. I encourage you to experiment to find a blend that works the best for you.

coaxing those natural sugar flavors out of the meat. Remember, that char or nice crust that you love is primarily sugar. Add a little oil, beer, or fruit juice and your dry rubs morph into web rubs.

Rubs are the most basic of seasonings and to some extent the most useful. They season the meat simply by their presence, and if left on the item for an hour to overnight (refrigerated of course), they become almost like a marinade, penetrating the meat. But it's on the grill that a rub's true magic takes place. When heated, a rub will form a beautiful, flavorful, crispy crust that adds perfection to most any food that you could possibly want to cook. The other thing about rubs is that they are instantly and infinitely adjustable to your own taste and mood. If you have a batch of basic rub or even a store-bought rub, a little addition of an extra spice can satisfy your whims.

It's hard to give exact amounts of how much rub to use. Some of it depends on the rub and how strong or spicy it is. It will also depend on whether you are coating a chicken breast or a rack of ribs. As a general rule, start with 1½ teaspoons or so for each side of a piece of protein, but go up to 1 tablespoon if necessary to coat the item thoroughly.

Developing your own rub is the first step in personalizing your grilling repertoire. Certain flavor elements are consistent in every great rub: Sweet, hot, and salty are the key elements, but you can add others. The chart on the facing page will guide you through basic combinations, and if something isn't listed there's probably a good reason—it just doesn't work. Try to keep your combinations within logical groups. Asian spices work better together, as do Mediterranean. That's not to say that you shouldn't cross-pollinate the spices, but go easy.

THE ELEMENTS OF A GREAT RUB

SALTY	SWEET	HOT	EARTHY	HERBY	SHARP AND SAVORY
Kosher salt	Granulated sugar	Prepared chili powder	Cumin	Thyme	Dried citrus peels
Sea salt	Light brown sugar	Pure chile powder	Coriander	Oregano	Granulated garlic
Smoked sea salt	Dark brown sugar	Black pepper	Paprika	Parsley	Granulated onion
Celery salt	Sugar in the Raw	White pepper	Smoked paprika	Rosemary	Dry mustard
	Maple sugar	Cayenne	Chinese five-spice powder	Marjoram	Mustard seeds
	Dehydrated honey	Crushed red chile flakes	Cinnamon	Fennel	Turmeric
		Hot paprika	Cloves	Sage	Curry powder
		Sichuan peppercorns	Nutmeg	Dill	Ground ginger
		Lemon pepper		Basil	
				Bay leaves	
				Cilantro	

I use an element of each of the categories in the chart above, starting with salty and sweet. Most of us think of some heat in rubs. Here's a guide to rubs with heat. Try 10 parts sweet to 4 parts salty, then add 1 part chili powder and 1 part paprika. Then add from other groups in ½-part increments to your taste. A part can be anything from a bottle cap to a cup measure, depending on how much rub you want to make. I start with a standard coffee measure as my "part," with ½ part being 1 tablespoon. Using this formula, you'll make enough rub for several recipes of ribs or other pig parts, chicken, or smoked brisket.

In blends where you are heading toward a specific taste, say Italian or Indian, go easier on the salt and sugar. Know that salt, sugar, and any hot ingredient you add will quickly become dominant. Start out low with the salt, sugar, and peppers, maybe 2 teaspoons of each to 1 tablespoon of everything else. And if you think you hit the winner with your first pass, call me. We need to bottle it.

Since a rub can also double as a flavoring marinade, on p. 280 are some guidelines for how long a rub should sit on various foods before cooking. Keep in mind that while you want to form a crust, a rub with a lot of salt and sugar can also pull enough moisture from meat to make the end result dry.

TIMING FOR RUBS

These are guidelines only; specific recipes may vary.

UP TO 15 MINUTES	UP TO 30 MINUTES	UP TO 90 MINUTES	2 HOURS TO OVERNIGHT
Shellfish Vegetables Delicately flavored fish fillets such as sea bass, catfish, tilapia, and grouper	Thin cuts of boneless protein such as boneless, skinless chicken breasts Pork chops (boneless and bone-in) Minute steaks Fish fillets and steaks like walleye, salmon, snapper, tuna, swordfish, and wahoo Pork tenderloin	Whole chickens Whole beef tenderloin Boneless beef roasts Standing rib roasts Boneless pork loins Bone-in pork loins Boneless leg of lamb Bone-in leg of lamb	Big and tough cuts of meat that you plan to cook low and slow Beef brisket Beef ribs Turkeys Racks of ribs Pork shoulders Pork butts Whole hams

STORING YOUR SPICES AND HERBS

If the majority of your spices and herbs are six months old, then get a bag, drop them in, and put them in the trash can. They have lost the potency they once had. Try to buy spices and herbs in quantities that you will use within three to six months. I know that it's sometimes hard to guess, but you know your taste buds and your family.

Protect your spices and herbs from heat and light, which cause them to deteriorate more quickly. Most of us store our spices and herbs in the cabinet directly above or next to our stove. While storing them elsewhere may mean extra steps, it will help them keep their flavor longer. I also have gotten in the habit of storing what I call the "red spices"—chili and chile powders, cayenne, crushed red chile flakes, and the like—in my refrigerator, which significantly increases their life. Remember, great flavor starts with good ingredients.

MARINADES

A marinade is simply a solution that contains some form of acid. Its purpose is to improve the flavor and to some extent the texture of foods—acids like vinegar, wine, and citrus juices are natural tenderizers and break down fibers. Most marinades also contain oil, which serves two purposes: It leaves a moist coating for your cooking, and it acts to protect the food when it is completely submerged so that you can extend the marinating times of some items. Beyond these two ingredients, mari-

THE ELEMENTS OF A GREAT MARINADE

ACIDS	OILS	DEFINING FLAVORS
Cider vinegar	Olive oil	Fresh and/or dried herbs
Distilled vinegar	Toasted sesame oil	Spices
Red wine vinegar	Canola oil	Minced aromatic vegetables such as onions, carrots, bell peppers, scallions, shallots
Balsamic vinegar	Vegetable oil	
Sherry vinegar		
Rice vinegar		Minced garlic
All types of citrus juices		Citrus zest
Wine, both red and white		Worcestershire sauce
Fortified wines like sherry, vermouth, and Madeira		Anchovies
		Tamarind paste
Plain (unflavored) yogurt		Ketchup
Buttermilk		Mustard
		Honey
		Molasses
		Bourbon
		Asian sauces like hoisin, teriyaki, and chili sauces
		Tabasco sauce

nades can include any combination of flavor ingredients. Salt, however, should always be used judiciously in a marinade because it can draw out too much moisture.

I'm a big fan of using zip-top plastic bags for marinating. I combine the food and marinade in the bag, close it, and squish the marinade all around. Most of the time I will place this package in a bowl or baking dish, which helps to keep the marinade in contact with the food and to contain spills. If you prefer, you can marinate foods in glass, plastic, or stainless-steel containers. Aluminum is an

absolute no-no since it reacts with the acids and can give a metallic flavor to the food.

Marinades, like all seasoning blends, are about balance. We've heard much about the primary flavor quadrangle of salty, sweet, bitter, and sour, and every marinade you develop should have a core of these flavors. There's a fifth taste sensation, umami, which in Japanese means "delicious." The term might be new to Americans, but it has been recognized in Asian cuisines for years, and you've probably encountered it whether you know it or not. The most familiar example of umami is

TIMING
FOR MARINADES
These are guidelines only; specific recipes may vary.

UP TO 15 MINUTES	UP TO 30 MINUTES	UP TO 90 MINUTES	2 HOURS TO OVERNIGHT
Most vegetables Shellfish Smaller fish fillets such as snapper, catfish, and tilapia	Meatier fish fillets and fish steaks like walleye, monkfish, sea bass, and grouper	Very sturdy fish fillets such as salmon, swordfish, wahoo, and tuna Boneless chicken breasts Pork chops Lamb chops Most steaks Pork tenderloin Chicken parts, including chicken quarters	Thick cuts of boneless meats Whole chickens Leg of lamb All roasts Flank steak Skirt steak Turkeys Ribs Whole hams Pork butts

Worcestershire sauce. You can also add other flavor profiles that are smoky or herbaceous to create a unique and tasty marinade. One caveat I have found is that you can't rely on that initial taste to see how a marinade will work. A marinade that tastes funky on your finger usually tastes great on meat.

You will not get sent to culinary hell for using prepared Italian salad dressing as a marinade. I know some people think that it's an absolute sin, but it's quick, it's tasty, and it works—take a look at the ingredients on the dressing, compare them to the ingredients in the chart (on p. 277), and it's easy to see why. I prefer making the dressing fresh with a powdered mix such as Good Seasons, but any of the excellent bottled Italian dressings will do. I've also been known to use Catalina and French dressing as all or part of a marinade. If you feel the need to report me to someone, do so. But in the meantime, I'll continue to use salad dressings for quick, no-brainer marinades.

Marinades react better with food at room temperature, but this can present food-safety issues. The rule of thumb should be that if something needs to marinate for longer than an hour, put it in the refrigerator. The exception is seafood, which should go in the fridge after 30 minutes.

Since all marinades are based on acids, you must be mindful when it comes to the marinating time. You don't want the marinades to break down the fibers of your food to the point that it becomes mushy, and fish in particular are highly susceptible to being over

THE ELEMENTS OF A GREAT SAUCE

SWEET	SOUR	SPICY	SALT	TOMATO	THE UMMM FACTOR
Granulated sugar	Cider vinegar	Horseradish	Kosher salt	Ketchup	Rendered bacon fat
Light and dark brown sugar	Distilled vinegar	Crushed red chile flakes	Sea salt	Tomato paste	Butter
Molasses	Balsamic vinegar	Black pepper	Smoked sea salt	Tomato puree	Wine
Light and dark corn syrup	Rice vinegar	White pepper	Worcestershire sauce	Tomato sauce	Beef stock
Honey	Wine vinegars	Cayenne	Soy sauce or tamari	Chili sauce	Liquid smoke
Maple syrup	Citrus juice	Hot pepper sauces	Asian fish sauce	Tomato juice	Your barbecue rub
Maple sugar	Mustards	Chiles	Anchovies		Soft drinks
Hoisin sauce	Beer	Most any spice or herb you can imagine	Capers		
Jellies, jams, and preserves	Wine				
Sorghum	Liquors				
	Coffee				

marinated. The chart on the previous page gives you a few basic guidelines.

Many folks like to use the marinade as a basting medium while cooking or as a sauce at the table. You absolutely should not use a marinade for either of these purposes without boiling the marinade after the meat has been removed for at least one full minute to kill any harmful bacteria. As with all grilling, be sure and pat the foods that you have marinated dry with paper towels before you place them on the grill.

SAUCES

Sauces are the final flurry of flavor. In a layering process that starts with a marinade or a rub, the sauce becomes the finish, the tie that binds everything together. Thicker sauces, which contain lots of sugar, should only be brushed on during the last 10 to 15 minutes of grilling so that they don't char from the heat of the grill as the sugar goes from caramelized to burnt. Thinner sauces that are based more on vinegar or other acids are called "mops," and they can be brushed on throughout the cook-

JUST AS WITH RUBS AND MARINADES, A GOOD SAUCE IS ABOUT BALANCE.

ing process. Condiments served at the table—steak sauces, dipping sauces, and let's not forget salsa—all add flavor to your meal through different avenues.

When we think of sauce and grilling, most of us think of barbecue, and most barbecue sauces are tomato based, although there are some regions that incorporate copious amounts of mustard in their sauces; and of course North Carolina is famous for its sharp and tart vinegar sauces. Other ingredients that show up in many southern sauces are colas, bourbon, and coffee.

Just as with rubs and marinades, a good sauce is about balance. It should have elements of sweet, sour, spicy, and salt in some balanced configuration. Sauces are also full of the fifth taste, umami, which is that savory, almost beefy deep flavor. Worcestershire sauce, soy sauce, and tomatoes are some examples of the umami side of the ledger.

When making your own sauce, think of one or two ingredients that will set it apart from the others. Also consider what you're going to use it for. Sauces for pork and chicken are fairly interchangeable but sometimes don't work well with beef. But sauces for beef might play nicely with duck, lamb, or venison. You get the idea. Some of my most fun days are spent in the kitchen, bottles of ketchup, tomato paste, and other ingredients jumping into pots and splattering the walls, in search of that ultimate, perfect sauce.

Think of yourself as a food artist or a potter. The chicken, beef, or seafood is your clay, and the rubs, marinades, and sauces are pigments and glazes. The grill becomes your kiln. Go create tasty, flavorful, and enduring art.

MY QUICK, SIMPLE, AND WONDERFUL ALL-PURPOSE RUB

MAKES ABOUT ½ CUP, ENOUGH FOR 2 RIB RECIPES, A COUPLE OF CHICKENS, OR A TURKEY

¼ cup packed light brown sugar

¼ cup paprika

1 tablespoon chili powder

1 teaspoon cayenne

1 teaspoon kosher salt

Freshly cracked black peppercorns (see sidebar, p. 111)

Rubs don't have to be complicated to be good. This recipe is the core of any rub. Start from here and devise your own if you wish. Most folks whom I have given this to love it the way it is.

Combine all the ingredients in a container with a tight-fitting lid. Shake to mix. The rub will keep for several weeks.

MORE-INTENSE BARBECUE RUB

MAKES ALMOST 2 CUPS, ENOUGH FOR 6 RACKS OF RIBS OR 8 POUNDS OF PROTEIN

½ cup paprika

¼ cup granulated sugar

2 tablespoons light brown sugar

2 tablespoons kosher salt

2 tablespoons freshly ground black pepper

1 tablespoon dry mustard

2 tablespoons chili powder

2 tablespoons ground cumin

2 tablespoons granulated garlic

2 teaspoons cayenne

If you want to stretch your flavor out a little more, here's the next step in a rub.

Combine all the ingredients in a container with a tight-fitting lid. Shake to mix. The rub will keep indefinitely, as long as you keep it away from heat.

TWO GREAT STEAK RUBS

These two rubs are adapted from Chef David Walzog, one of New York City's nouvelle steak masters. They're both fun rubs to have around the house, and they complement much more than just steak—ribs, lamb, chicken, and seafood all improve with a dose of one or the other of these rubs. Ancho chile powder is made just from ancho chiles—if you typically use something labeled "chili powder" it's most likely a blend of several chiles as well as spices like cumin—and because it is a pure chile powder, it tends to burn more quickly than a blended powder will. Lower the heat slightly when using this rub and add an additional minute or two to the cooking time.

For either of these rubs, combine their ingredients in a container with a tight-fitting lid. Shake to mix. Store away from heat and they will last for several weeks.

FOR THE CHILI RUB

MAKES ABOUT ¼ CUP; USE 1 TEASPOON PER 12-OUNCE STEAK

1 tablespoon ancho chile powder

1 teaspoon ground cumin

1 teaspoon ground coriander

1 teaspoon garlic powder

1 teaspoon cayenne

1 tablespoon kosher salt

FOR THE HERB RUB

MAKES ABOUT ⅓ CUP; USE 1 TEASPOON PER 12-OUNCE STEAK

1 tablespoon dried thyme

1 tablespoon dried oregano

1 tablespoon ground fennel

1 tablespoon kosher salt

2 teaspoons dry mustard

1 teaspoon onion powder

2 teaspoons paprika

TUSCAN-STYLE DRY RUB

**MAKES ABOUT 1³/₄ CUPS;
USE ¼ CUP PER 5 POUNDS
OF PROTEIN**

½ cup dried oregano

5 tablespoons kosher salt

4 tablespoons Spanish paprika

4 tablespoons ground fennel

3 tablespoons granulated garlic

3 tablespoons granulated onion

2 tablespoons cayenne

4 teaspoons sugar

This is a versatile seasoning with a taste of the hills of Tuscany. Use on any grilled vegetable, chicken, flank and skirt steak, shrimp, or, surprisingly, lobster. Drizzle any of those items with a little olive oil and you're good to go.

Combine all the ingredients in a container with a tight-fitting lid. Shake to mix. Keep in a cool, dark place for up to 6 months.

PHILIPPINE BARBECUE MARINADE

**MAKES ABOUT 1¹/₂ CUPS,
ENOUGH FOR 2 TO
2¹/₂ POUNDS OF PROTEIN**

1 cup ketchup

¼ cup Chinese oyster sauce

3 tablespoons honey

2 tablespoons fresh lemon juice

1 tablespoon tamari

This recipe went through a lot of hands to get to me. I'd had some Philippine barbecue decades ago and thoroughly enjoyed the taste but could never seem to get a recipe. Finally, one of the creative designers at the *News and Observer* in Raleigh, North Carolina, got this recipe from her grandmother's aunt, who still lives in the Philippines. I love this on pork and on poultry, but it also is a unique marinade for salmon and tuna. Let your meat marinate for at least 2 hours and up to overnight, but don't marinate seafood for longer than 2 hours.

Combine all the ingredients in a medium bowl. Use immediately, or store in an airtight container in the refrigerator for up to 2 days.

HONEY MUSTARD MARINADE

If you're looking for a fat-free marinade, your search is over. This is wonderful when used on a turkey breast or lean, boneless pork chops. Marinate your meat for at least 4 hours or overnight.

Pour the honey into a small saucepan and place over medium-low heat. As the honey gets loose, stir in the mustard, tamari, cumin, and garlic. Remove from the heat and let cool before using. Use immediately, or store in an airtight container in the refrigerator for up to 2 days.

MAKES ABOUT 1³/₄ CUPS, ENOUGH FOR 2¹/₂ TO 3 POUNDS OF PROTEIN

¾ cup honey

¾ cup Dijon mustard or a good-quality brown mustard

½ cup tamari

2 tablespoons ground cumin

6 garlic cloves, minced

IN THE KITCHEN

An easy way to deal with measuring honey is to spray your measuring cup lightly with vegetable cooking spray. You might even want to spray your spoon to help you get the honey out of the measuring cup as well. (Just don't dip the sprayed spoon into the honey jar.) It just goes a whole lot faster, and you don't leave any of the honey in the cup.

CARNE ASADA MARINADE

MAKES 1 CUPS, ENOUGH FOR 2 TO 2¹/₂ POUNDS OF PROTEIN

1 tablespoon chili powder

1 tablespoon onion powder

1 tablespoon garlic powder

1 tablespoon dried thyme

½ tablespoon dried oregano

½ tablespoon freshly ground white pepper

½ tablespoon freshly ground black pepper

1 tablespoon hot pepper sauce

1 tablespoon salt

½ cup olive oil

1 cup fresh orange juice

This recipe is adapted from the fajita marinade used at the Flying Burrito restaurant, in Durham, North Carolina. And while it's exceptional for fajitas, it also works well as a marinade for flank steak, strip steak, chicken, pork chops, and even lamb. Use it any time you want a little south-of-the-border or Tex-Mex influence in your food.

Combine all the ingredients in a medium bowl. Whisk until well combined. Use immediately, or store in an airtight container in the refrigerator for up to 2 days.

AT THE GRILL

To use, place the steaks in a large zip-top plastic bag and pour the marinade over them. If necessary, mix in enough additional orange juice to cover the steaks. Squish until the steaks are completely covered. Refrigerate for at least 1 hour and up to 24 hours. Grill the steaks and serve with warm flour tortillas or soft corn tortillas.

SPICY YOGURT MARINADE

For a little Middle Eastern flair, try this tart and spicy marinade with grilled chicken, pork chops, and even salmon. It also serves double duty as a sauce once your grilled beauty hits the plate. This keeps for 3 or 4 days in the refrigerator.

1. In the bowl of a food processor, combine all the ingredients. Process until smooth.

2. Reserve half of this marinade to serve as a sauce at the table. Keep covered and in the refrigerator. Combine the rest with pork, lamb, fish, or chicken, and marinate any of these for 30 minutes to 1 hour at room temperature. When you remove the protein from the marinade, be sure to pat the marinade off so that it doesn't burn on the grill.

MAKES ABOUT 1²/₃ CUPS, ENOUGH FOR 2 TO 2¹/₂ POUNDS OF PROTEIN

1 cup plain low-fat yogurt

1 small onion, quartered

3 garlic cloves, peeled

One 1-inch piece fresh ginger, coarsely chopped

1 tablespoon fresh lemon juice

1 teaspoon ground cumin

1 teaspoon kosher salt

½ teaspoon ground turmeric

¼ teaspoon ground cinnamon

¼ teaspoon ground cloves

¼ teaspoon ground nutmeg

¼ teaspoon cayenne

EAST TENNESSEE–STYLE BARBECUE SAUCE

MAKES ABOUT 3½ CUPS

1 cup ketchup

One 8-ounce can tomato sauce

1 cup packed light brown sugar

1 cup apple-cider vinegar

1 tablespoon Worcestershire sauce

1 tablespoon paprika

1½ teaspoons onion salt

1 teaspoon dry mustard

1 to 2 teaspoons hot pepper sauce
   (use your favorite)

When eastern Tennessean Belinda Ellis challenged the greatness of North Carolina barbecue at a Southern Foodways Alliance symposium I decided to go see what she thought was great barbecue. What I found was barbecue that was very similar to North Carolina's Lexington-style 'cue, with two exceptions. First, eastern Tennessee folks cut their meat into slightly larger chunks, and second, ketchup has found its way into their sauce in a big way. That being said, east Tennessee barbecue sauce is darned good stuff. Thicker than North Carolina sauce, it still has that vinegar bite that symbolizes North Carolina sauces. Not only is this good with smoked pork shoulder, but it is also much better than any store-bought sauce for other pork cuts and chicken. It's okay with beef brisket, but I prefer Virginia Pruitt's (see the facing page) for that. The sauce keeps nicely in the refrigerator for a couple of weeks.

Combine all the ingredients in a small saucepan. Cook and stir over low heat until the sugar melts and the ingredients are blended. Lower the heat and simmer for about 10 minutes. Pour into an airtight container and refrigerate for up to 2 weeks.

VIRGINIA PRUITT'S PERFECT BARBECUE SAUCE

Perfect barbecue sauce? That sounds pretty arrogant. With all the brands and homemade recipes out in the world, can one really be that good? Well, put it this way: If you can get a bunch of vinegar-loving good ol' boys from North Carolina to go gaga over a sauce, then I think it has some validity.

Now, Virginia Pruitt, of Bonner Springs, Kansas, is way too modest to proclaim this sauce much beyond just "good." This is a family recipe that has roots in several states, with a little experimentation over 50 years. Ms. Pruitt got the recipe from her aunt-in-law, Ruth Reed, who lives in Denver. The original version came from Ruth's mother, who was reared in Kentucky.

The sauce is a great blend of sweet, tart, tang, and clingability. I have tried it on ribs, brisket, smoked pork butt, and grilled chicken with fabulous results. If you want a one-stop barbecue sauce, this may be the one.

Mix all the ingredients together in a medium saucepan. Place over medium heat and slowly bring to a boil. Reduce the heat slightly and cook until thickened, about 10 minutes. Thin with water if it gets too thick. Serve on anything your heart desires. Pour into an airtight container and refrigerate for up to 3 weeks.

MAKES ABOUT 2 CUPS

1 large onion, chopped

1 cup sugar

1 cup ketchup

½ cup distilled white vinegar

¼ cup yellow mustard

½ teaspoon freshly ground black pepper

½ cup Worcestershire sauce

EASTERN NORTH CAROLINA–STYLE BARBECUE SAUCE

MAKES ABOUT 3 CUPS

1½ cups apple-cider vinegar

1½ cups distilled white vinegar

1 tablespoon sugar

1 tablespoon crushed red chile flakes

1 tablespoon freshly ground
 black pepper

1 tablespoon kosher salt

1 tablespoon hot pepper sauce

This is the sauce that will pucker your taste buds, and when most folks come to North Carolina this is the one they seem most anxious to try. Both styles of North Carolina sauces are heavy on the vinegar, but west of Greensboro, some ketchup slides into the sauce. You can also use this as a "mop" or basting sauce while smoking a pork shoulder or whole hog.

Mix all the ingredients together in a medium bowl. Store in an airtight container at room temperature for up to 2 months.

LEXINGTON-STYLE BARBECUE SAUCE

MAKES ABOUT 3 CUPS

2 cups apple-cider vinegar

½ cup water

½ cup ketchup

2 tablespoons light brown sugar

1 tablespoon hot pepper sauce

2 teaspoons crushed red chile flakes

2 teaspoons kosher salt

1 teaspoon freshly ground
 black pepper

This is the dividing line for North Carolina barbecue. In the Piedmont, which includes Lexington, pork shoulders are smoked and the sauce features some ketchup and sugar, but more sugar than sauces from eastern North Carolina and less ketchup than sauces from western places like Memphis and Kansas City. Use the "dip" to toss with any pulled pork, chicken, or turkey; it makes an excellent table sauce as well. People who prefer predominantly dry, Memphis-style ribs might like to use this sauce as a mop during the last few minutes of cooking.

Whisk all the ingredients together in a medium bowl until the sugar and salt dissolve. Use immediately or store in an airtight container in the refrigerator for up to 4 weeks. Shake before using.

SURPRISING KANSAS CITY–STYLE SAUCE

Kansas City sauces are typically thought of as sweet, thick, and tomato based, which is true to a certain extent, but some also have a little bite. This recipe sort of hits a middle ground. Slather it on chicken, ribs, pork chops, beef brisket, or even salmon, or use it as a dipping sauce for grilled shrimp.

Combine the tomato paste, water, and vinegar in a medium saucepan. Place over medium-high heat and stir until blended together and smooth. Add the remaining ingredients and cook, stirring, until the sauce just reaches a boil. Reduce the heat and simmer for 10 to 15 minutes. Use immediately, or let cool and store in an airtight container in the refrigerator for up to 2 weeks.

MAKES ABOUT 4 CUPS

One 12-ounce can tomato paste

2 cups water

1 cup distilled white vinegar

1 tablespoon celery juice

½ cup barbecue seasoning blend, store-bought or homemade (use your favorite)

½ cup granulated sugar

½ cup packed light brown sugar

2 teaspoons cornstarch

1 teaspoon liquid smoke

FRANK'S SAN FRANCISCO BARBECUE SAUCE

MAKES ABOUT 3 CUPS

3 cups lower-sodium beef broth

One 6-ounce can tomato paste

¼ cup Dijon mustard

¼ cup brown or grainy mustard

½ cup Worcestershire sauce

¼ cup distilled white vinegar

1 cup loosely packed light
   brown sugar

2 tablespoons chili powder

2 teaspoons crushed red chile flakes

1 tablespoon hickory-flavored
   liquid smoke, or more to taste

Frank Bartoni, a crabber and fisherman for over 40 years in northern California, shared this barbecue sauce recipe with me. He swears that he got it from a fireboat captain in San Francisco Bay. Wherever it came from, it's a delicious sauce that's different from the ones I grew up on in the South. Try it on beef ribs or roasts, as well as on whole roasted chicken, grilled swordfish, or grilled salmon. You probably will need a loaf of sourdough bread to complete that San Francisco feeling.

1. Combine all the ingredients in a medium saucepan. Place over medium-high heat and bring to a boil, stirring constantly until the sugar has dissolved. Reduce the heat and simmer for 1½ to 2 hours, stirring occasionally.

2. Taste and adjust the seasonings, if necessary. Remove from the heat and let cool. Use immediately, or store in an airtight container in the refrigerator for up to 2 weeks.

SLOW-COOKED MEMPHIS-STYLE BARBECUE SAUCE

Memphis's location allows the barbecue meisters to pull inspiration from three different directions—the vinegar of the Carolinas, the sweet of Kansas City, and the spice of Texas. This sauce incorporates all those flavors into a truly authentic Memphis-style barbecue sauce. While you can cook this sauce on a stove, I've found that throwing all the ingredients in a slow cooker makes for easy work. Just cover and cook on low for about 4 hours, and then uncover and cook for about 2 more hours. Use with just about any kind of pork cut, whether it be smoked barbecue, ribs, loins, or chops, and it's equally at home with chicken. Keep some of this in your refrigerator at all times.

1. Combine the ketchup, water, vinegar, both sugars, pepper, granulated onion, and mustard in a medium saucepan. Place over medium-high heat and bring to a boil, stirring to dissolve the sugar.

2. Reduce the heat to low and simmer for about 1½ hours, stirring the sauce occasionally during this time. Add the lemon juice and Worcestershire, and cook for an additional 30 minutes.

3. Remove from the heat and let cool. Pour into an airtight container and refrigerate for up to 3 weeks, though I doubt it will last that long.

MAKES ABOUT 4 CUPS

One 24-ounce bottle ketchup

1½ cups water

½ cup apple-cider vinegar

⅓ cup packed light brown sugar

⅓ cup granulated sugar

2 teaspoons freshly ground black pepper

2 teaspoons granulated onion

2 teaspoons dry mustard

1 tablespoon fresh lemon juice

1 tablespoon Worcestershire sauce, preferably Jason Smith's (see p. 296)

APRICOT BARBECUE SAUCE

MAKES 2¹⁄₃ CUPS

1 cup ketchup

½ cup apricot preserves
(peach, pineapple, or blueberry
preserves or orange marmalade
work well too)

½ cup apple-cider vinegar

1 small onion, finely chopped

2 garlic cloves, finely chopped

1 tablespoon Worcestershire sauce

Brush this barbecue sauce liberally over pork or poultry like duck, chicken, turkey, or quail during the last 10 minutes of its grilling time. You probably will want to divide the sauce in half so that you can have some to pass at the table.

Combine all the ingredients in a medium saucepan. Place over medium-high heat and bring to a boil. Reduce the heat to medium-low and simmer, stirring occasionally, for about 10 minutes or until the sauce has thickened slightly. Use immediately, or store in an airtight container in the refrigerator for up to 1 week.

JAMAICAN-STYLE MANGO RELISH

MAKES ABOUT 1¹⁄₂ CUPS

2 tablespoons olive oil

1 onion, finely chopped

1 green bell pepper, seeded and
finely chopped

1 scallion (white and green parts),
finely chopped

One 1-inch piece fresh ginger, grated

6 garlic cloves, minced

1 fresh jalapeño chile, seeded and
finely chopped (wear gloves to
prevent irritation)

2 ripe mangos, peeled, pitted, and
chopped

Juice of 2 limes (about ¼ cup)

1 teaspoon kosher salt

This biting condiment is a perfect partner to lamb chops. It also adds an excitement factor to grilled chicken pieces or pork chops. It will keep for about a week in your refrigerator, covered tightly.

Place a medium skillet over medium-high heat. Add the olive oil, and when it begins to shimmer, throw in the onion, bell pepper, scallion, ginger, garlic, and jalapeño. Cook until the vegetables have wilted, about 4 minutes. Add the mangos and lime juice and stir until combined. Sprinkle with salt. Transfer to a bowl and let cool. You can use the relish at this point, but the flavor will improve overnight. I like it at room temperature, so if you refrigerate it, let it come to room temperature before serving.

TZATZIKI SAUCE

This Greek yogurt and cucumber sauce can bring life to a lot of recipes. Not only is it good with Dad's Americanized Greek Kebabs (p. 54), but you can spoon it over any of the lamb burgers in the book as well. Don't hesitate to use it any time you want a cool, tangy juxtaposition to a hot and spicy grilled item. Heck, it's pretty good just as a dip with veggie sticks.

Stir all the ingredients together in a small bowl. Cover and refrigerate until nicely chilled, or for up to 4 days. Serve cold.

MAKES ABOUT 1 CUP

½ cup plain whole-milk yogurt, preferably Greek

¼ cup peeled, seeded, and chopped English cucumber

¼ cup snipped fresh dill

2 tablespoons chopped fresh mint

PEANUT SAUCE

Peanut sauce is a lovely condiment from Southeast Asia. Mainly used with satays, it's also great with grilled fish.

1. Heat the oil in a heavy-bottomed saucepan over medium heat. Add the garlic and cook for 2 to 3 minutes or until lightly browned. Reduce the heat to low and stir in the soybean sauce, tomato paste, fish sauce, and chili paste.

2. In a small bowl, combine the peanut butter, sugar, and water. Stir into the soybean mixture. Bring to a boil. Reduce the heat to low and simmer for 2 minutes, stirring constantly. Pour the sauce into individual serving bowls and sprinkle with the sesame seeds and peanuts. Serve at room temperature.

MAKES ABOUT 1 CUP

1 teaspoon peanut oil

3 garlic cloves, minced

¼ cup soybean sauce (not soy sauce; available at Asian supermarkets)

1 tablespoon tomato paste

1 tablespoon fish sauce

1 teaspoon chili paste

1 tablespoon peanut butter

½ tablespoon sugar

1 cup water

1½ tablespoons sesame seeds, toasted

10 to 15 dry-roasted peanuts, coarsely chopped

JASON SMITH'S HOUSE-MADE WORCESTERSHIRE SAUCE

MAKES ABOUT 4 CUPS

2 tablespoons olive oil

4 large yellow onions,
    coarsely chopped

5 fresh jalapeño chiles, chopped,
    with their seeds (wear gloves
    to prevent irritation)

Two 16-ounce bottles light corn syrup

One 16-ounce bottle dark corn syrup

1 cup vinegar

2 cups water

Six 2-ounce cans flat anchovies,
    drained

6 garlic cloves, minced

1 tablespoon molasses

1 teaspoon whole cloves

½ teaspoon freshly ground
    black pepper

1 cup drained prepared horseradish

2 cups veal stock or lower-sodium
    beef broth

Juice of 4 lemons (reserve the rinds)

IN THE KITCHEN

You may want to thin this sauce to use in marinades. Just stir 1 part hot water into 3 parts sauce. This will get you close to a commercial Worcestershire sauce viscosity.

Jason Smith is chef-owner of 18 Seaboard, a casual-to-upscale restaurant in Raleigh, North Carolina. I've known Jason for a long time, and he has always intrigued me with his adventuresome spirit. He's traveled in some not-so-normal circles to develop his cooking skills, including spending a winter in Antarctica cooking for the scientists and crew. I like this recipe because, with fewer ingredients than in most Worcestershire sauce recipes, he still develops a big Worcestershire flavor. Take the time to make this once and I think you will be hooked on having your own house-made Worcestershire to liven up any dish you might cook. The ingredient list may look a bit jarring with some of the amounts, but forge ahead.

1. Take a 5-quart Dutch oven and place over medium heat. Add the olive oil. When the oil begins to shimmer, pour in the onions and jalapeños. Cook, stirring occasionally, until the onions have taken on some color and both vegetables are soft, 5 to 10 minutes. Now pour in both corn syrups, the vinegar, water, anchovies, garlic, molasses, cloves, pepper, and horseradish. Stir the ingredients to combine, and keep at a simmer until it has reduced by about one-half, which could take as long as 2 hours. Keep a close eye and stir occasionally to prevent anything from sticking to the bottom of your pot.

2. Add the broth, lemon juice, and the reserved rinds. Stir well to combine, and keep at a simmer for approximately another hour, or until the sauce is reduced, coats the back of a spoon, and is a bit syrupy. Strain the sauce through a fine sieve, discarding the solids. Let cool slightly, then taste and add salt or more lemon juice as you see fit. Let cool completely and store in an airtight container in the refrigerator indefinitely.

HOUSE-MADE STEAK SAUCE

Here's another chance to leave the bottled stuff on the shelf. Now while I'm not a big proponent of putting steak sauce on a really great grilled piece of meat, that's just me. Evidently there's a good portion of you out there who like the extra zip that a steak sauce can bring. The sauce is even better if you're using Jason Smith's House-Made Worcestershire Sauce (see the previous page), but regardless, I think you'll find this interesting and delicious. If you thin this sauce with 2 tablespoons of canola oil and 2 tablespoons of distilled vinegar, you'll have a pretty darned good marinade for a steak.

Whisk together the ketchup, horseradish, honey, maple syrup, mustard, and Worcestershire in a medium bowl. Taste and season with salt and pepper. Pour into an airtight container and let sit in the refrigerator for at least 1 hour before using. The sauce is much better at room temperature or even slightly warmed than it is straight out of the refrigerator. Kept tightly sealed, the sauce will last for about a week in the refrigerator.

MAKES ABOUT 2 CUPS

1½ cups ketchup

½ cup prepared horseradish, very well drained

2 tablespoons honey

2 tablespoons pure maple syrup (not pancake syrup)

1 tablespoon Dijon mustard

1 tablespoon Worcestershire sauce

Kosher salt

Freshly ground black pepper

LIQUID/DRY MEASURES

U.S.	METRIC
¼ teaspoon	1.25 milliliters
½ teaspoon	2.5 milliliters
1 teaspoon	5 milliliters
1 tablespoon (3 teaspoons)	15 milliliters
1 fluid ounce (2 tablespoons)	30 milliliters
¼ cup	60 milliliters
⅓ cup	80 milliliters
½ cup	120 milliliters
1 cup	240 milliliters
1 pint (2 cups)	480 milliliters
1 quart (4 cups; 32 ounces)	960 milliliters
1 gallon (4 quarts)	3.84 liters
1 ounce (by weight)	28 grams
1 pound	454 grams
2.2 pounds	1 kilogram

OVEN TEMPERATURES

F°	GAS MARK	C°
250	½	120
275	1	140
300	2	150
325	3	165
350	4	180
375	5	190
400	6	200
425	7	220
450	8	230
475	9	240
500	10	260
550	Broil	290

index